CW01394897

Sophie from Romania

RORY CELLAN-JONES

Sophie from Romania

A Year of Love and Hope with a Rescue Dog

SQUARE PEG

1 3 5 7 9 10 8 6 4 2

Square Peg, an imprint of Vintage, is part of the Penguin Random House group of companies whose addresses can be found at global.penguinrandomhouse.com

First published by Square Peg in 2024

penguin.co.uk/vintage

Typeset in 11.4/16.25pt Palatino LT Pro by Jouve (UK), Milton Keynes
Printed and bound in Great Britain by Clays Ltd, Elcograf S.p.A.

The authorised representative in the EEA is Penguin Random House Ireland, Morrison Chambers, 32 Nassau Street, Dublin D02 YH68

A CIP catalogue record for this book is available from the British Library

ISBN 9781529918588

Penguin Random House is committed to a sustainable future for our business, our readers and our planet. This book is made from Forest Stewardship Council® certified paper.

For all the world's rescue dogs and the
brave souls who care for them

Contents

Welcome

There is a moment in just about every conversation I have with anyone I meet these days when they ask the same question. Sometimes it is the very first thing they say, perhaps shouting it across the street as I hurry to the station. Some slip it into the middle of a conversation, a little embarrassed – 'I hope you don't mind me asking but . . .' Others wait right until the end, often insisting, 'I can't let you go without asking . . .' or 'my wife/husband/daughter/boss would never forgive me if I didn't ask . . .' I never mind this question, partly because it's the same thing I ask my wife when I call home from a trip away: 'So, how is Sophie getting along?'

Welcome then to all those who have ever asked that question and to the thousands who follow the adventures of our Romanian rescue dog Sophie. This book is for you, a way of thanking you for your interest in our beautiful pet and for the kind words of encouragement you have sent us as we try to take her on a journey away from fear.

If you had told me a few years ago that one day I would write a book about a dog, I would have been certain that you had me mixed up with someone else. No, as the Technology Correspondent of the BBC, my job was to think about the latest smartphones, developments in artificial intelligence and quantum computing, the battle against disinformation and online bullying. I might write about the occasional robot dog, and with the advent of Covid lockdowns, I began to make regular mention on social media of our beloved Collie cross Cabbage, my daily companion for walks, until her death in January 2022. But what expertise did I have to write a whole book when I could barely tell a Whippet from a West Highland Terrier?

Then, in December 2022, twelve months after I left the BBC after a forty-year career, Sophie came into our home. It quickly became clear that she was going to be a very important part of a post-retirement life that was already far busier than I had anticipated. I started keeping a daily diary recording her progress – or lack of it – and documenting the emotional rollercoaster of living with such a nervous animal.

And because I made the choice to talk about Sophie on social media, creating the hashtag #sophiefromromania, she has also attracted a hugely loyal and supportive audience on Twitter (or X as it became known during the writing of this book) and Instagram. Soon, I was finding that if I had not posted a new photo of Sophie by 9 am, her vast community of online fans was getting anxious.

As a very early user of Twitter, I already had a large following but I watched in amazement as my audience grew by more than 100,000 in the six months following the arrival of our new dog – and they weren't there for my views on the latest gadgets or pictures of my sourdough loaves. It was a similar story on Instagram where I started with a much lower follower count of around 5,000 and saw it climb tenfold in the year after I began posting photos of Sophie.

So you will hear plenty in this book about how this devoted

online community reacted to each moment in the story of our Romanian rescue dog. I make no apology for that because in the era before Twitter and Instagram came along, the whole story would have been very different. We would never have met our wonderful dog behaviourist Si Wooler who first contacted me via a Twitter direct message. Television and radio programmes around the world would not have beaten a path to our door because they would never have even heard of Sophie. And instead of being buoyed up and unfailingly supported by warm and lovely messages from hundreds of thousands of Sophie fans, ready to rejoice at every sign of progress and commiserate with every setback, we would have felt we were very much on our own.

I am sure that our friends would have tried to be supportive but, with very few dog people among them, I am equally certain that most would have asked themselves what on earth we were doing, persevering with a dog that was terrified of visitors and would never go out. Without the daily moral support and interest of you, Sophie's fanbase and followers, who knows whether we would have persisted with our beautiful but painfully anxious rescue dog?

You will also hear from some of the thankfully few negative voices on social media, those whose apparent purpose in checking in for Sophie updates was to be relentlessly critical of what we were doing. They thought – and had no qualms in letting us know – that we were going down the wrong path with her and should just 'get on with it' – clip a lead on her collar and drag her out to the local park. While I was clear that the patient approach advocated by our advisor, Si Wooler, was the right one, these messages served to undermine my resolve and feed my anxiety that Sophie would never be able to experience the things 'normal' dogs enjoy, such as going for a walk or chasing squirrels in the park. It is important to recognise that there is still an ongoing debate amongst animal experts about the best way to treat a fearful dog, even while Si's methods reflect what is now mainstream.

Because much of my desire for a canine companion was informed by the medical imperative to be more active, what you will also encounter in these pages is a lot of talk about Parkinson's disease. We acquired Sophie around four years after I had been diagnosed with the incurable degenerative brain condition. I was coping with my symptoms pretty well at the time but my hope was that a new dog would act as an important support in helping me maintain my physical and mental health, by making me get out early each morning for a walk. Sadly, that did not happen – in 2023 at least – and I became a little more hindered by my Parkinson's as the year progressed.

Nevertheless, I knew I could not blame Sophie. Indeed, as the months progressed the bond between us grew deeper, as I came to understand just how frightened she was by the world she found herself in, so different from the one she had inhabited for the first year of her life. Because of her, I sought out, met and learned from the owners of other Romanian rescue dogs whose stories are scattered through this book.

As in any relationship, there have been ups and downs for me and Sophie: moments of joy as she made some big breakthrough, such as offering me a paw or snuggling up in her bed for the first time; moments of deep frustration, even despair, on my part when she retreated back into her shell and refused to engage with any of us. This book will give a sense of all this too. Above all, however, this is a story about loving patience and what it can achieve, and about how three of us – me, my wife

Diane and Si – managed over time to show Sophie she was safe and had finally found her home.

Like many a good love story, this one began just before Christmas, when a stranger from far away arrived at our home in the dead of night . . .

Rory Cellan-Jones

Chapter One

Special Delivery

Meeting Sophie Cellan-Jones

'Love the dog you have, not the dog you thought you wanted.'

Instagram user @pembertonlismore

17 December 2022

It is just after midnight on the Saturday before Christmas and, despite going to bed several hours earlier, I am wide awake and checking my phone for the latest updates on a delivery we are expecting. When my wife Diane and I had gone to bed at 10 pm, we had been told to expect it around 5 am but I see now that the schedule has been updated – we should now be ready, we are told, at the ungodly hour of 0300 hrs. I peer out of the bedroom window onto our quiet street in a West London suburb. Christmas lights are twinkling in a number of the houses, and a few windows are lit up as part of a street Advent calendar organised by one of our neighbours.

Giving up on sleep, I slip on some jeans and a sweater over my pyjamas on this freezing night and, careful not to wake Diane, head downstairs to wait. So, what is it that has got me, a man in his sixties with a tremor in his right hand and knees that creak as he descends each step, as excited as a six-year-old waiting for Santa Claus? No, not a model railway or a games console. The much-anticipated delivery that has me sitting now on the bottom stair, checking the time on my phone every five minutes, is of a dog. A dog called Sophie.

That was not her name when we picked her out at the end of November, some three weeks earlier, from the pet profiles on the website of a Romanian rescue charity. The dog that Diane zeroed in on was a one-year-old with a very sweet, rather sad face; below her photo was a caption that read, 'Seven loves everybody and is just looking for her forever home.' 'Exactly what we need,' I thought, as we filled out the application papers. Like Diane, I thought she seemed perfect except for one thing: her name. I could not imagine myself running around the park after her shouting, 'Seven! Seven!', like some over-excited judge from *Strictly Come Dancing*. We had a family meeting to choose an alternative, and my daughter-in-law suggested Sophie, after the loveable if somewhat undisciplined mongrel rescue dog her parents had owned until she died of old age a couple of years previously. It seemed ideal, with an Eastern European flavour about it – and so Seven became Sophie. We'd been told in the interim a little about her background – she had been discovered abandoned with other puppies by the roadside in a Romanian village. The vet who had found her handed Sophie and several of the other abandoned puppies over to her elderly father who kept them in a barn for several months. We 'met' Sophie via a video clip in which she seemed pretty lively, jumping up at what appeared to be the sleeve of the man caring for her.

At the beginning of December we signed a form promising to look after her well and return her to the rescue organisation if things didn't work out, and then uploaded a couple of pictures of our garden to show it was suitable for a dog. The paperwork complete at our end, we were told that getting together the various documents needed to satisfy the Romanian and British authorities would take a couple of weeks, but that we should have Sophie before Christmas. A week on came the news that she would arrive on Thursday, 15 December. A few days before this 'due date', we included a visit to a pet store in our round of Christmas shopping and bought food, a harness, and a lovely new bed. When our old dog Cabbage died at the beginning of the year we were so grief-stricken, we threw everything of hers out. Since then, the house had felt strangely empty but now Sophie's bed was installed next to the Christmas tree, and we could not wait to see it occupied.

In the end the schedule slipped a little, as we were told that there'd be a couple of days' delay, but that Sophie had now been picked up from the farm in a remote part of rural Romania which had been her temporary home. From there she was taken to Bucharest to join around fifty other dogs being taken in three vans to new homes in the UK. We then joined a WhatsApp group where we got updates on her progress from the young team escorting the dog convoy. By the morning of Friday, 16 December they had reached the Eurotunnel depot at Calais. Then came the joyful news that all the dogs had passed their health checks, along with a photo of them lined up in front of bowls tucking into a meal. We couldn't see Sophie, but all her companions looked pretty cheerful despite the rigours of the trip.

It was early evening before we learned that they had arrived in Kent, with the escorts promising to give us an ETA update once they had had something to eat. When it came through, we learned that our rescue was going to be dog number eight of twenty-one to be dropped off, arriving at our home at around 5 am after the van had been across Kent and Surrey, up to Milton Keynes and Bedford and then back down to West London.

It is now 2.30 am and, having learned that the schedule has accelerated, I wake Diane who comes downstairs, groggy but as excited as I am, to welcome a new member of the family. Before long there is the noise of an engine outside on this cold still night. We open the front door to find a sleek-looking vehicle parked in the middle of the road, quite unlike the battered Transit van I had imagined. A man has emerged from it to check that they have found the right house and he quickly returns to the dog transporter to collect a bundle which he places in my arms. He steps back, gets out his phone to take a picture, and then within seconds both he and the van are gone, heading for the next drop-off twenty-five miles away in Maidenhead. Sophie has arrived at her forever home!

The photo which the driver sends us twenty minutes later is one we will scrutinise time and again over the next year. It shows me grinning broadly, despite the early hour, but the creature in my arms is looking sad and terrified. She appears much smaller than we had imagined, her ears are floppy, and she is curled up as if trying to hide from the world. We retreat inside and I put her down on the wooden floor of our hallway where she promptly does what a dog needs to do in several places. We are prepared for this: our last dog came to us at about the same age, also not toilet-trained, so we are well equipped with antiseptic wipes and poo bags. We know that at the age of one, Sophie is still an adolescent and accidents can happen. So we're expecting another delivery later that day – a bumper pack of absorbent puppy pads to be placed at strategic spots, which should be rather more effective than the sheets of the *Financial Times* we had spread out over our rugs for our beloved Cabbage fifteen years earlier.

We usher Sophie through the door into the combined living room and kitchen that serves as our main living space, little knowing that she would not dare venture back across the threshold to other parts of the house for many months to come. We manage to persuade her to have a couple of gulps from the water bowl we have put out, then Diane retreats upstairs to try to get a few hours' sleep.

I stay downstairs and stretch out on the red leather sofa where our last dog used to join us whenever we watched television; I shut my eyes, knowing that I will get no sleep but pretending that I might. For the next couple of hours I keep Sophie company, but she shows no inclination either to come close to me or to explore her new home. Her main aim seems to be to find as small a space as possible to retreat to: first she squeezes herself under the bottom shelf of a bookcase, then in a corner next to the sofa. Soon after 6 am, Diane decides she cannot sleep and comes downstairs to see how we are doing. We start to prepare a cooked breakfast but first we have an important task to attend to.

Both Diane and I are enthusiastic users of Twitter, using the social media service as a work tool but also, somewhat cautiously, for some of our personal interests. I was a very early adopter, joining in 2007 for the purposes of reporting on the new phenomenon of social media for BBC Radio 4's *Today* programme. In the early years most of my tweets were about technology news, sharing stories and connecting with other techies but soon I began tweeting about more personal things – my love of baking, particularly sourdough bread, and my daily walks with our dog Cabbage. When Cabbage was alive – before her kidnapping as a fifteen-year-old dog, her eventual return and then rapidly declining health – I left home every morning before 7 am, rain or shine, for a forty-minute circuit of our local parks. I tried to keep it going after her death but somehow when I peered outside and the weather was bad, it seemed foolish to get drenched for no reason, and I soon became a fair-weather walker.

As one of the UK's leading economists and now a Professor at Cambridge University, Diane had been a little sniffy initially about my Twitter habit. But she eventually realised that many of her peers were using the service to discuss economics and promote their research, and it has since become an invaluable place for her to network with other academics; slowly but surely she had built a platform of 30,000 Twitter followers which, post-Sophie, has now doubled. Diane is a more serious person than I am, with a more work-focused Twitter feed, but she does tend to tweet about two subjects other than economics – dance and dogs. Dance, because she has been taking ballet classes twice a week for nearly forty years and is an obsessive *Strictly Come Dancing* fan, tweeting out her scores for the contestants, and getting impatient when the great British public backs a loveable klutz at the expense of a better dancer. And dogs, because she is a huge dog lover, delighting in videos and photos of amusing or soulful pets. Such was her devotion to Cabbage that her Twitter profile still features a picture of our beautiful Collie cross.

So, first things first. Diane wants her network to know that we have a new dog, and so at 0617 hrs on that December morning she tweets the photo of me standing on our doorstep clutching Sophie along with this caption: 'Meet Sophie, here greeting @ruskin147 when she arrived last night. She's tired & nervous after a long journey but we're looking forward to settling her in to her new home.'

We get on with the job of making a breakfast of scrambled eggs on my homemade bread with bacon and tomatoes, and hoping that, just as Cabbage had been, Sophie will be an enthusiastic snaffler of leftovers from our plates. But since she is still cowering in a corner, she misses out on some tasty morsels of bacon fat. No matter, the big moment I have been waiting for all this year is about to arrive – our first walk.

Now on a bright frosty Saturday morning, I am ready to resume the old routine. We decide to take it gently and let Sophie roam our small London garden first for a short time before introducing her to the suburban streets of our area and the dogs of our neighbours. But the moment we get her outside she dives under a garden table and hides, cowering behind some flowerpots. Diane has to drag her out and we put a lead on her. By this time I have downgraded my expectations of this first walk to a few circuits of the lawn but even this proves impossible. Sophie digs in her heels, refusing to budge an inch. We give up and take her back inside where she makes her way to her spot behind the red leather sofa.

We tell ourselves this is disappointing but not really surprising. After all, the poor creature has been uprooted from the barn in rural Romania which was her home, transported across Europe in the confined space of a noisy van with a dozen strange dogs for three days, and then dumped in the unfamiliar environment of a house with two weird humans who seem to want to be her friends. No wonder she is traumatised but, we reason, once she has had a few days to decompress and get used to her new home she'll realise she has lucked out and all will be well.

I set off for the walk on my own – I have missed my regular Saturday morning exercise class, so I need to put some steps in if I am to meet the daily activity targets set by my Apple watch. When I get to the park, I post a photo on Instagram which is supposed to have a dog in it, adding this caption: 'Solo walk this morning – new dog Sophie too tired and scared after her long journey to accompany me. We're taking it slowly and hopefully in a while we'll settle into a new morning routine.'

The rest of the day passes in a blur, so tired and emotionally worn out are we by the events of the early hours and the anxious wait for Sophie to arrive. I slump in front of the TV for the World Cup third place play-off, then we have dinner on trays watching the final of *Strictly Come Dancing*. Sophie, meanwhile, remains in the narrow space between the red sofa and a radiator. It is quite restful really, it occurs to me – though not quite how we had expected our first evening with the new dog to be.

Before heading upstairs to bed that night we place some puppy pads on the living room rug and by the back door into the garden. 'Night, night, Sophie,' we say, closing the living room door and leaving her to spend her first night in this strange house on her own. We would have loved to take her upstairs to sleep in our bedroom as Cabbage did, but it was pretty clear that was not going to happen just yet.

After a patchy night's sleep, I wake on Sunday soon after 5 am and lie in bed for more than an hour, listening intently for any sound from downstairs. As you may already have gathered, early waking has been a rather trying feature of my life ever since the onset of my Parkinson's disease. Insomnia and disordered sleep patterns are common symptoms of the condition unfortunately, and something which all the friends involved in a Parkinson's podcast we have started (more on this later) struggle with too. Suffice to say for now that, while I am excited and unsettled by the arrival of Sophie in our lives, my frequently broken nights around this time aren't entirely down to that. The downside to waking up hours before everyone else is that you have a lot of time to ruminate about all kinds of things, which isn't always helpful . . .

As I lie in bed on this Sunday morning, I keep wondering what I will find when I get up – will Sophie have gone on the rampage, tried to chew her way through the door to escape or knocked down the Christmas tree? Or will she have found her nice cosy bed, had a good sleep and be ready to make a fresh start with her new family? At 6.30 am I finally creep downstairs to make a cup of tea and gingerly open the door to the living room. Where I find . . . Nothing. Well, apart from one wet patch on a puppy pad which is the only evidence of Sophie having been out and about. A glance behind the sofa confirms that she is still there, looking up at me with fearful eyes.

And that's where she remains for the whole day. This means she misses out on another activity I'd been really looking forward to having her with me for. Every Sunday morning I drive a couple of miles to Hanwell to meet my personal trainer Wendy on the towpath of the Grand Union Canal. Wendy is a small fiery woman who by her own admission prefers animals to people, her great love an ageing horse whose care seems to take up much of her income and a lot of her time. When I was training for half-marathons Wendy used to cycle alongside me on 10K runs up and down the canal between Brentford and Southall. These days, however, we tend to just do a few stretches, a bit of power walking, and then she puts a pair of pink boxing gloves on me and peppers me with amiable insults as I essay a few jabs and hooks.

Until the beginning of this year, Cabbage was a constant companion on these outings, racing ahead of us in the early days, towards the end of her life barely keeping up. She and Wendy, who always turned up with a bit of chicken or a sausage as a treat for her, adored each other; when she died Wendy was heartbroken, tearing up for a long time afterwards every time I mentioned Cabbage.

But in recent weeks Wendy has been excited by the news of a new dog, and eager to meet her. So when I turn up alone this Sunday morning, I can see the disappointment written all over her face. But never mind, we agree, give it a few weeks and Sophie will be bounding ahead along the towpath urging us to keep up.

Back at home, the situation has not changed. Sophie is still in the only place where she feels safe. Diane does tempt her out briefly by putting a leftover fish finger on a plate at the entrance to her den. Sophie grabs it and retreats with it to her dark, warm spot between the sofa and the radiator. That evening, neighbours we have known for twenty-five years come over for the regular get-together we have at each other's houses every Sunday. They are of course eager to meet our new dog but we have to disappoint them, explaining that she is too shy at this stage and trying our best to dissuade them from leaning over the back of the sofa to say hello.

We had known, even before Sophie arrived, that Monday was going to be a potentially tricky day for our bonding process with the new member of the household. The week always starts with a 5.15 am alarm call and Diane departs for Cambridge and her job as Professor of Public Policy, returning on Wednesday evening. But on that particular Monday I have one of my regular appointments at Moorfields Eye Hospital, an hour's tube journey away in East London. In 2005, after the discovery of a malignant melanoma behind my left eye, I had undergone an operation which had seen a radioactive plaque inserted behind the eye. Ever since, they have kept a close eye on my tumour, occasionally blasting it with a laser if it shows signs of growing again, and in 2019 sending me for proton beam therapy at a specialist centre on Merseyside. That has been very successful and the tumour now appears dormant – but a side-effect of what I had described in a BBC video as 'having a small hadron collider fired into your eye' is the threat of painful glaucoma. My doctors have decided that to try to avert this I should undergo a course of laser treatment accompanied by injections into the eye as the best option, and that Monday was to see my first session in the laser room.

The terror I had experienced back when I was diagnosed with cancer has faded, to be replaced by a weary resignation at yet more uncomfortable, if not painful, treatment. But the week before, the question had loomed – who was going to look after the new dog? She would, we assumed, be tearing around the house chewing up anything left on the floor or maybe barking pitifully at being deserted by her new family. So we have asked our second child, who lives just a couple of tube stops away, to pop over that morning to do a bit of dog-sitting. In the event, this will prove to be a far from arduous task – our new dog remains behind the sofa the whole time and does not emerge either when I return from the hospital at lunchtime after an uncomfortable session staring into the laser machine.

Later that afternoon, as I sit alone in the kitchen feeling a bit sorry for myself, Sophie does briefly wander out and put her nose in her food bowl. I quickly grab a picture on my phone.

By now, on the third day of her life as a Londoner, our new dog is becoming something of a social media celebrity. Diane's Twitter post showing her in my arms on our doorstep has attracted a record number of 'likes' and my first tweet about Sophie with a picture of her brief visit to the garden and refusal to come for a walk gets an even bigger reaction. Since then my phone's screen has been continually alight with notifications, all about Sophie and how cute she is. It seems that the faithful band of online supporters who followed us through the last years of our beloved Cabbage are now gripped by the drama of our very nervous Romanian rescue dog, and thousands more have joined their number.

Knowing how a hashtag can be a way of forming a community around a subject and help it to go viral, I sit and think about what might work for Sophie. Then I add a caption to my photo of her at her food bowl: 'Immensely cheered after a rather trying morning at the hospital to be able to lure #sophiefromromania out from behind the sofa briefly for a snack.' I post it on Instagram which means it is automatically reposted on Twitter via an automation app called If This Then That. Soon, it has accumulated 700 likes on Instagram – about ten times as many as I'd normally get for a post – and more than 7,000 on Twitter.

Comments on Instagram tend as a rule to be longer and more insightful than on Twitter. And now, yes, there are lots of responses saying how beautiful Sophie is, but there are also plenty from experienced rescue dog owners offering advice. A number of these are recommending that we get a harness as well as a lead on our fearful dog as soon as possible – because otherwise there is a danger she will bolt when we walk her. Others offer words of reassurance: 'Everything must be so frightening to her,' says one. 'Just be near and with her. She'll get it soon and will be your best dog.'

Over the next few days I continue to use the #sophiefromromania hashtag and the audience continues to grow. In that week before Christmas the weather is damp and gloomy, and the news, whether it is the cost-of-living crisis or the war in Ukraine, appears universally grim. People seem desperate to be distracted by some good news and for a while it feels as though Sophie might deliver that both for us and for her growing army of fans. Eager to know what she gets up to overnight once we have gone up to bed, not long after her arrival I set up what I call my 'nature-cam' in our kitchen cum living space. I had originally used this cheap motion-triggered infrared camera to get shots of foxes which would cavort in our garden and attack the food waste bins. Now, by placing it near the fridge looking back towards the red sofa, I can be sure to get a view of most of the space she occupies when she emerges. She is confined – or rather has confined herself – to the knocked-through living room, dining area and kitchen we created not long after we moved in, in 1992. Beyond the door to the rest of the house lie the hall and the front room, which is home to the piano, and is mainly used when we have guests at the weekend. But to Sophie so far, this and the bedrooms and study on the first floor – let alone the loft conversion – all remain alien territory.

The next day when I come down in the morning Sophie remains behind the sofa but when I extract the memory card from the nature-cam and put it in my computer, I discover that she has not been there all night. Instead, the black-and-white video clips show her striding confidently around the kitchen, even stopping to have a sniff at the camera as if to say, 'Who's spying on me?' When I chop together a few of these clips and post them on social media, this – the first footage of Sophie – is viewed nearly 300,000 times.

People continue to leave lots of messages of support or advice on how to treat her.

'This is a gripping story. She is so lovely. Good luck. Watching her progress and wishing you all well,' and, 'She walks around with tail up, so feeling confident in the space,' are among more than 170 comments on the video. Wow – I usually try to respond to comments but with as many as this, it would take all day!

Over the next day, Sophie continues to hide away for most of the time but then on the Tuesday evening, the fourth day after her arrival, she pops out briefly while we are sitting watching television. Then as she tries to squeeze past the Christmas tree she knocks an ornament off, panics and dives back behind the sofa. The following day, as if she is recovering from some traumatic incident, Sophie is once more a recluse and we barely see her. This is something of a disappointment to another regular caller to our home – our cleaner, Halina, who's from Poland. Halina first came to us twenty-five years ago barely speaking any English; now she is a successful businesswoman with buy-to-let properties as well as her cleaning enterprise and able to negotiate any situation she needs to with ease. Over the years, she has helped us with childcare, and has been to a family wedding and a funeral, so she feels like part of the family by now. She adored Cabbage and has been eagerly anticipating the arrival of our new dog since she heard the news. She desperately wants to stroke and pet Sophie as she did Cabbage.

So that day and for a long time to come, Halina has to manage her own disappointment about a situation she admits she doesn't completely understand. And the fact that each time she visits she brings with her a very noisy vacuum cleaner, which will be used in every room in the house, means that an appearance by the recluse behind the sofa is even less likely than when other visitors appear. Sophie is truly terrified of the sound of the vacuum cleaner, and will remain so for many months, and naturally enough, she comes to associate Halina's visits with the appearance of this vociferous monster.

Thursday, the day before Christmas Eve, also starts quietly

on the Sophie front, although the nature-cam shows she has been out a number of times during the night. But then that evening as we watch the news, she is out and roaming freely around the kitchen for long enough for me to grab some footage. I post it on Twitter and Instagram and the internet goes bonkers. On Instagram the commenters can barely contain their delight: 'Look at her getting a bit braver'; 'Well done, Sophie!'; 'She is getting there'; 'This is such positive progress.' On Twitter nearly half a million people watch the video, with almost 300 making comments. I seize on this one and the encouragement it offers: 'This is the heartwarming tale Christmas needs. Look at her, she'll be scoffing turkey at the table with you all come Sunday.' Later that night, #sophiefromromania trends on Twitter for the first time. It is exhilarating to see so many people excited and involved in this story and we bathe in a warm glow of online love.

Christmas has arrived, a time we love to celebrate in our own home with friends and family. On Christmas Eve, a Saturday and a week to the day since Sophie's arrival, I bake sausage rolls as I always do while listening to the Festival of Nine Lessons and Carols from King's College Cambridge, in preparation for the arrival of a dozen or so neighbours as well as our son's family for early evening drinks. But what to do about Sophie? She is still really scared of me and Diane most of the time: how will she react to a crowd of strangers clumping noisily around the space she has spent a week in and is perhaps beginning to regard as home, or at the very least, a safe space for the time being?

It turns out to be pretty simple – the moment the doorbell rings and the first guests troop in, she retreats behind her sofa. Among the early arrivals are our son, his wife and their two children, a girl, who's nearly four, and a two-month-old baby boy. Our granddaughter has been hugely excited about meeting the new dog but has to be dissuaded from peering behind the sofa, and that applies to the adult guests too. Sophie remains in her safe space throughout the party, and she is still there when we go to bed.

Christmas Day dawns and I creep downstairs to find no physical signs of overnight activity, though the nature-cam does show that Sophie has ventured out in the small hours. Our Christmas Day festivities are more low-key than normal, as our son and his children will be celebrating with his wife's parents. There are just five of us gathered round the table as I carve the turkey, and I look hopefully towards the sofa: surely the delicious smells will tempt Sophie out? Not a chance – she stays where she is and remains there for the rest of the day.

Over the next couple of days, I feel a stab of worry as we see very little of the dog we had hoped would be at the centre of our Christmas celebrations. Every now and then she is tempted out by a piece of turkey skin or some bacon, but she is mostly 'Sophie-behind-the-Sofa'. The day after Boxing Day I come downstairs in the morning to find, for the second night running, no sign that she's been out. After another day when we don't seem to be getting anywhere, I'm feeling a little gloomy and in the evening I retreat to the loft to watch a football match, hoping to take my mind off the subject which now feels like it's dominating our lives.

Downstairs Diane, no football fan, is watching *Countryfile* in the living room. Suddenly my phone pings and there's a photo of Sophie standing in front of the television, then another of her peering out from behind another sofa. I come downstairs and cautiously sit down next to Diane, while Sophie continues to stroll around, sniffing at the scented candle and the rug, exploring her territory. I sneak off to grab a piece of sausage from the fridge, then sit back down and wait with it in my outstretched hand. The dog looks at me, carefully approaches, and then ever-so-delicately removes the sausage from my hand.

This feels like a tremendous breakthrough, and when I post a short video on social media of her taking a second piece of sausage, the internet goes completely mad. A million people watch the footage on Twitter and there are nearly 1,400 comments. 'The perfect Christmas story, Rory. Well done!' writes @paulwaugh. 'Our whole family is following her progress,' tweets @micky_kilburn. 'My daughter just shouted "Mum, the Twitter dog has come out from behind the sofa." Well done, #sophiefromromania, your new chapter begins.'

Even before the sausage-eating incident, mainstream media outlets have begun to notice this emerging social media phenomenon. *The Sunday Times*, the *Daily Telegraph* and the *Daily Mail* all get in touch, as do a number of broadcasters. On the Thursday morning after Christmas Day I appear live from the kitchen on BBC Radio 5 Live and *BBC Breakfast* talking about Sophie. Earlier when I came downstairs first thing to make tea, I found the Christmas tree toppled sideways onto a bookcase, so I imagine there has been a middle-of-the-night shock for the roaming resident of behind-the-sofa.

Sitting in front of my laptop with the corner of the sofa in the background I hear the presenter of *BBC Breakfast* introduce the item: 'You might have had lots of visitors over the festive period, some of them more trouble than others, but not many will have been as shy and retiring as the guest who arrived in the home of our former BBC colleague Rory Cellan-Jones a week before Christmas.' They use some of the video I have shot of Sophie, including the breakthrough moment of her eating out of my hand the previous night. I tell the story of the last ten days and then a dog behaviour expert in the BBC studio up in Salford has some advice for dealing with dogs like Sophie: 'Don't feel like you have to interact with them. They are taking their time to decompress and just get used to feeling safe. Once they feel safe, you'll see a different dog. And the joy of bringing one of those dogs around is the best thing you can imagine.'

Throughout the piece I try to strike a positive tone – despite the fact that the star of the show remains determinedly out of shot – but I also feel the need to introduce a gentle note of warning: 'I think there is a bit of a cautionary tale here about being aware of what adopting a dog from Romania or other foreign country means.' The interview ends in an upbeat way, however, with me leaning back and addressing our invisible dog with a statement of encouragement and hope: 'Sophie, sooner or later we'll be going for a nice long, gentle walk.'

Immediately afterwards there is an extraordinary and heartwarming response from huge numbers of viewers, who contact the programme to wish us the best or tell stories about their own rescue dogs. Some are even able to share their experiences with dogs brought over to the UK from Romania, just like Sophie. These latter stories are of particular interest to me and Diane of course, and I find myself resolving to follow them up and seek out others – part of my journalistic instinct, I suppose, but also because of a need to have some points of reference for our own efforts to help Sophie settle in.

After the success of the *BBC Breakfast* item and huge outpouring of public support, we are feeling upbeat again, confident we are on a steady upward trajectory towards that first walk. The mood doesn't last, however. Over the coming days, Sophie's appearances get rarer. It probably does not help that on New Year's Eve we have a big family lunch with a dozen of us around the table just feet from her hiding place, then later in the run-up to midnight there is as always a constant fusillade of fireworks all over our West Ealing neighbourhood, which seems to get louder every year.

In the days that follow, we seem to have got into a rather disheartening routine. Each morning, after a broken night's sleep, I creep down the stairs and open the door to the living room. Reasonably often I find a puddle or something more solid on the puppy pads, but the food in her bowl is usually untouched and on many occasions there is no sign of any activity at all, including on the nature-cam. As the day unfolds, we see very little of Sophie and if she does come out, any rapid movement or the arrival of a guest or casual caller sends her scuttling back behind the sofa.

Ever since we started talking about her on social media, people have been mentioning the '3-3-3 rule' for adopting a rescue dog. Apparently it takes three days before the animal's feeling of being completely overwhelmed by the experience of arriving in a strange new home starts to wear off; three weeks before it can really begin to settle in, and three months before the dog will be completely comfortable with its new owners. But by Saturday, 7 January, three weeks after her arrival, Sophie is still extraordinarily nervous with us and does not seem to have 'settled in' to anything other than spending nearly all her time hiding in her safe space.

I feel discouraged and even a little cross. Just a few days after Sophie's arrival, I decided to start keeping a diary about her progress, in which to record the highs and lows of each day's happenings. I think I assumed there would be mostly highs, but as my diary attests, three weeks in, I feel that I'm on 'an emotional rollercoaster' on a daily basis, with each small step of progress being followed by an inevitable lurch downhill. Much of the time our new dog remains in her shell and reluctant to emerge – literally and metaphorically – and while the supportive messages on social media keep flooding in, there are others, especially from some describing their own experiences with rescue dogs, which frankly get me down, as one of my diary entries at the time reflects: 'One person tweeted this about their dog: "Lara is great now but wouldn't leave the house for six months . . ." Six months?! I couldn't stand that.'

I had imagined that by now the two of us would be starting each day with a walk in the dark before 7 am, followed by a hearty breakfast where Sophie would beg for scraps of bacon from my plate. Then later, perhaps, Diane and I would put her in the back of the car and head off to somewhere like Burnham Beeches for another winter walk, followed by lunch in a cosy pub where our new dog would snooze under the table. Then we would head home and in the evening Sophie would join us on the sofa, not behind it, while we'd watch television. Later, she would follow us upstairs and soon be snoring gently on a cushion in the corner of our bedroom. This after all was what Cabbage had done. Why couldn't she be a proper dog like Cabbage?

When I share some of these reflections with Diane, she reminds me of a couple of things. The first is that I seem to have forgotten how much time Cabbage herself needed all those years ago to settle down and feel at home when she came to us as a young dog around the same age as Sophie. Secondly – and most importantly perhaps in this instance – Diane points out that I've always been a naturally impatient person, while this situation – helping a terrified rescue dog to find her feet in a completely unfamiliar environment – is one that is going to require a huge amount of forbearance from everyone. Well, one thing I can't dispute there is my natural lack of patience, instances of which over the years have become the stuff of family folklore.

There was, for example, the famous Ikea Wardrobe Incident,

which goes back over thirty years to a time when Diane and I were living in our first house together. On this occasion I became so wound up as I tried to make sense of the indecipherable instructions and the endless components of the flatpack we'd taken delivery of a few days earlier, that Diane wisely sent me out for a walk. A while later, having channelled my anger into several brisk rounds of the local park, I came back to find that in my absence, my wife had managed to put together the wardrobe seamlessly in her usual calm, level-headed way. Needless to say I was delighted that I wouldn't have to enter into the fray with it again myself. DIY does tend to bring out the worst of my impatience – I am the guy who never reads the manual or sorts out all the parts before assembling something, or bothers with that boring prep stuff before painting the ceiling.

As I mull over all this, and the need to be patient, I find myself scrolling back to look at some of my first Twitter posts about Sophie. When I return to that very early photo of her in our back garden, digging in her heels and refusing to budge, I see that many new comments have been posted below it since I last looked. Among them is one on Instagram from @pembertonlismore with a very apt if sobering message:

> 'Things my dog has taught me: Love the dog you have, not the dog you thought you wanted. You are not her owner but her carer. It's not about what you want, but what she needs. Don't [put] your timeframe on your dog but take steps forward when she shows she is good and ready. Some dogs build trust and confidence quickly, some take time. Be patient and be guided by your dog.'

Maybe the sender is on to something.

Chapter Two

A Man's Best Friend

In Loving Memory of Cabbage Coyle

'Grief is the price we pay for love.'

Queen Elizabeth II

I was never a dog person. Or at least, I wasn't until I was well into middle age. I spent my childhood in a cramped one-bedroom council flat on the borders of Camberwell and Dulwich where there were strict rules forbidding the ownership of pets. Now it is true that on this rather posh council estate, which was among the first to be sold off, some tenants chose to ignore the rules. I remember sharing the malodorous lift one day with an elderly woman clutching what I saw then as a nasty yappy little Pekinese to her chest, both of them looking offended to be locked in close quarters with me. You could just about get away with a small dog or a cat as long as they did not make a nuisance of themselves.

But my mother had no interest in us acquiring a pet of any kind. She had arrived in the flat in the mid-1950s with her thirteen-year-old son, my half-brother Stephen, after leaving her husband and spending five years in desperately shabby bedsits or boarding houses in Maida Vale. To both of them, the flat must have seemed like a paradise – their own small but warm and comfortable living space with no prying landlady or shared bathroom along the hall. Why on earth would they risk everything by breaking the rules about keeping pets? Then, just as sixteen-year-old Stephen was preparing to spread his wings and make a career in the theatre, I came along, the result of a love affair between my mother and a much younger BBC colleague. So in her mid-forties, she became a single mother all over again.

Money was tight and the idea of sharing our living space with a pet was simply out of the question. Besides, she didn't even like dogs, which she'd refer to as 'nasty smelly creatures'; meanwhile, she thought there was something creepy and arrogant about cats. And, as with every other matter in my early years, I agreed with Mum. When it came to dogs, I found them either annoying or frightening. In the first category was Buster, the Yorkshire Terrier belonging to my childminder, Mrs Gregory. With Mum out at work as a secretary in the BBC drama department, I spent a lot of my childhood in the bigger but much more crowded flat on a rougher council estate, which was the home of Mrs Gregory – 'Auntie' to me – along with her disabled husband and what sometimes felt like dozens of kids (she was an emergency foster mother as well as a childminder), and Buster the dog.

It was a noisy environment – the TV was always on, the kids were hollering, especially when 'Auntie' gave them a smack – but Buster seemed equally determined to make his voice heard. He raced around the living room barking furiously at anything or anyone that got in his way, at a volume that seemed extraordinary coming out of such a tiny bundle of fur. These days, I might find that cute – but back then, Buster, the first dog in my life, just seemed like a pain.

None of my wider family owned dogs, and on the rare occasions when I was taken by aunts, uncles or godparents on country walks, any dogs we encountered – slavering hounds straining at the leash or pressing their jaws against a garden gate – were a source of terror for me. What I particularly hated were the ones that decided they wanted to get up close and personal. 'Stay calm, he means no harm,' their owners would say, which I didn't find reassuring in the least as Samson or Fang tried to climb all over me.

Mind you, there was one significant person in my life who was crazy about dogs – my dad. The trouble was that although my mother had told me about him at an early age, I didn't get to meet him until I was in my twenties. By the time I was ten, in the early 1970s, my father James Cellan Jones was beginning to make a name for himself as a television drama director. After he directed much of the huge 1960s hit series, *The Forsyte Saga*, he appeared in various newspapers, including the *Daily Mirror*, Mrs Gregory's paper of choice. When she showed me a photo they'd published of him, I didn't have a clue what to say, so I simply remarked on the dog sitting on his lap – a Boxer, which to me now looks rather sweet with soulful eyes but back then appeared vaguely threatening. 'Poor little tyke,' I recall Mrs G murmuring to her husband, and she wasn't referring to the dog.

As the years passed and I grew more interested in my dad and his career, I couldn't help noticing that just about every television drama he directed, from Shakespeare's *A Midsummer Night's Dream* to Sartre's *Roads to Freedom*, featured a dog at some point. Even as recently as last year in fact, quite soon after Sophie's arrival in our home, the BBC repeated Dad's landmark series, *Fortunes of War*, starring Kenneth Branagh and Emma Thompson. One night, as I watched an episode set in Romania, in which Ken and Em prepare to flee a regime friendly to the Nazis, I found myself grabbing the remote control and spooling back a few frames. There, hiding out on the roof of their apartment with a dissident wanted by the police, was a dog – a German Shepherd* the spitting image of Sophie.

It was only in my mid-twenties, when I got to know my dad and my Cellan-Jones family, that I really understood how big a role dogs played in all their lives. When I first rang the bell at the large Edwardian home where Dad lived in Kew, the next thing I heard was a thump and a fusillade of barking as two dogs crashed into the door. It opened to reveal the whole family stood there, with my new half-brothers and sister gripping the collars of two slobbering Boxers, shouting, 'Down, Max! Stop it, Daisy!!' It looked to me as though these dogs wanted to tear me limb from limb, but at least they served as an icebreaker as I handed a pot plant to my stepmother, Maggie, while my half-brother, Simon – who had contacted me several weeks earlier and extended the invitation to the house – introduced me to my new half-brother Din and half-sister Vinny, who had only learned of my existence relatively recently.

Jim, as I took to calling my dad, and my stepmother Maggie had decided that Boxers were their kind of dogs and usually had a couple of them. They were utterly devoted to these rambunctious and energetic creatures in a way that, before I became a dog owner, I struggled to comprehend. Even Diane, who had grown up with a dog, found Max and Daisy and their successors a little tiresome at times. Before a visit with me to Kew she'd often change into her oldest jeans – 'They're only going to get slobbered over,' she'd say. And when the dogs inevitably

* From early on, we always assumed Sophie was a German Shepherd, possibly encouraged by a few people who said she looked like their dogs. But recently someone said she looked like a Dutch Shepherd, something we'd never heard of. We could get a DNA test but don't fancy getting a blood sample or a swab inside her mouth.

climbed all over us, my dad would shout at them, 'You stupid beasts!' but in a tone of immense affection which suggested that it would be silly to be too annoyed with them.

Over the years, I got more comfortable with my Cellan-Jones family's dogs – Simon at one stage had a loveable Labrador called Desmond – without ever wanting one in my life. That all changed in 2007 and I'm still not entirely sure how we ended up owning a dog called Cabbage. That autumn we were having a few disciplinary issues with our younger child, and there was talk of good behaviour being rewarded with a dog at Christmas. The child, excited by this prospect, began to scour the website of the rescue charity, Dogs Trust, and took to lecturing us that 'dog ownership is rewarding but has its responsibilities'. Yes, we said, as long as you realise those responsibilities include picking up poo . . .

It was in November 2007 when our search for a dog began in earnest with a visit to the Dogs Trust rescue centre a few miles away on the outskirts of London. One caught our eye, a Collie cross about a year old, nervous after apparently having had a difficult start in life. She was a pretty creature, not too big, not too small – I really didn't have the vocabulary to describe dogs – but I was a bit alarmed by how jumpy she was. And she was called Cabbage – what a ridiculous name!

We drove home with the kids chattering happily about the dog, while I silently wondered whether this was such a good idea. A few days later, I flew with a camera crew to Nigeria to shoot a story about an organisation called One Laptop Per Child, which aimed to bring computers to children in underdeveloped countries. We travelled from our hotel in the gleaming modern city of Abuja out to a dusty village without running water or electricity. The hope was that the little white and green laptop recharged by solar power at a school where there were fifty to a class would help close the digital divide both within Nigeria and with the rest of the world, leapfrogging children into a more prosperous future. I couldn't help noticing a couple of skinny dogs scavenging for food amongst the rubbish heaps – here in the early 2000s, they were pests, not pets.

The filming trip was such an intense experience that I did not think much about our quest for a pet. So it was a shock when I walked through the front door of our Ealing home and found our household had a new member. Cabbage, who had arrived the night before, roamed the living room skittishly, then jumped up at me, planting her paws on my midriff. 'She wants a walk,' said Diane, handing me a lead with a smile, as if to say, 'Your turn now.'

Still bleary-eyed from my overnight flight home, I clipped the lead to Cabbage's collar – after Diane had shown me how – and set off on my first dog walk. It took a bit of getting used to as Cabbage first dragged me forward along the tree-lined avenues on a grey autumn afternoon, then forced me to halt as she inspected a lamppost or relieved herself under a tree. But I soon got the hang of it and began to ask myself some questions. Like, how come we had got a dog in November when it was supposed to be for Christmas? Was she house-trained? And could we possibly change that daft name, so that we didn't attract ridicule by sounding like a greengrocer touting his wares when we summoned her back to us?

The answer to the third question was a definite 'no' when we had a family meeting about it – our youngest told us that Cabbage had already had enough trouble in her life without the trauma of learning a new name. The sight of Diane covering the living room rug in newspaper told me all I needed to know about the dog's toilet habits and for a few weeks we had to deal with a number of overnight accidents.

And I gradually came to understand why we had got Cabbage well before Christmas – it was Diane who had really wanted a dog. She had often talked about Lassie, the Alsatian her mum and dad had when she was born in the Lancashire mill town of Ramsbottom. The youngest of four children by ten years, she was never allowed to walk the dog. Lassie died when Diane was six and when she asked whether they could get a new dog, her mum and dad said no, it was too much bother. 'We got a budgerigar and a goldfish instead,' she told me glumly when we first discussed getting a pet. So it turned out that she had wanted a dog ever since and it quickly became evident that she and Cabbage had a special bond – when we registered her at the vet's, she was listed as 'Cabbage Coyle'.

But I too soon came to love our energetic rescue dog. Friends had told us we were mad to get a Collie because they needed so much exercise – three walks a day. But that turned out to be a good thing for a man in his late forties with a bit of a beer belly. I did the first walk of the day, leaving home before 7 am, winter and summer, rain or shine.

A few months on I took up running, and three times a week my early walk with Cabbage became a run, a three-mile circuit with the dog starting on the lead and pulling ahead, then unleashed at the entrance to one of Ealing's many parks. While she was never a well-trained dog, she mostly behaved herself in the park – unless someone was foolish enough to be playing football. Then she would race onto the pitch, apparently convinced she was a star striker. On at least one occasion there was the embarrassment of a burst football.

But I quickly became addicted to the early walk, a time to think about the day ahead and to chat with other dog walkers. In a London suburb, stopping and chatting to complete strangers would normally have them running away terrified from the madman – but a dog changed everything. You quickly learned which dogs were sociable and up for a bit of bottom sniffing, and which were nervous or aggressive and to be avoided – and much the same applied to their owners, minus the bottom sniffing.

Take Luna, for instance, a large, shaggy, and rather moody dog – my knowledge of breeds then, as now, was pretty sketchy. At first we steered well clear of her and her owner, a pleasant woman who lived in one of the rather grand houses on an elegant treelined street nearby. When we did encounter them, Cabbage always shrank back as Luna made it clear she had no time for other dogs and was quite prepared for a fight if that was what we wanted. But gradually the dog calmed down, and Diane and I on our separate walks both began to chat to her owner. Julie – a tremendously warm and chatty French woman who had married an Englishman many years ago and settled in Ealing – told us that Luna too was a rescue dog. We became friends and Julie was to become an invaluable source of advice and help when we got Sophie.

We never learned the name of one elderly lady or the dog she walked daily in our park. The dog, an amiable mongrel, was friendly enough but its owner's disgruntled look every time Cabbage came near deterred us from even an exchange of pleasantries. Then, after some weeks when I'd noticed the pair had been absent from the park, I suddenly encountered owner and dog out walking again, and found myself talking to the elderly lady as we and our dogs negotiated a treacherous stretch of black ice on a February day. She said in a gruff Scottish accent that she had not been well and then, pointing at her dog, confided in conclusion: 'It's only *this* one that keeps me going . . .' We saw the two of them a couple more times and then no more.

Far keener to engage in conversation was an American

gentleman who, like Julie, lived in the locality. Cabbage and I saw him out early each morning, grappling with two enthusiastic Golden Retrievers which looked fully grown but were apparently still puppies in spirit and temperament. He was one of those East Coast Americans – a New Englander perhaps – who seem to have stepped straight out of the nineteenth century, and was always extremely polite and solicitous, even as his two dogs tried to haul him off into the distance. He always referred to our Cabbage as 'your pup', even when she was pushing fifteen. Perhaps this is why his own dogs retained their puppy-like antics well into their adult years. (When I showed him a photo of Sophie shortly after her arrival he became gripped by her story. 'How's that fine pup of yours – out for a walk soon?' he asked.)

My walks with Cabbage were not limited to Ealing. She turned out to be eminently transportable, snoozing on the back seat of the car. We took her on holidays to the Lake District, where she hauled us up mountains, to Cardigan Bay in West Wales where our morning walk was along a coastal path with stunning views; we even got her a pet passport and took her to Brittany where she frolicked on the beaches, pursuing a ball right up to the water's edge but never quite overcoming her fear and taking a swim. On those occasions when we flew abroad, we never had to put her in kennels because she would always stay with Diane's ballet teacher, an animal lover whose house seemed to be overflowing with dogs, cats and even a pet magpie. Cabbage loved going there, returning several pounds heavier and looking at the contents of her food bowl as if to say, 'Is that it? I'm used to steak!'

Cabbage arrived in our lives just as the smartphone and social media era was getting underway. As the BBC's Technology Correspondent, it was my job to be an early adopter – I had joined an infant social network called Twitter in May 2007 and that November when the first Apple iPhone arrived in the UK, I splashed out on the gadget that was going to change the world. The first of thousands of photos I captured of Cabbage was shot with the very primitive camera of that original iPhone. She made her debut on Twitter in 2008 when it was still a niche social network derided as the place sad hipsters went to tell the world (well, their half-dozen friends) that they had just had a cappuccino. I'm afraid many of my early contributions were like that, but on that day in June my tweet did reveal a little about how my attitude to dogs was changing: 'Seem to have got used to shouting "Cabbage" across the park at 7.45 on a Sunday morning . . .'

Meanwhile my running had become quite serious – yes, Cabbage and I were out pounding the park before 8 am on a Sunday. When in 2012 it was announced that Ealing was going to have its own half-marathon I entered and trained with Cabbage by running along the towpath of the Grand Union Canal from Brentford to Southall. But soon both the dog and I were slowing down. In 2016 I ran my fifth Ealing Half, starting with what I thought was just a niggle in my lower back. Within half a mile it became clear that the niggle was something a lot more serious. I was in terrible pain but having raised a hefty sum in sponsorship for the Alzheimer's Society I felt obliged to carry on, walking the second half of the course and crossing the finishing line in a sorry state.

Greg, the friendly Aussie physio I visited, patched me up but I soon began to realise that my running days were drawing to a close. Which must have been a relief to Cabbage – we were both getting too old for this game. She was losing her hearing – a boon on Guy Fawkes night when she used to be in a perpetual state of terror – and her eyes were clouding over.

In the summer of 2018, on holiday in Italy, Diane noticed that I kept dragging my right foot. At first she made light of it – 'Pick your feet up, man!' – but then we began to worry. I went to see Greg the physio again, hoping he'd order me to do a few exercises that would sort it out, but he looked perplexed and a little concerned, suggesting I book an appointment with my GP.

When I eventually got around to that, I was seen by a young trainee doctor who pulled my limbs in various directions, then left me briefly to consult someone more experienced. When she returned, it was to say that it would probably be best for me to book an appointment with a consultant neurologist. That, of course, turned out to be four months later, in early January – but very quickly I got a clue from elsewhere about what might be wrong. An academic neurologist had watched me doing a live broadcast on *BBC Breakfast* from Jersey in the Channel Islands. I was holding a length of fibre optic cable to illustrate the ultrafast broadband connections islanders were now getting – the neurologist noticed that my hand was shaking, and then wrote to the BBC suggesting that I should get this checked out, as this kind of tremor could be a symptom of Parkinson's Disease.

So it was hardly a surprise to be told when I finally got to see a junior doctor at St Mary's Paddington that I was exhibiting 'symptoms of Parkinsonism'. It is never great to hear that you have an incurable degenerative brain disease but I was reasonably calm. Perhaps this was because I was thinking back to December 2004 and what had seemed a far more frightening diagnosis – being told that I had a malignant melanoma behind my left eye. My father, then in his late eighties, had Parkinson's so I knew a bit about it and it did not appear to be imminently life-threatening. I was, however, keen in my journalistic way to understand the condition and how it could be treated. I quickly went on a course of the dopamine replacement drug, Sinemet, but this and other drugs merely mask the symptoms rather than arrest the progress of Parkinson's. But as I talked to doctors, researchers and other people with Parkinson's, one thing became clear – exercise was the most reliable way to keep your symptoms under control.

And for me, the easiest and most reliable form of exercise was my daily walk with Cabbage. For a while I kidded myself that nothing had really changed, that the effects of my Parkinson's were invisible to most people, certainly in my professional life. I had told a few close colleagues, reassuring them that although I would no longer be so keen to carry the camera crew's tripod (frequently the reporter's job), I would still stand my round in the pub.

But one May morning in 2019 after I had appeared live on *BBC Breakfast* demonstrating the new 5G phone network that was launching that day, my producer asked me a question as we travelled by train to Birmingham to do more filming on the same story: 'Have you ever thought about going public about your Parkinson's?' She then told me that my tremor had been very apparent as I'd waved a phone around on the TV that morning. Later, I looked back at the broadcast and it was immediately clear she was not exaggerating.

In fact my producer was pushing at an open door in suggesting that I tell the world. I wanted everyone to know so that I could get on with my life. To break the news, I did what now came naturally to me – I tweeted. On 31 May, I posted a message, saying that a few viewers had noticed my hand shaking, so now was a good time to reveal my condition; I concluded: 'I'm getting good treatment and the symptoms are mild right now – so I'm carrying on as normal. Onwards and upwards.'

The reaction was swift and overwhelmingly positive, with thousands of people sending me kind messages and wishing me well – and only one saying I had probably got Parkinson's from standing too close to 5G phone masts(!). I appeared on the radio talking about my diagnosis and the *Mail on Sunday* ran a sympathetic double-page spread – unusual for a paper normally hostile to the BBC. I have to admit I got a buzz from all the attention – and it was a useful distraction because I was going through a hard time on a different front. After lying dormant for several years, the malignant melanoma behind my left eye was showing signs of growth again – this was when my doctors recommended the proton beam therapy. So I then spent a week in June on Merseyside being treated at the only UK centre specialising in proton beam for the eye.

Meanwhile, I was, perhaps unsurprisingly, suffering two frequent symptoms of Parkinson's: depression and insomnia. Diane knew about my trouble sleeping, but I never really told her about the black cloud that descended on me at night or any time I was alone with my thoughts. So, given all this, the publicity generated by my disclosure that I had a Parkinson's diagnosis was welcome, especially as it also gave a higher profile to Cabbage. In a number of media interviews, I mentioned that she was an integral part of my daily exercise routine, which made our online community grow some more. Around this time, I became involved in fundraising with the charity Parkinson's UK, committing to walk sixty-six miles in a month – not difficult as long as we kept to our daily routine – and Cabbage and I raised over £1,000 by taking part in a 5K walk around Richmond Park.

But in March 2020, everything changed. Suddenly, walks had to start and finish at our front door. The first Covid lockdown saw Boris Johnson order us to stay at home – apart from thirty minutes' daily exercise. For me and Cabbage that meant an early stroll to the nearest park, a rather uninspiring rectangle of grass with views of the A40 and Pinner. It was not the most promising scenic material, but I started taking a picture each day – usually featuring Cabbage – and then posting it to Instagram and Twitter. 'I think the dog and I are still allowed out – anyway, it's essential therapy for both of us,' was the caption on one of those first photos. What I did not reveal was one – for me – hugely positive effect of the pandemic: quite suddenly the depression that I had been suffering for the past year lifted. Perhaps this was because figuring out how to do my job from home had given me a new sense of purpose – aside from that, I haven't yet come up with any other explanation.

In those strange, disconcerting times, when a miasma of fear and boredom spread across the land, it soon became clear that people really liked to share a moment via the daily photo and built it into their routine. A British journalist marooned by lockdown in Hong Kong contacted me to say it was his daily reminder of home, while others seemed to like the mundane nature of the photos because they reflected their own lives. And when restrictions were eased and I said I might stop posting quite so often, there was a chorus of commenters urging me to carry on.

By now Cabbage had become a minor online celebrity with a select audience. My social media activity was mainly focused on my work as the BBC's Technology Correspondent, with occasional mentions of my sourdough baking habit. But I couldn't help noticing that the tweets about my dog were among the most popular; for a fetching picture of her on the sofa on International Dog's Day, I'd receive ten times more engagement than my other posts. But it would be an incident in November 2021 that propelled Cabbage into the mainstream.

Before this, however, in spring 2021, I decided that after a forty-year stint, it was time for me to leave the BBC. There were a lot of factors which fed into this decision, but at the time my Parkinson's diagnosis wasn't one of them – I genuinely didn't feel it was affecting my work. In hindsight, though, it's possible that somewhere at the back of my mind was the thought that it might in the future, and that I'd better get on with other things I wanted to do while I could. No – the main reason I left was because in April, BBC management informed me and the rest of my colleagues working in technology news and on the *Click* programme that our jobs were being moved to Glasgow. For those who did not want to go or chance their arm bidding for a job in a different field in London, there was a reasonably generous voluntary redundancy deal, and nearly all of us took it. That was a really difficult time for younger people with kids at school, and I felt for them. As for me, after the initial shock, I quickly realised that this could be a good opportunity to try a few new things with the cushion of my pension and the redundancy payment.

But back to our beloved Cabbage, and the series of events that November which would catapult her to online fame. While Diane and I walked her morning and evening, we had for a couple of years employed a dog walker to take her out in the middle of the day. Brett was an ebullient South African who would collect half a dozen dogs in his shiny new Ford Transit van and take them off for a two-hour romp on Wormwood Scrubs or some other West London open space. One Friday morning I was at the home of a veteran television director – talking to him about the BBC drama department in the 1950s for a memoir I was writing about my family history – when my phone rang.

It was Diane – she was at an economics conference when she'd received a panicky call from Brett to tell her that Cabbage had been stolen. It was a confused tale. It seemed that Brett had stopped for some reason to knock on a door, then turned around to see the van, with the dogs in it, disappearing into the distance. At first Diane and I were dumbstruck, then distraught. It immediately seemed likely to me that we would never see our lovely dog again. She was worth nothing to anyone but us and if her kidnappers were only interested in the van, they might dump her and the other dogs in the middle of a busy road or find some way of doing them mischief. That thought was unbearable – Cabbage was more than a pet, she was part of our family.

I apologised to the TV director and rushed out to my car to drive home, my mind racing, my heart beating so fast that I felt ill. But as I put the key in the ignition, I stopped, and thought about what was most urgent if we were to have a hope of getting our beloved pet back – telling the world. A decade ago, that would have meant printing leaflets and sticking them to trees – now it meant mobilising a social media crowd which cared deeply about dogs. So, as I sat behind the wheel, I composed a tweet: 'Something terrible has happened. Our dog walker's van with our dog Cabbage in it has been stolen while he was picking up another pet. Please look out for a black Ford Transit reg XXXX YYY. Take a photo and DM me or just ring the police.'

Now I soon learned the tweet was not entirely accurate – it turned out that Brett hadn't been picking up another dog but had stopped at a relative's house in Acton to see if she wanted to help walk the dogs, foolishly leaving the key in the ignition. But the reaction was instant, with thousands of people retweeting the message or getting the news out on other platforms, some even creating 'Missing' posters with photos of the dogs.

'Save Cabbage!' the cry went up, and messages poured in from people I knew and many I didn't. 'Rory I'm so sorry. I feel like we all know Cabbage from your daily walks. Wishing everything for a speedy return xxx,' wrote the novelist JoJo Moyes. As I drove home, I heard my friend the broadcaster Adrian Chiles doing his show on BBC Radio 5 Live. I stopped the car and sent him a WhatsApp message. Half an hour later, I was sitting at my kitchen table, listening to Adrian close his show with a brief mention that our dog had been stolen.

Next, I spoke to Brett who by now had teamed up with the owner of one of the other stolen dogs. In her car they were combing the streets of Acton, trying to spot the van. That sounded a hopeless task – surely it would be miles away by now – but, feeling helpless myself, I understood their need to do something, anything. Soon, Diane came home, and sat playing endless games of Solitaire on her computer, as we both silently wondered if we would ever see Cabbage again.

By now, I was taking calls from newspapers, TV and radio stations – this was becoming a big story. Then there was a knock at the door – an enterprising young reporter from the *Daily Telegraph* had decided to turn up at our house. Admiring her persistence, I invited her in, talked her through the story and made her a cup of tea. Then she asked whether I could put her in touch with Brett. I said I wasn't sure he would want to talk but when I got him on the phone, he was only too eager to help, perhaps wanting to make amends for having left the van unattended. Soon, he and the dog owner were dropping by to pick up the reporter so she could join the hunt.

As darkness began to fall, we started to lose hope. I googled the statistics on the growing crime of dog theft, and they were not encouraging. Less than a quarter of the nearly 1,700 dogs stolen in 2020 had been returned to their owners. Some breeds were fetching record sums, with Covid lockdowns making dogs desirable. At first, we had assumed that this was an opportunistic theft of quite a valuable van, with the thieves then startled to find they had acquired half a dozen dogs too. But then we became aware that sitting up front in the passenger seat had been Bafi, a cockapoo. This cross between a Poodle and a Cocker Spaniel can fetch as much as £2,000 on sites like Gumtree.

Late in the afternoon I was contacted by Ford's UK press office. They had spotted the hullabaloo on social media and wanted to let Brett know that his Transit van was modern enough to have a feature allowing him to track it using a smartphone app. Brett, still scouring the Acton area with the pet owner and the *Telegraph* reporter, said he knew about the app but had forgotten his password. Once he had managed to get a new one, bingo – he was sent details of a location for the van. Just as I was preparing to talk to Radio 4 and then ITV London news, I got a text from Brett, saying they were heading for Park Royal, one of London's few industrial zones and just ten minutes from where the van was stolen. 'Be careful,' I texted back and switched my phone off for the broadcasts.

Twenty minutes later I switched it back on, expecting to find a message. There was nothing and eventually we called Brett. The news wasn't good – they had found no sign of the van or the dogs. Gloom descended once more.

Then quite suddenly, just before 7 pm, everything changed. First Brett called again to say the app had suddenly updated and given him a new location for the van, a mile or so from the first one. Then Diane's phone rang. It was a man telling her that he had come across a number of dogs wandering along a residential street in Park Royal, and one of them had a tag on its collar with the mobile number he had just rung.

We leapt into our car and headed through the Friday night traffic for the address he gave us just off the Hanger Lane roundabout a couple of miles from our house. I still could not quite believe the nightmare was over until I saw our dog, safe and well. By the time we got there the caller had gone, having handed over the dogs to Brett who had headed there after we alerted him. There in the back of the car which had led the hunt sat four dogs including Cabbage, all of them looking slightly confused. A fifth soon turned up – but there was no sign of Bafi the cockapoo.

We took our bewildered old dog, posed briefly for a photograph for the *Telegraph* reporter who had got her scoop, and headed home. There, Cabbage munched up some sausages and drank what seemed like a gallon of water but seemed none the worse for her ordeal. I tweeted a picture of her, captioned 'Cabbage is home!' which ended up getting 66,000 'likes', but I also appealed for people to look out for Bafi. Late that night came the excellent news that the cockapoo had been found, miles away across the river in Roehampton. Perhaps Bafi's captor had taken him there to sell, and then seen the social media firestorm and decided the dog was too hot to handle.

Over the weekend the man who had rung Diane's mobile got in touch with me. Vishal Patel had been walking his black Labrador Leo when he saw what he at first thought were two foxes crossing the road. 'I then realised they both had leads on so they were not foxes,' he said. 'And all of a sudden, a beagle came out of nowhere.' He told us that the dog, which he now knew to be Cabbage, had been friendly but looked very anxious: 'Her tail was between her legs.' He had noticed the dog tag on her collar and called the number on it, at first getting no answer and then trying again. Thank goodness . . .

So presumably, I asked him, he had heard about the missing dogs on social media that afternoon? 'No, nothing at all,' he said, despite being on both Twitter and Instagram. He'd been out for a long time with his own dog and was just thinking of getting them both something to eat. It was a useful reminder that social media may be powerful, but a Good Samaritan like Vishal – who does not walk on by when they see a person or animal in trouble – is even more valuable.

Autumn became winter and while Cabbage's ordeal made her a bit of a celebrity, and we were occasionally greeted on our walks by admirers, things soon returned to normal. Well, not quite – she seemed even slower and more frail than before and some mornings we turned around only a few hundred metres up the tree-lined avenue to the park and headed back home. Still, as my photos show, she remained an integral part of our family Christmas, lying on the rug surrounded by wrapping paper or in her favourite spot on the sofa, just about tolerating the exuberant affections of our two-year-old granddaughter.

I got my first bout of Covid just after Christmas 2021 and had to isolate for a week. I resumed our walks on dark and murky January mornings, but then midway through the month Cabbage caught a gastroenteritis bug which seemed to be affecting many dogs, with outbreaks across the country. Our vet warned that although the bug usually responded to treatment, for a dog as old as ours any illness could be dangerous. Having been cheerful until recently, Cabbage – now deaf and blind – was put on a drip, and with the vet's surgery too busy to accommodate her, she was sent to a nearby animal hospital to spend a couple of nights under observation.

She seemed a little better when we picked her up, but back home she went off her food, rejecting even sausages. After a few days of illness, things turned from worrying to alarming and I began to feel that mixture of fear and irritation one experiences while caring for an ailing elderly relative. One evening, with

Diane away from home, I found myself near to tears, shouting, 'Just eat the bloody sausage . . . *Please*!' At this point Cabbage needed carrying upstairs and down, and her back legs kept giving way when she tried to stand. Worst of all, she seemed miserable, finding no joy in life any more.

So, one Friday morning in January we carried her ever so carefully out of the front door, placed her on the back seat of the car and set off on a journey, knowing that she was unlikely to return home with us. At the surgery, we had a conversation with the extremely sympathetic vet who knew Cabbage well. She made it clear that, while there was no immediate threat to her life, her condition was unlikely to improve. We decided it was time to let her go and sat on the floor stroking her as she quietly slipped away.

Chapter Three

Stay-at-Home Dad

'The one absolutely unselfish friend that a man can have in this selfish world – the one that never deserts him and the one that never proves ungrateful or treacherous – is his dog.'

George Graham Vest

It took us a long time to get over the loss of Cabbage and think about getting another dog. Every morning there was a reminder for me of our loss when I instinctively headed for the front door for the first walk, only to realise I would be on my own. The thing about trying to keep up the old routine but now without Cabbage at my side was that it only served to make me more keenly aware than ever that she was gone. Taking the same route around the park, retracing our steps of old, meeting the other dog walkers we used to pass the time of day with – all of it made me long for her reliable presence and companionship even more, especially in the early months.

On those first forays on my own, when I crossed paths with those familiar faces, they were resoundingly kind and sympathetic – 'So sorry to hear you lost your pup,' the American intoned with concern, while Julie and Luna made a point of stopping each time they saw me for longer than they would have previously, just to commiserate about Cabbage and check in to see how I was doing. But even though I knew they understood very well, it felt like I was somehow no longer of their number or part of the club. Which of course I wasn't. And so within a couple of months, I had given up on the early outing and no longer met or had regular chats with other dogwalkers.

As the spring of 2022 made way for the summer months, both Diane and I were doing our best to adjust to life without Cabbage. But it wasn't easy – she'd been such an integral part of our everyday world, and such a key presence in our home. Diane kept finding reminders of her around the house even after we had thrown out her bed, leads and feeding bowls, and each time her eyes would fill with tears. Friends with dogs or cats understood our grief but I sensed others did not really get it – just as I would have been sceptical myself, before Cabbage taught me how close a bond you can have with a pet and how painful it is to lose them.

Archaeology suggests that the relationship between humans and dogs goes back over 15,000 years. In 1914, in Germany, the earliest remains of a dog were discovered buried alongside two humans, although at first the bones were thought to be of a wolf. It was not until the 1970s that researchers concluded that it was a dog and that the humans must have kept it as a pet. The remains showed signs of the dog having suffered canine distemper – a serious and often fatal viral illness – for a period before its death, so its owners must have kept it alive even when it was of no practical use.

Of course, until modern times most dogs were kept as working animals rather than pets, but the idea of a special bond goes way back. In Homer's *Odyssey* it is only his beloved dog Argos that recognises Odysseus when he returns from his travels. In Victorian times the idea of a unique bond between dogs and humans really took hold, reflected in stories like that of Greyfriars Bobby, a Skye Terrier which reputedly spent fourteen years guarding the Edinburgh grave of his owner. In the United States a courtroom speech in 1870 by a lawyer, George Vest, representing a farmer whose dog had been shot, included one of the most quoted sentences in legal history: 'The one absolutely unselfish friend that a man can have in this selfish world – the one that never deserts him and the one that never proves ungrateful or treacherous – is his dog.'

It was only in the twentieth century that scientists showed that the idea of a unique bond had some validity, as we will hear later on. Until recently, it was commonly assumed that it was vital for the human to be 'top dog' in the relationship, imposing their will on the inferior creature and punishing any disobedience. Over the last thirty years, mainstream dog behaviourists have moved away from that view, urging dog owners to use rewards rather than punishment in training, aiming for a friendship built on love rather than fear.

While I was always clear that I wanted another dog, for a few months after we lost Cabbage poor Diane began to well up every time we talked about the subject. Besides, her university work meant she travelled a lot, often to the United States, and if we were going to get a new dog, she wanted to be home for a good stretch to help bed it in. I should explain here, however, that with this pet it was going to be my turn to stay home and look after the new family member. I owed that to Diane. After all, in the early years of our marriage she put her career on hold for three years to look after our first child. When we met I was a TV reporter for the BBC in Wales and, having completed a PhD at Harvard, she was two years into a job as an economist for a research company in London. While I began competing for and eventually got a BBC reporting job in London, she decided that she too would like to try a career in journalism.

When our son was born, she had a good job as a reporter on the *Investors Chronicle*, known to be a great training ground for financial journalists on what we still called Fleet Street. But she chucked in the job so that she could combine doing freelance work from home with looking after our baby boy. I took only a few days' paternity leave before heading off on assignment in Ireland for *The Money Programme*, the first of many overseas trips in the first couple of years of our baby's life.

Diane told me later that she found being a stay-at-home mum both lonely and tedious. 'I thought my brain was turning to mush – I would write down things I heard on the radio, so that I would have something interesting to say to you when you came home from your glamorous job.' But when she did return to work with a job on the City pages of the *Independent*, her career took off like a rocket. Within three years she was the paper's Economics Editor, earning more than I was. Later, after just a brief pause to have our second child, she started her own economics consultancy and was appointed to the BBC Trust, the corporation's governing body, rising to become Vice Chairman. After that, as one of the UK's most prominent economists, she was recruited first by Manchester University then Cambridge as a professor.

Now, the roles are going to be reversed – I'm going to stay at home looking after the youngest member of the family, our new rescue dog, and Diane has a hugely busy job which often takes her abroad. But in this hyper-connected world I am going to be able to combine dog-sitting with podcasting, writing and all sorts of other activities in a way that was not available to Diane in the early 1990s. And what I was expecting to be just a moderately busy retirement has quickly evolved into far more than that.

After I left the BBC, by autumn 2021 I had four days a month working as a consultant for two PR companies, I had started a newsletter combining my interests in health and technology and I was trying to get a contract to write a memoir based on the thousands of letters my mother left behind for me when she died. Just a year later, I had found a publisher for the book, signed the contract and had a tight deadline to get the first draft written. I'd also taken on a monthly podcast for my wife's Bennett Institute at Cambridge, a regular column for the *Which Computing* magazine, and the occasional piece of journalism for *The Times*. So I was quite busy enough – and then another project began to evolve which would in time become very exciting and threaten to crowd out almost everything else.

In late 2020, a year after I had 'come out' about my Parkinson's, I got a call from Edward Stourton, the very distinguished BBC broadcaster and a man I barely knew. He wanted me to meet a man he described as his oldest friend, who had recently been diagnosed with Parkinson's and was in a really bad way. So it was that, when lockdowns permitted, I found myself sitting in a Chelsea pub with Sir Nicholas Mostyn, a High Court judge. While his symptoms included nightmares and hallucinations which were seriously affecting his sleep, he did not seem to be in a particularly bad way. In fact, Nick, who was to become a good friend, is one of the most ebullient and optimistic people you could hope to meet, determined not to let Parkinson's get him down.

Over the next eighteen months we started meeting regularly in the pub and a few days before our third meeting, Nick called me and asked, 'Do you mind if I bring Jeremy Paxman along too?' I gulped and said that was fine – while I had worked on the same programmes as Jeremy a few times, I did not know him and was rather in awe of 'the Grand Inquisitor' who had recently revealed his own Parkinson's diagnosis. I assumed that he and Nick were old pals but it soon emerged that the ever-confident judge had just phoned him on spec.

Jeremy turned out to be good company, far more gentle and amiable than I had imagined, although he was understandably depressed by the severity of his symptoms. 'I keep on falling over,' he told us sadly. By early 2022 we'd taken to meeting in his local pub in Notting Hill, Paxman often arriving accompanied by his dog, a Springer Spaniel called Derek with a sweet temperament, acquired from Battersea Dogs Home. I would sit stroking her and find myself thinking about how much I missed Cabbage.

We were soon joined by others in what the judge began to refer to as our 'support bubble'. Jeremy brought along the comedy scriptwriter Paul Mayhew-Archer – a lovely man as upbeat about his Parkinson's as Paxman was gloomy. Then there was Gillian Lacey-Solymar, a former broadcaster, academic and businesswoman both Jeremy and I had worked with years ago at the BBC. Still in her fifties at the time, she was the youngest of our group but the one who had been living with Parkinson's the longest and whose symptoms were proving so debilitating she had agreed to the major surgery involved in placing a DBS (Deep Brain Stimulation) unit inside her brain. And finally I brought along Mark Mardell, the recently retired BBC foreign correspondent and presenter of programmes such as *The World This Weekend*. Mark was the most recently diagnosed of us but, cruelly, his main symptom was a severe weakening of his voice, his most important professional tool.

Very early on, when there were just four of us, Judge Nick began to talk of turning our bubble into the basis for a book. '*Four Men in A Boat*, we could call it,' he said to the bemusement of us all and a withering verdict from Jeremy Paxman: 'Worst idea ever.' Undaunted, Nick suggested we look instead at starting a podcast and kept badgering us about this idea. Knowing a bit about podcasting – but pretty sure this one would never happen – I agreed to help him research how to go about it. So this was another project which was just beginning to take off and would soon become both exciting and highly absorbing.

In November 2022 Diane and I decided we were at last ready to start looking for a new dog – our hope was that we might be able to welcome it into our home by that Christmas. We signed up to a number of British rescue organisations including Dogs Trust, where we had got Cabbage back in 2007. But as we scrolled through their lists of dogs online, we struggled to find many that we felt drawn to and could see in our home. There seemed to be dozens of 'Staffies' – we were, however, perhaps unfairly, prejudiced against them – and the organisations seemed determined to put us off many of their other dogs with warning labels. 'This dog must be muzzled on walks', 'This dog is not comfortable with children,' or even, 'This dog cannot live in a home where there are frequent visitors.'

I decided that the next step would be to sound out Battersea Cats and Dogs Trust, the best-known of the many rescue organisations in the UK, which do a vital job of taking in unwanted or abandoned pets and finding them new homes. I had a long phone call with a very sympathetic woman at Battersea. But while I had heard news reports saying that record numbers of dogs had been abandoned as lockdown restrictions eased and people tired of the pets they had acquired when forced to stay at home, she told a different story. They had 25,000 people on their waiting list and new dogs were being snapped up like Glastonbury tickets the moment they were listed. We did apply for one dog but were told it had already gone and in any case the animal did not like men, so could not have been given to us.

For the first time in fifteen years, we went in person to the Dogs Trust rescue centre at Harefield to see what was on offer. The answer was – not much. Only around half a dozen dogs, many of them Staffies, did not have 'reserved' labels next to their pens. Some months later, I spoke to Adam Clowes, operations director for Dogs Trust, and he gave me a pretty convincing story about why it is tough to find a UK rescue dog. His organisation cares for around 14,000 dogs a year, finding homes for 11–12,000 of them – sadly some dogs never find people willing to adopt them. But while at any one time there may be 2,000 dogs in its rescue centres, there will be around seven people looking for each one.

The trouble, he explained, is that once people decide to get a dog, they want to have it within four to six weeks. They often have pretty fixed ideas about the kind of dog they want – if they have had a Collie before, they want one again – but the charity knows that every dog is different and works hard to fit the right one to the right owner. 'If the rescue home doesn't have the type of dog you want within those four to six weeks, then that's when we start seeing that people start to look elsewhere.'

That was us – looking back, I can see how impatient we were. We were beginning to despair when I ran into Sadaf, a neighbour and former BBC News colleague, on the street. She had with her a charming little Terrier with an injured front paw which didn't seem to slow her down too much as she hopped, skipped and jumped along the pavement. 'Cookie, wait,' Sadaf ordered, as the dog seemed eager to continue the walk.

When I told her of the problems we were having finding a

new dog, she told me that Cookie had come from Romania. Before we got Cabbage, I might have laughed at the Terrier's name, and wondered why anyone would go to the trouble of importing a disabled dog from far away. Now I got it though, and felt both envious of Sadaf's obvious connection with Cookie and excited to find out more about how she had found her.

Sadaf had nothing but praise for the organisation which had brought her dog to the UK, a charity called Friends Indeed. Sadaf explained that it had been set up by a Romanian couple who had settled near Peterborough about twenty years ago, and they were passionate about their mission to save dogs and give them loving homes in the UK. This was no fly-by-night organisation, Sadaf insisted, the couple had really integrated into British life. Their daughter was now a deputy head teacher at a primary school and had married a policeman. What is more, they wanted an ongoing relationship with the new owners of their dogs and she had even paid them a visit with Cookie, leaving the dog in their care for a couple of hours while she went on a work assignment nearby.

I went home and had a look at some of the dogs Friends Indeed was advertising online. This was more like it – they'd all had a tough start in life but they were eager for a new beginning, with no nonsense about being intolerant of men or hating visitors. Typically, the ads would describe them as, 'a lovely boy for a loving home', or, 'a beautiful and kind girl looking for a forever home'. I called Adrian, the owner of Friends Indeed, and he explained how it worked and that if we did not get on with the dog we chose, the charity would take it back. All very reassuring.

So I sent Diane a link to some of the dogs on offer and she emailed back from Cambridge with her choices: 'Max, Ella, Jack, Molly, Seven, Lassie – Lassie was the name of my childhood dog'. Then, later: 'Seven looks lovely . . .' So we settled on Seven, renamed her Sophie, and on 17 December our 'loving and kind girl' arrived in her new home. It did not take us long to find out that she was a lot more complicated than the advert had suggested and that we were going to need some professional help. Lots of it.

Chapter Four

The Dog Whisperer

Canine Psychology 101

'There's no such thing as "too slow" with classical conditioning . . .'

Si Wooler

By now, I am beginning to understand just how beautiful a dog we have living with us. Diane has said that from the first day, but I've been less sure, perhaps because Sophie is obviously part German Shepherd – or Alsatian as we had called them when I was growing up. As a boy, it's a breed I had always associated with aggression, after seeing news reports showing such dogs deployed by police to control protests in America's Deep South or in apartheid South Africa. But there is no aggression in Sophie, just fear in those liquid brown eyes coupled with a look in that beautiful face that says, 'Please be kind to me.' It is her ears, however, that have won me over, along with a legion of online fans. Often they are the first we see of her in the morning – those distinctive furry triangles peeping out from behind the red sofa. Her hearing seems to be her primary sense and those ears are in constant motion, scanning the horizon for any sound that might pose a threat – even a relatively quiet, harmless noise like me dropping a newspaper too suddenly on the kitchen table sends her scurrying back to her safe place.

It's the beginning of January 2023, three weeks since Sophie's arrival in our home, and it's becoming clear that she's going to be spending a lot more time in her safe place behind the sofa than we could possibly have imagined. Our hopes – that relatively quickly she would come through the understandably disorienting experience of arriving in a strange house with strange people after three days locked in a van, and begin to settle in – have faded. Instead, there are entire days when she doesn't break cover at all, even to eat or drink, and certainly not to pee or poo on the puppy pads which still cover the floor in her immediate vicinity. It's so difficult to know what we should do and even Diane admits that it's all very worrying. The only positive thing however is that we are not alone in this ordeal – a man called Si is with us every step of the way.

Almost from the day Sophie arrived, people were giving us advice. Some of this came from well-meaning friends – 'Oh, I am sure if you just put a lead on her and tell her she's going for a walk, it'll be fine' – but the vast majority of it was from the thousands now following her on social media. Many were very kind, often from people wanting to share their own experiences: 'As a serial adopter I can attest that the first two weeks are always the hardest, and it's at exactly the point when you think, "I can't do this" that then things get better – every time.' Or: 'Has anyone suggested you put something that you have worn in beside her? As long as you don't mind not getting it back, it may calm her . . . '; or then again: 'Does Sophie like smooth liver paté? If so, maybe spread some on the tips of your fingers to encourage her to physically connect with you for a bit longer than just the time it takes for her to quickly snatch a piece of cheese out of your hand?'

Hmm, I'm not so sure I want to smother myself in liver paté – or peanut butter, as someone else suggested. But we did try putting my old Wales rugby shirt in the safe place behind the sofa – however It didn't seem to make the dog any more comfortable in my presence.

Meanwhile, quite a few people were sending us private messages offering their suggestions and advice, some claiming to be experts in the field of canine behaviour. While we greatly appreciated everyone's efforts, it was all becoming very confusing because everyone seemed to have a different view on the best way forward. But very quickly we zeroed in on one man.

Si Wooler got in touch via Twitter Direct Message on 23 December 2022, just six days after Sophie's arrival. A qualified dog trainer and behaviour consultant – he provided some details of his professional credentials – he said he'd be more than happy to jump on a Zoom call with us some time (without obligation or fee) if it would be helpful, as he had some tried and tested strategies we could try with Sophie. He then rather diplomatically said that while I was getting some good advice on Twitter, some of it was wide of the mark.

When I replied, thanking him for his kind offer, Si came back quickly and in the exchange of messages we then had, he offered some really interesting initial insights. 'With fear and anxiety cases it's important to keep dogs like Sophie under their fear threshold. That means going at their pace rather than trying to push progress . . .' Some of the key techniques he used, he explained, involved Pavlovian conditioning, 'Making positive associations between the scary thing and something the dog already likes such as a favourite food.' This is apparently very different from the idea of rewarding an animal for good behaviour because in this case, the only thing that triggers the reward is the presence of the scary thing or situation. 'This might seem counterintuitive because people often think that by introducing the treat at this time, you are "reinforcing" the fear but this isn't how it works.'

As far as Sophie was concerned, his suggested approach would be to allow Sophie her safe space behind the sofa and wait for her to make a move – then and only then would be the time to offer her some tasty treats, always from a distance, however, even by simply throwing them in her general direction. 'As you help Sophie form a positive association between you being around and the good stuff being produced, her anxiety will subside.' Si summed up by warning that changing a Romanian rescue dog's behaviour can take time but offered some much-needed encouragement: 'You're doing a great job.'

Well, this seemed like a plan based on expertise and while we didn't understand all the terminology we decided we liked the cut of his jib. So the next morning we got on a Zoom call with Si – the first of many over the next year – and began to get to know him. It turned out that he was living in Portsoy on the Aberdeenshire coast in a cottage overlooking the beach. He and his partner Nina had moved there from Wiltshire in 2021, and he did much of his work as a dog behaviourist remotely.

In the course of that conversation Si would explain that he had spent much of his working life as a sound engineer, hired for rock gigs and conferences. His change of career happened after he acquired a dog from an RSPCA shelter in Bath: 'He was a Rottweiler with all manner of issues. He was scared of people. He was scared of dogs. He was scared of plastic bags drifting across the road. But he exhibited that fear in aggressive behaviour.' Si also thought the dog's name, Tyson, was a problem. 'I think it was just the thing that you called Rottweilers at the time. I imagine it was because of Mike Tyson, a boxer, and given that he had a reputation for biting people's ears off I didn't think it was a very good image for a dog that was already troubled enough as it was.' Instead, he opted for Thompson, a name near enough to what the dog had been accustomed to hearing but without the ear-biting connotations.

Next, Si decided he needed to find out what he could do to help the dog but was unimpressed with the methods he found: 'A lot of them are about applying punishment, and it didn't sit well with me.' But then he found an online course run by US psychologist Jean Donaldson, who had spent years as the lead behaviour consultant for San Francisco's Society for the Prevention of Cruelty to Animals. He became one of the first students on her two-year course: 'It was a degree-level kind of course, and it involved a lot of video submission. You were also sent a lot of video demos to watch – huge numbers of really scientifically based webinars that were all about behaviour and how it functions.' By 2014 he was ready to put all he had learned into practice as a behaviour consultant, specialising in aggressive or fearful dogs.

By the end of that first Christmas Eve Zoom call, we felt we could put our trust in Si Wooler to show us the way forward. While he thought it was possible that Sophie just needed to decompress after her long journey, his key message was that we needed to go at her pace, rather than trying to hurry her. That doesn't sound too bad, I thought, I can be patient if it's just for a few weeks.

Si, Diane and I set up a Sophie WhatsApp group, where he gave us advice almost daily. It was a huge comfort to be able to share our questions and concerns with someone so sympathetic and knowledgeable. Si was also an ally as a close observer of our social media accounts, and the comments, genuinely well-meaning or otherwise, which flooded in with every update about Sophie. Much later, he'd tell me that, as he and his partner Nina took it in turn to carefully monitor the online feed, they'd come up with a game they called 'Sophie Buzzword Bingo', with points being awarded for the most popular suggestions. These included: 'learn to speak Romanian'; 'get down on the floor at her level'; 'introduce another dog', and so on.

From the start, he was keen to dissuade us from following the advice of those who wanted us to move faster: 'A quick tip regarding the suggestions to drop the food further into the room: resist. If Sophie is doing commando strikes to get the food and then dashing back, she isn't ready for the bigger step.' He started sending us quite detailed instructions on how to use food to change Sophie's behaviour:

'Goal: To get Sophie comfortable with being closer to you and further away from her safe place (but in tiny incremental steps) by reliably associating you with good things.

'Procedure: Station yourself on a chair at a distance that Sophie seems comfortable with and wait for her to appear. When she does, throw some treats aiming for them to land close to her. Continue to do this (throwing each time to roughly the same distance from her) until you see some sign that she is anticipating the next throw – looking at you or at the treat source are the most likely. Throw the next treat a little closer to you and further away from her. Repeat this until you see the same response as before.'

When I was slow to understand the theory behind his methods, Si would always take me back to the story of Pavlov's dogs. Every time they were due to be fed, the Russian scientist rang a bell immediately before the food appeared: he did this so consistently over time, that eventually the dogs would salivate at the mere sound of the bell, before they sighted the food. In the same way, he explained, he wanted Sophie to start to associate us – potentially scary things – with the appearance of good things, in the form of tasty snacks. It was what he called 'classical conditioning'. Any time he mentioned this strategy, he always followed up by repeating the same line: 'There's no such thing as "too slow" with classical conditioning . . .'

From the off, there was something about this mantra that made me feel uneasy. No such thing as too slow? That's not exactly music to the ears of a famously impatient man. Weeks, ok. Months, maybe. But years? That's too slow – for me, at any rate.

Because now, my sense of urgency isn't just about me being me – the man who in the later years of his BBC career was often barred by his producer from a TV news edit suite, on the grounds that he was making everyone nervous. I couldn't stand how, when we were cutting a report for the next news bulletin and there were just minutes to go before we were due on air, the editor would endlessly faff around trying to get one shot change just right, or even worse, trying to engage me with their views on technology. '*Can we just get on with it!*' I'd urged on more than one occasion at two minutes to 6 o'clock when ours was the first report on the programme.

No, now my need for things to happen quickly on the Sophie front comes down to this: I am a man in his mid-sixties with a degenerative brain disease and even though for the moment I am coping well and doing lots of interesting new things after leaving the BBC, who knows what I will be like a year from now? Will I even be up to walking a vigorous young dog?

But Si is able to soothe my fears with some very heartening words: 'I know how important it is for you to be out and about with her. I'm increasingly confident we'll get there sooner rather than later. In cases like this you tend to see significant progress just as you are beginning to lose hope . . . Hang in there and give her the space to make her own choices. You're doing better than you might imagine.'

Okay – we can do this. We'll certainly give it our very best shot.

Among the many people who contacted us right from the very start of our time with Sophie were those who had faced similar experiences with Romanian rescue dogs. It was always enormously comforting to talk to them and realise that we were not alone as we navigated life with a deeply anxious dog. That's why I made it my mission at an early stage to find out more about some of these 'Rommie' owners and their dogs, and to share their stories. The first of these stories is a tale with the happy ending we are all seeking when we get a new dog.

ZOE FROM ROMANIA

Jane and her partner, Neil, applied to adopt Zoe (then named Meadow), a Husky cross, through a rescue charity in December 2020 but had to wait for some months for Covid restrictions in the UK to be lifted before being able to collect her at a Maidstone service station. By the time they got her she was a year and ten months old. As Jane recalls, 'We had no idea what state she would be in, or what her temperament would be like.'

Zoe had had a traumatic life – first living as a street dog, then ending up in the kill shelter from which she was rescued. 'For the first week after she arrived, either my son Alex or I slept on the sofa to be with her during the night. For the first forty-eight hours she whined almost constantly and was obviously very nervous and badly needed reassurance. She also smelt horrible.'

Fairly quickly after her arrival, Zoe needed an operation when the scar from a sterilisation procedure in Romania became infected. This meant she had to wear a cone for ten days, which she hated. 'She wanted lots of attention and stroking, and still does,' Jane tells me.

'And she wasn't trained at all. So we gradually trained her to do her business outside, and to sit, each time giving her rewards afterwards.'

Having been warned by the charity that Romanian rescue dogs will try to escape, Jane's partner Neil fitted a child gate in the hall and they only let Zoe off the leash in fenced dog parks, which was 'very frustrating for everyone'. Having also heard that huskies have a reputation for stubbornness, they tried recall training in a safe dog park. 'But she wasn't that interested and the only thing that seemed to work occasionally was giving her chopped up frankfurters as a reward. Zoe disembowelled numerous soft dog toys at home and we finally settled on giving her antlers (naturally shed antlers which you can buy online) to chew, to let off some energy.'

Two-and-a-half years on, Zoe is allowed to run free in certain open spaces well away from roads: 'She mostly comes back, enticed by high-value treats.' According to Jane, much of the secret to managing their rescue dog has been for her to focus on building up her own courage and trying to take her partner's advice not to be so afraid of Zoe escaping.

At this point, Zoe loves running around and playing with other dogs her own size. But she knows when to back off and is very gentle with dogs that are shy. She'll happily chase everything from cats to squirrels and even birds in flight – but when she comes back home after a run or a play, she doesn't like too much stimulation and wants to curl up for a sleep on her bed. When on the lead, she'll bark a little at certain dogs but not others. According to Jane, the only other time she barks – and it's only one bark – is when people come to their door.

'Zoe is still very frightened of bins, lorries, vans, kids' scooters and, for some reason, tall, dark-haired men. She cowers when any of those pass us by, and needs reassurance . . . On the other hand, she loves the attention of children who come up and ask to meet her. Meanwhile at home she still needs lots of reassurance and stroking – and she gets very jealous when we are on the phone and demands attention.'

Jane concludes by saying that while it has been a slow process, it has been a very rewarding one too: 'All in all Zoe is now a happy and contented dog.' She tells me Zoe looks very much like Sophie. I can only hope that if we show as much patience as Jane and her family, we will be able to achieve similar results.

It's now the second weekend in January and as I wake on the Sunday morning, I am not in a good way. For one thing, it is 4 am and I know I am not getting back to sleep. For another, my heart is racing and I'm feeling truly apprehensive. I have no idea what I will find when I go downstairs and open the door into what I am coming to think of as Sophie's room. Despite my best efforts to stay calm and relax, by 5 am I can bear it no longer and go downstairs.

I open the door to the kitchen and find . . . nothing. The food bowl is untouched, the rug and the puppy pads are clean, and Sophie is still behind the sofa. By my calculations she has now been there for thirty-six hours – without eating or drinking anything. I wait until a slightly more civilised hour and send Si a WhatsApp – when he replies, for the first time ever he sounds worried himself. She could be ill, he says, and if that is the case we'll have to get her to the vet: 'Never mind the training regime, the animal's health comes first.'

In the late afternoon, we put yet another a bowl of fresh food next to the entrance to her sofa den, taking the untouched one away. After a while Sophie pokes her nose out cautiously and scoffs the lot before retreating out of sight again. Phew! Though at some stage surely that has got to come out of the other end.

I have another very poor night's sleep, waking at 4 am again, worrying this time about how on earth I will get Sophie into the car to take her to the vet if that proves necessary. Diane's alarm goes off at 5.15 am – after the holidays she is back in her normal routine, heading off to Cambridge until Wednesday evening, leaving me alone with Sophie until then. When I come downstairs soon after 6 am, I feel something close to despair when I check and realise that nothing has changed – the dog is still behind the sofa, with no evidence that she has been out overnight.

At 8 am, I'm sitting at the kitchen table eating bacon and eggs – food has always been my way of coping – when Sophie slinks into view, does a circuit of the kitchen and then circles back behind the living room sofa. My view is obscured by the wall which still acts as a divider in the middle of our knocked-through kitchen-living room but it's not long before I hear that she has come out again and there's a slight scrabbling noise coming from the puppy pads on top of the rug. For ten minutes I sit absolutely motionless and silent, trying to interpret the sounds coming from the other side of the wall. Then, hearing her depart I go and take a look. I almost punch the air – never has anybody been so pleased to see a pile of poo and a lake of pee! I clean up cheerfully, whistling as I work in the knowledge that the immediate crisis is over.

That afternoon I have a long Zoom call with Susan, head of the dog behaviour team at the Dogs Trust, the rescue organisation where we got Cabbage. While we are happy with the advice from Si, we think it might be wise to get a second opinion. And while Si has in fact just promised to pop in to our house for a short time this Friday during a visit down South to see his mother, we can see the advantage of having an advisor based in London rather than 500 miles away.

What is really encouraging is that Susan agrees with just about everything Si has told us in terms of moving at Sophie's pace: 'The less-is-more approach is definitely the right one and it will help you achieve the results you want more quickly than trying to push her beyond her comfort zone.' Susan then outlines what one of her in-house dog behaviourists would do if we signed up for their services. The process would start with some initial consultations via Zoom, and then, once Sophie is a little more settled generally, they'd do one or more home visits to assess the best way forward and help us to identify three goals which we want to work on in the first instance – for example, getting her to go outside for her toilet needs, and so on. 'Our service is about helping you by helping Sophie to become the best that she can be, so that you can enjoy living together. We do that first and foremost by helping to build her confidence, so that she can become the kind of dog you would like to have.'

The services of a Dogs Trust behaviourist are not inexpensive by any means – the charity can't be seen to be undercutting the private sector. But when Diane and I talk about it that evening, we agree that it would be well worth it if we can end up with a Sophie I can take for a walk, or cuddle up with on the sofa watching TV on those nights when I am alone in the house. We then wonder whether having Si on WhatsApp and the Dogs Trust doing the occasional visit might be a good combination.

But when we later run this idea past Si, he makes it clear that it risks not really working – it's tricky to have two advisors, even if they hold similar views. He says that he does however completely understand our thinking, and is happy to withdraw if we decide we want to work with a Dogs Trust behaviourist, especially a locally-based one. This leaves us in a quandary. We have already developed a strong bond with Si, and he's available virtually 24/7 via WhatsApp to soothe our worries – and after all he is coming to see us that Friday. We end up deciding to stick with him for the moment and see how we get on.

On Wednesday evening that week I go to the BBC's Broadcasting House, my former work site, for the leaving do of Beaty Rubens, one of my oldest friends and a distinguished radio arts producer. The Council Chamber where the party is taking place is packed with admirers of Beaty from the arts world, including the classicist Mary Beard. But it seems that she and many others I speak to at the gathering have one subject alone on their mind – 'How is Sophie?' is what they all want to know. As I leave at 9 pm a familiar figure is standing outside Broadcasting House – it's George the *Big Issue* seller, who I'd often exchanged a few words with when leaving the building to head home after work. 'Hello Rory,' he calls now, 'How's Sophie?'

Meanwhile on social media, interest in her story continues to grow – since Sophie's arrival a couple of weeks prior, my Twitter followers are up 70,000, now totalling 280,000. Now, traditional media organisations also begin taking a keen interest in our dog, and not just in the UK. French and Italian newspapers both carry stories on the poor little rescue dog who is afraid of everything. 'Four weeks behind the sofa', says the headline in the *Corriere della Sera*, going on to describe her as 'the four-legged orphan'. And France's *La Voix du Nord* describes Sophie as, 'this dog rescued from the streets which fascinates British internet users'.

Soon after, my phone rings, and it is the BBC news presenter Sophie Raworth wanting to come and meet her namesake for a report for the *Six O'Clock News* on Friday. She explains that she – along with many of my other former colleagues in the newsroom – is obsessed with Sophie's story and convinced the nation wants to know all about it. I warn her that she is extremely unlikely to see the shyest dog on earth, while telling her that Friday isn't a bad day to come because the man I've taken to calling our 'dog whisperer' will be paying his first visit.

But on Thursday I wonder whether I have been over-cautious about our little Greta Garbo and her desire to avoid the limelight. While I'm out at a meeting in town, Sophie emerges, takes food from Diane's hand, puts her front paws up on the kitchen counter and practically demands a stroke. While she is much more cautious when I get home, this feels like another big leap forward.

Friday begins with an interview with the *Today* team, once a regular part of my morning routine when I brought the audience news of the latest cyberattack or advances in AI. Then I was often given an early slot just after 6 am and would be sitting in my pyjamas in the front room, having fired up the ancient broadcasting equipment I kept there. But today I am on in primetime at 7.45 am, telling the BBC's flagship news programme about a matter of global importance – the emotional state of our rescue dog.

While it is a radio interview, I am using the Zoom video conferencing system to communicate with Broadcasting House, propping my laptop up on the kitchen table with a view over my shoulder of the corner of the sofa, behind which of course Sophie is hiding. Just before they get to me, out she pops as if on cue, to 'oohs' and 'aahs' from the production team. Then throughout my interview with Amol Rajan and Nick Robinson, she stands there motionless as if she is aware that she's on camera. I tell the story of how we got her and then we speculate as to why she has proved to be such an internet and media sensation. My theory is that at a dark time – both literally and figuratively – in the depths of winter, with the Ukraine war grinding on and a cost-of-living crisis gathering pace, people are desperate for a bit of good news. And Sophie – we all hope – can provide it.

Around 10 am there is a gentle knock on the door which immediately sends Sophie back behind the sofa and Sophie Raworth, a producer and a cameraman have arrived. Shortly afterwards Si is on our doorstep, fresh from Gatwick Airport. I put everyone in our posh front room, away from the living room and kitchen where Sophie has her home. We need to come up with a plan which will result in a nice piece for the news without raising the dog's already sky-high anxiety levels.

The cameraman, Bhas Solanki, is a BBC veteran I have worked with many times – a calm, courteous man about as far from the sweary hard-drinking (and occasionally accurate) stereotype as you can imagine, but also someone who has spent much of his career covering wars and natural disasters. So I am somewhat embarrassed to have to ask him to be as sensitive as possible when filming our pet.

I have already managed to capture a lot of decent footage of Sophie on my phone and I've supplied this to the producer, along with some night-time shots from my 'nature-cam', so there isn't too much pressure – but I know Bhas will still be eager to capture some shots of his own. We creep into the kitchen and start in a low-key way, with Sophie Raworth interviewing me as I stand with my back to the now legendary sofa – whose reclusive resident inevitably stays put. Then there's an interview with Si, who turns out to be a TV natural – or at least that is my impression watching from the sidelines.

By now they have enough material for a decent news package, but they still want to get something of Sophie if possible. Bhas films me and Sophie Raworth peering over the back of the sofa, then gets one quick shot from the side looking at the dog while she stares back balefully. When he starts to go about getting some more shots, I tell him gently that I think the canine Sophie has had enough and he stops. The news team pack up their equipment and head off around noon.

Which leaves me and Diane, back home by this time, to get to know Si over lunch at the kitchen table. In the flesh he is just as calm a presence as down the line on Zoom, and we feel safe in his hands. What's more, the three of us seem to instantly feel comfortable in each other's company and the conversation flows in an easy and unstilted way. After we've eaten, Si has a couple of hours to spare before setting off to see his mother in Wiltshire – and so he gets to work with Sophie. He prepares some treats, small slices of sausage and cheese, then places a chair a few feet away from the entrance to her den and sits patiently, waiting for her to emerge. Two hours later, precisely nothing has happened – which is exactly what Si had predicted. We are impressed by his Zen-like composure, if slightly disappointed that our little diva has refused to grace any of our distinguished visitors today with her presence.

When the *Six O'Clock News* comes on, Diane and I are round at our son's house, watching with our grandchildren. Our four-year-old granddaughter is excited that her grandpa and the new dog she has yet to meet are on the television. Sophie's story is the last item and it has been given a generous amount of time. The other Sophie – Sophie Raworth – introduces the package standing in front of some of my photos of her namesake, then we see the story of her arrival at our house and her disappearance behind the sofa. I explain how important it is for me to go for a walk with my dog and my disappointment that this isn't happening – but go on to talk enthusiastically about the amazing interest in her online: 'It's like nothing I've ever experienced.'

Then Sophie Raworth asks Si how confident he is that everything will turn out well in the end. 'I'm very confident,' he says. 'It's not always the case with fearful dogs – you can't always be sure how far you're going to go with them. But looking at her lately, and knowing what we know about her I've got no doubt that she's going to be a smashing pet . . .'

Diane and I don't quite high-five each other but we are both immensely cheered by Si's prediction.

'Well, Sophie from London didn't really get to meet Sophie from Romania this time. It's going to be a slow, but hopefully successful journey,' is the newscaster's final line, after which we take the family to the pub across the road to celebrate. Scrolling through my feeds while sipping a pint of London Pride, it is clear that the piece has had a big impact – and again, one which extends well beyond this part of the world: 'Hello from Australia,' someone posts on Instagram, 'we just saw Sophie on the TV – beautiful!'

What a week it has been, starting with feelings of despair about our poor frightened dog, ending with real hope that we are turning a corner, cheered on by besotted fans around the globe. And over the weekend things are about to get even better.

Saturdays in our house are never an excuse for a lie-in. As part of my plan to control my Parkinson's symptoms through exercise, I took up Pilates a few months after my diagnosis. I managed to find a weekly class in our area being run on a Saturday at 8.15 am. Then mid-morning, piano teacher Theo comes to the house to give me and our daughter a lesson. When more than twenty-five years ago our son Adam started piano lessons, aged six, I decided that I would give it a go too, having never learned an instrument at school. Adam soon gave up but I have carried on ever since, acquiring Theo as a teacher about twenty years ago now. After getting as far as Grade 5, I decided not to pursue exams any further, given the serious daily practice that involves, but I continue to enjoy my weekly lessons where we discuss all manner of things and even try a little Chopin or a jazz piece.

All of which means Diane and I usually grab a light breakfast soon after 7 am, and on this Saturday too we stick to that routine. Sophie doesn't appear particularly lively though she does poke her nose out cautiously shortly before I leave the house. I find myself wondering, for at least the hundredth time, at how much of her time our star spends doing absolutely nothing – just snoozing behind the sofa and showing no interest in the outside world. But unbeknownst to me, today while I am out at Pilates, that is about to change . . .

The class is just a mile or so from home – I tell myself I'll cycle but usually end up just jumping into the car. I am the oldest there by about twenty years and often the only man. Still, it is always an experience I emerge from with a virtuous glow – even though I can't be sure it has any effect on my Parkinson's. After a quick warm-up, for the remaining fifty minutes the Pilates teacher will take us through a series of stretches and contortions which might look easy to the casual observer, but are surprisingly strenuous – as is confirmed by the sign on the wall above where she stands throughout the class: 'If it isn't hard, it isn't Pilates'.

About twenty minutes in, my phone pings. Sneaking a glance at the locked screen lying next to my mat, I can only see that it is a message from Diane, and I spend the rest of the class wondering, slightly anxiously, why she needs to contact me when I will be home within the hour.

The moment the class is over, I open the message – to find a photo of Sophie out in our back garden. Wow – this is a big moment! It's the first time she has been outside since that Saturday of her arrival just four weeks ago, when after breakfast she dug her heels in and refused to contemplate going for a walk with me. I have to bite my tongue to stop myself from sharing the news with the rest of the class, who are pretty much complete strangers and might look askance at the old guy staring at his phone, shouting 'My dog is in the garden!'

I rush home to find Sophie is now back indoors, but Diane gives me a full account of the earlier events. She explains that she opened the French doors to the garden on this chilly but bright January morning – just to give the dog a sniff of the fresh London air – and then, with very little hesitation, Sophie headed outside and began to get to know her new domain. Of course, for the rest of Saturday she is pretty quiet, as if to tell us not to get ahead of ourselves, but we are still bubbling with excitement. On social media, joy is unconfined – according to the app's metrics, Diane's tweet with the picture of Sophie in the garden is viewed by 1.6 million people.

But if we thought Saturday was good, Sunday is, as described in that day's entry in my dog diary, 'Huge!' Sophie comes out from behind the sofa during breakfast, circling back to her safe place repeatedly until she feels more confident, and then she hangs out in the kitchen with me while I make bread. Even better, aided by Diane's comforting presence, she allows me to stroke her properly for the first time, and then when I go into the back garden, she follows me out. She stops in the middle of the lawn to take her first outdoors dump – and yes, this time I do actually punch the air in delight.

Once more, this development is greeted with a wave of love and approval from our online community. The audience, who have followed Sophie for four weeks, have decided two things. Firstly, that they love what we are doing – by we, I mean me, Diane and Si – and secondly, that they think our approach is working. Someone on Twitter posts joyously with their theory about what is going on inside Sophie's head: 'Oh wow!!! It's like #sophiefromromania has finally thought: "Sod it, they're nice. I'll trust them. They pet me, feed me steak, use kind voices & have a garden. Like 'em!"' She just wants to share this moment: 'I literally shouted to my husband, "Sophie has ventured out to the garden! Not our youngest daughter but #sophiefromromania."'

While the rest of January does not provide smooth or linear progress, the general direction of travel seems good. Sophie still leaves the occasional puddle or worse on the floor but by the end of the month, she is just about house-trained which means a major improvement to the air quality in the house. There is even a week when she does not retreat behind the red sofa to sleep, choosing instead to kip on the stone tiles in the kitchen. But then one day Halina our cleaner makes a scary noise – though of course all noises are scary to Sophie – when fitting a new bag to the wastebin and our diva dives back into her safe space, which once again becomes her home every night and for much of the daylight hours too.

In a WhatsApp conversation after another such incident Si provides both reassurance about the speed at which she recovers from setbacks, and hope that further progress is on the near horizon: 'On the bright side, it looks like Sophie's recovery time is pretty short now. It's not so long ago that it could be nearly two days before she'd emerge again after an upset,' he writes. 'The time is coming when I imagine you'll want to discuss what your next priorities are for her. My suggestions are: the harness (naturally); some quiet walks; seeing how she reacts with other dogs; and an introduction to your dog walker. Would that be accurate, or would you have a different list?'

My reply finds me being a little more cautious than I might have been before our experiences over the last four weeks with Sophie: 'All of that is exactly what I would like – but it feels like she needs to get more comfortable with both of us first.'

'Yes – absolutely,' Si agrees. 'It's not time yet but still well worth thinking and talking about. You're over the biggest hurdle now and things will pick up pace.'

As January draws to a close, I reflect on what feels like a fairly tough six weeks since our frightened little dog arrived. I have felt very discouraged at times, especially in the early part of each week when Diane is away in Cambridge. Last year, when after Cabbage's death I was alone in the house for the first time, I had looked forward to the companionship a new dog would bring. Instead, it is clear that for now Sophie is far more comfortable when Diane is around: when she isn't, our new dog and I are effectively strangers, sharing the house but only interacting briefly at mealtimes. Or that's how it feels to me anyway. Thank goodness, then, for Si. As I continually tell him, he is as much a therapist for me as for the dog. So when he tells me that we are over the biggest hurdle, when he talks of some quiet walks, and things picking up pace, I feel a weight lifting from my shoulders.

Chapter Five

Sleepless Nights, Restless Dog

'The important thing is to go at their pace. Because it's about fear. This isn't about her choosing to be stubborn or difficult. It's about her being frightened of everything.'

Si Wooler

It is clear now, in early February, that we have a superstar on our hands. My Twitter and Instagram accounts are pinging so constantly with messages about Sophie that I have to dive deep into my phone settings to turn off notifications, while more people are stopping me on the street with the inevitable question, 'Has she been for a walk yet?' Meanwhile at work in Cambridge and even on occasion abroad, Diane now finds she is best known for her dog: 'I haven't had a meeting since Christmas which hasn't started with someone asking, "How's Sophie?" . . . And yesterday in Cambridge a complete stranger came up to me in the street and inquired after her too!'

Meanwhile Sophie is certainly making some progress – which is good, because a major milestone is fast approaching whereby she'll have to cope with being looked after by someone else – albeit for just a few days. In early March I am heading off to the French Alps for a week-long skiing holiday with a group of old friends. This will be my second visit to the slopes since my Parkinson's diagnosis and feels like a big deal. Last year, although I tired easily, I managed to ski better than I had expected, but since then my symptoms have worsened. So, will I still be able to get down the mountain?

And of course the other question very much on my mind in relation to my trip is, who will look after Sophie on the Monday and Tuesday of that week, when I'll be away and Diane will be in Cambridge? We have long assumed this would be Elaine, Diane's ballet teacher, who always had Cabbage to stay when we were away from home. Elaine has been desperate to meet Sophie since she first arrived. Even that hasn't been possible as yet, so the prospect of our fearful recluse coping easily with staying over at Elaine's is hard to envisage right now. However we still have some time – four weeks – to get her ready to face the world beyond our house, and given the progress she's been making even in the last few days, we are hopeful.

In the first few days of February, we continue to break new ground in small increments. Going into the garden seems to be second nature now for Sophie, and she's on the verge of being house-trained. I stand by the open back door shouting, 'Sophie – garden!', and she approaches me very nervously, as if it must be a trick, then dashes past. Once outside, she is in her element, exploring every corner of our small London garden, diving into bushes, digging holes in the flowerbeds and disappearing behind the shed.

Sophie has no collar on these days – one day in January, Diane leaned over the back of the sofa and removed it, concerned it was proving uncomfortable – and we haven't managed, or seriously tried, to put it back on since. This means that if our dog somehow got out of the garden there would be no easy means of identifying her. I think back to the dramatic day when Cabbage was stolen, and how the tag around her neck with Diane's mobile phone number was the key to us getting her back. And so now, as I watch Sophie racing around the garden with increasing confidence, I'm feeling a tad anxious. Every so often she puts her two front paws up on the wall separating us from our neighbours and I tense up, thinking she might manage to climb over. It is a relief when she comes up to the door, and after a cautious sniff, decides to come back in.

It soon becomes evident that out in the garden, she is a different dog – holding her tail up, sniffing the air, doing 'zoomies' back and forth, up and down the twenty-metre lawn. We recently noticed pieces of chewed-up plastic flowerpot lying strewn around the garden, so we've now left out a few toys – a couple of balls and a frisbee – for her to play with instead. At first she ignores them – but then one day something magical happens . . .

I'm at the kitchen window filming on my phone when Sophie comes bounding up to one of the balls, sinks her front legs down in front of it, bounds back up and races away with it. While I think to myself that this is a cute moment and post a clip on Twitter with the caption, 'Is she beginning to learn how to play?', I don't quite get the significance of what I've just seen. Very shortly afterwards, we get a call from Si, sounding excited and rather breathless, and quite unlike his usual calm self. 'I've seen the clip!' he begins. 'Do you realise what just happened? That's a play bow! Your Sophie has just done a play bow . . .' I have no idea what a play bow is, but one thing that is very clear from Si's reaction is that this is a *huge* moment in her development.

A quick Google search tells me that a play bow is a dog's way of communicating that it wants to engage in play – when a dog meets another dog for the first time, it assumes this position, which is like a canine semaphore to signal, 'I'm here for fun, not to fight.' Even if that play might involve a lot of rough and tumble, both animals now know that it is nothing serious. It can also be a sign to a human that their pet wants to play, and one website even tells me how I can reciprocate: 'Get down on all fours, stretch your arms in front of you, lean on your elbows, and stick your rear end in the air.' Let's not get ahead of ourselves, I think, and not just because I don't particularly relish the idea of suddenly assuming this position on our back lawn, which several of our neighbours can get a good view of from their upstairs windows if they happen to be looking out . . . No, the point is that Sophie's first play bow has been directed at a ball rather than at another dog or a human. But it is definitely a start.

Unlike me, it seems our online community is well aware of the import of this moment, because the clip becomes the latest Sophie video to go viral. One person comments that the play bow is another testament to our patient and gentle approach, which I'll admit leaves me and Diane feeling proud of what we have achieved, and very grateful to Si for his wise advice.

A couple of days later, Twitter swoons again when I post a clip of Diane and Sophie having a long cuddle in the kitchen. Our famous dog likes us – well, she likes Diane anyway – and she is beginning to settle in to her new home. I allow myself to hope that we may soon be visiting other homes with her and that I can stop worrying about my trip away in March.

Meanwhile, I want to understand a bit better where Sophie comes from, and get to grips with the wider story about Romanian dogs. Given the fact that our sweet but scared dog has turned out to have such challenges, I feel a little guilty that I did not do more research before we got her. On social media everyone quite naturally assumes that she has been through the same sort of horrors that we have all come to associate with Romanian rescue dogs. One follower observed how nervous she still is, and speculated that she must have been badly abused in Romania, echoing what seems like a generally held consensus that Sophie must be deeply traumatised after brutal treatment in her country of birth.

But that does not really match up to what we've been told, although at first that was a little sketchy – that she had been abandoned by the roadside, and rescued by someone who looked after her for a few months, keeping her in a barn.

Then a call from the British Veterinary Association (BVA) makes me realise I needed to know more. A few vets have noticed the publicity being generated by Sophie and have expressed their unease about it. It seems that UK vets have been unhappy for a while about the number of dogs coming in from Romania, their main concern being that these animals might bring diseases into the country with them.

I make the point to the BVA caller – who is, I should say, conciliatory throughout our conversation – that as far as we could tell, when Sophie first came to us, she had had her jabs and passed successfully through the animal welfare checks at Calais – so what is there to worry about? But he has an answer to that, which he sums up in one scary word: brucellosis. Also known as undulant fever, Malta fever, and Mediterranean fever, this is a bacterial infection which mainly affects cattle, swine, goats, sheep and dogs but can be transmitted to humans, meaning that in the UK it is classed as 'a notifiable animal disease'. Brucellosis is extremely rare in this country, and was entirely absent in the UK from 2004 until 2018, when it was detected in a number of dogs imported from Eastern Europe. In 2022, however, there was a particularly dramatic case which was widely reported in the media, when a woman from Stoke-on-Trent, Wendy Hayes, became infected with the disease, thought to have been transmitted by a dog from Belarus she was fostering. All five of her dogs had to be put down and she called for a ban on imports.

The man from the BVA does concede that the disease is still very rare over here, and that the risk is greater amongst street dogs and animals that have not been neutered – whereas, as I confirm, Sophie has been spayed and was not a stray. Nevertheless, he tells me, the Association recommends that I get her tested for the disease if that hasn't been done already.

All of this is yet another reason I feel I should find out more about Sophie's back story, starting with the man who introduced us to our newest family member – Adrian Tataru, who runs Friends Indeed, the charity which brought her to the UK and delivered her to our door last December. Realising I know so little about him and his organisation, I get in touch with Adrian on the number we were given when Sophie arrived, and told we should use anytime to contact the charity if in need of advice or support. In the exchanges that follow, I get a much fuller picture of him and his wife Maria, who works alongside him. What's clear very quickly is that this couple are no fast-buck merchants. I find out more about what Sadaf told me before: Adrian is a drilling engineer – the family moved to the UK from their native Romania in 2007 when he was offered work here. They settled near Peterborough, with Adrian travelling constantly to work on rigs. It's evident to me that he and Maria are absolutely devoted to the welfare of dogs – not least because they had been working with rescue organisations in Romania for over twenty years before setting up their own charity in 2020.

Adrian is also a passionate man – and when I message him to tell him about the concerns expressed by the British Veterinary Association regarding brucellosis, he is quick to make his own stance clear, and in no uncertain terms. He simply doesn't believe there is anything to worry about on this score when it comes to dogs from Romania: 'Romania is not a Mediterranean country and we have had, for example, no rabies there for decades now.'

When I ask him directly if Sophie has been tested, he tells me that she hasn't, because there have been no cases of brucellosis reported for a very long time in the area where she was found. In any case, he points out, there are dozens of other things you could test any rescue dog for before brucellosis, since it is so rare. And he's upfront about the fact that for his organisation, the financial outlay involved in getting each rescue exhaustively tested in such a way would make the cost of their whole operation prohibitive: 'Our costs would be somewhere around £1,500 for each animal. At the moment, we are spending around £750 per dog (including the transport here) on average, and we are heavily losing money. Who would pay £1,500 for a Romanian rescue?'

We paid £550 for Sophie – which, given the cost of transporting her across Europe, did not seem unreasonable, compared with the £225 we would have paid to adopt a dog from our local Dogs Trust rescue centre. But I'd still assumed it was a modestly profitable business for the charity. I later find out that the transport of such dogs to the UK is often contracted out to external private companies; when I hear this, I remember the sleek-looking vehicle which dropped Sophie to our door back in December and I realise it's likely that these transport service companies are not offering concessions for charities. A few months hence, in June 2023, when I visit Adrian and Maria at their home I will see for myself that what he has said about losing money is true – and it's clear that their operation is not necessarily in a financially healthy situation.

Given that Sophie wasn't a street dog but led a sheltered life in Romania – and is now a recluse – Diane and I decide at this point not to worry too much about brucellosis. But we do want to know more about her back story, such as where in Romania she has come from, and what can possibly have made her such an anxious dog. When I talk to Adrian about this, he says that we really need to speak to the vet who found her – Ana-Maria, who'd been mentioned to us before. And so over the course of several phone calls with Ana-Maria, where Adrian translates, and then an exchange on Facebook Messenger, we're just about able to piece together the story in more detail.

Sophie was found near Focsani, a city of 66,000 people in the Francia region, some 190km north-east of the Romanian capital, Bucharest. Ana-Maria was called to a vineyard where seven puppies had been dumped, four of them (including Sophie) with very similar brown and black markings, three with grey fur. Ana-Maria took them all to her father who kept them in a barn. She insists they were all looked after well by him – and certainly the video clip we saw of Sophie leaping up at him enthusiastically did not indicate a traumatised dog. So, what, we asked Ana-Maria, could have gone wrong to turn her into such a fearful creature?

Ana-Maria taps out her reply on Facebook Messenger: 'She wasn't frightened here with us, only a little shine [shy]. I think the transport made her to be so frightened, because when [for the start of her journey to the UK], I transferred her from my dad's to me in the car, she was very very scared. But after a few hours, she was again the happy dog that we ever knew! She was a puppy when my dad found [had?] them, my dad even he couldn't offer them the best food or place [but] he love[d] them all, he plays with them every single day, and the dogs love him too!'

The people – Adrian, Maria and Ana-Maria – who had rescued Sophie and brought her to our home seem sincere, but I am now beginning to ask myself serious questions as to whether getting a dog from Romania was a little rash. Maybe I should have done just a bit more research before taking the leap. A little late perhaps, I try to dig out some facts and figures.

It seems that Romania has long had a problem with stray dogs and we can lay the blame at the door of President Nicolae Ceausescu, the ruthless Communist leader of the country from 1965 until he was killed in the 1989 uprising. In the 1970s his determination to industrialise Romania saw a mass movement of the population from the countryside to the cities where cramped apartments left no room for pets. As a result thousands of dogs were abandoned on the streets, where they formed packs and multiplied fast.

After the fall of Ceausescu, dealing with stray dogs was not a priority in a country in turmoil, and the streets of Bucharest and other cities became ever more overrun with hungry, sometimes aggressive animals. There were periodic culls of strays, coupled with the building of rescue homes – but neither of these measures truly addressed the problem, and the rescue centres simply could not cope with the sheer numbers of dogs being brought to them. A tragic incident in 2013 brought things to a head. A four-year-old boy was set upon and killed by a pack of dogs in Bucharest, a city estimated at that time to have 64,000 strays on its streets. Amidst the public uproar that followed, Romanian MPs voted overwhelmingly for a law enabling the state to euthanise stray dogs if they were not claimed within two weeks of being picked up on the streets.

Hence the emergence of the emotive term 'kill shelter' for dog pounds, which effectively became like Death Row for the country's strays with a maximum stay of fourteen days. Rescue organisations in Romania began offering dogs for adoption abroad, tugging on the heartstrings of potential adopters with warnings that Fido faced death if someone did not offer him a home soon.

Meanwhile, in 2012 the UK harmonised its regulations on pet imports with the rest of the EU, making the process a lot simpler. As a result the number of dogs coming to the UK soared. Over 67,500 dogs were brought legally into the UK in 2020, with nearly half of them from Romania. There has also been a boom in Romanian rescue organisations operating in the UK, with 101 listed on the Charity Commission website. Friends Indeed is one of the bigger operations, with the 2022 accounts showing it raised just over £100,000, whereas some of the other charities have very little income from fundraising. But the accounts of Friends Indeed also show that the charity is spending most of what it earns – with over £50,000 going just on the cost of transporting dogs to the UK – and it has negligible reserves. In the 2022 financial year, Adrian Tataru is listed as supplying Friends Indeed with an interest-free loan of £4,744 to assist with short-term cash-flow requirements.

Recently, there have been suggestions that Romania's problems with stray dogs are easing, with fewer on the streets in big cities. In one of our conversations, Adrian tells me, 'In the civilised cities like in Bucharest and Cluj Napoca in Transylvania, they don't even put down dogs anymore and there are no kill shelters.' He does stress, however, that in rural areas people still just dump unwanted puppies, as had happened with Sophie. This is very sad of course, though it's unfortunately something which continues to happen here in the UK also. So while I'm glad that Sophie and her siblings weren't left to die on the roadside where they were abandoned, the question remains for me whether we have been too hasty in deciding to import a dog rather than get one from a local shelter.

Given this further general background about the plight of Romania's rescue dogs, it seems like the right juncture to look at another of our Rommie rescue case studies here. This time the story is one which has me nodding along as I recognise in it so much that is similar to our own experience.

BELLA FROM ROMANIA

Lorna told me how Bella – '42kg of matted, smelly fur' – had arrived in her family's home in November 2022, just before Sophie came to us:

'We didn't know much about her history other than she had been saved from a kill shelter by a local charity. The charity delivered her at 10 pm after a long two-day journey and we had no idea if she was house-trained or whether she would get on with our cat. We literally knew nothing about her, other than she needed a loving home and we had lots of love to give. Our beloved family dog had died five months previously. A relative of mine enquired as to whether – if we were ready to think about getting another dog – we would be interested in adopting a rescue from Romania. Our children were grown up (although still living at home), so we all sat down as a family to discuss the pros and cons – but really it was just small talk, because it was something everyone wanted to do, and we were all up for the challenge . . . And a challenge it has been!'

So the story of Bella's adoption already has quite a few similarities to our story with Sophie: a family seeking another dog after the loss of a beloved rescue pet; the trauma of a long journey for the new dog before coming to their home; having very limited information in advance about its background. But at least Lorna and her family seem to have gone into this with open eyes and an awareness right from the beginning that it wasn't necessarily going to be easy.

'Bella was and still is wary of everyone, particularly men. We suspected that she had been chained up for a very long period – she had no fur on her front "elbows" (and still doesn't), presumably from lying for so long on concrete or some other hard surface. We could not get a collar on her for the first few weeks. During that time too she'd lie hidden in the bushes in our garden for hours on end whatever the weather (and this was in December); she was too afraid to come out. Every time someone spoke to her, she exhibited submissive behaviour – shying away, keeping her tail between her legs, avoiding direct eye contact . . .'

Fortunately, Lorna's husband, Mike, was working from home for the first month after Bella's arrival, while Lorna was recovering from a major operation. 'During this time, Mike was able to build some trust and slowly, with a *lot* of patience, we managed to get a collar on her, take her to the groomer's (this didn't go well) and to our local vet for a check-up.

'We have to admit, there have been a handful of times when we thought that it was not going to work out for us with Bella. It is still very much a work-in-progress. After a second failed attempt at the groomers, we now have to groom her at home. But she no longer sleeps outside and she loves going for walks on a harness. We still cannot get her into a car although this is getting better. She has just started to play with us but only with a rope – she's not interested in balls or squeaky toys – yet, anyway. She is still wary of other people but is getting better with that too.

'We have all worked together as a family. And our social lives have been slightly curtailed. We all say Bella is a low maintenance dog, i.e. she just really eats, sleeps and has occasional fusses . . . However the truth is that she is pretty high maintenance, for one thing because we all accommodate our diaries around her. We often say to friends she is a difficult dog to love, as she is not very affectionate but we *do* love her – if in a totally different way to our previous family dog. The change in her personality over the last nine months has been small – but also huge . . . If that makes sense!'

Once more I can relate to much of what Lorna is saying about life with Bella. We too are finding that we have to accommodate our diaries around Sophie. However, she is just beginning to show signs of giving and receiving affection, and we are certainly finding it easy to love her – even if her constant anxiety around us can be exasperating at times. But that's what love is like, isn't it?

By mid-February we still feel we are making progress with Sophie, although it sometimes seems that we take two steps forward and two steps back. One weekend she frolics in the garden with Diane, beginning to show her playful side. And she doesn't immediately retreat behind the sofa in fear or bark loudly when Theo arrives for our regular Saturday morning piano lesson – whereas on previous weekends she has seemed both terrified and outraged by his arrival. But then in the early part of the next week when Diane is in Cambridge as usual, our dog becomes a recluse again, often with just one brief foray into the garden first thing, followed by a retreat behind the sofa for the rest of the day and evening.

Meanwhile I'm beginning to realise that I am literally losing sleep over Sophie. The fact is that since my Parkinson's diagnosis in 2019, I've rarely been able to sleep more than four hours a night – and even that isn't usually in one unbroken stretch. Poor sleep is something everybody in my Parkinson's support bubble – bar one – struggles with and it's comforting and helpful to be able to discuss this kind of shared problem.

Nick the Judge, as I call him, suffers from terrible nightmares which he sometimes finds himself acting out – something which can understandably be very alarming for his wife at times, when she wakes to find he has his hands tightly around her throat. Gillian Lacey-Solymar doesn't suffer from bad dreams but has grown painfully accustomed to spending long periods of the night awake. Meanwhile, for Paul Mayhew-Archer, the knowledge that he'll have difficulty falling asleep has led to a nightly ritual which he now feels compelled to stick to: 'For some reason, I've decided that two o'clock in the morning is a perfect time to do Sudoku – I don't know why . . . So I finally get off to sleep about 3.30 am.' Mark Mardell too finds it difficult to get enough sleep at night, and as a result suffers from excessive somnolence during the day. Jeremy Paxman is the one exception in our group – he tells us he 'sleeps like a baby' – however it later emerges that his doctor has prescribed him a heavy-duty sleeping pill which fortunately is very effective – such medications have as yet proved of no help in my case.

One of the many things I've tried to help tackle my sleep

problems is the cognitive behavioural therapy app, Sleepio, which was devised by Professor Colin Espie, who is Professor of Sleep Medicine in the Nuffield Department of Clinical Neurosciences (NDCN) at Oxford University. In 2021, the year before we got Sophie, I signed up to Sleepio and found that it definitely helped improve matters, when I adopted some of the key recommendations – for example, reducing my sleep window to 11 pm to 5 am, and when getting into bed, turning the lights out straight away rather than reading or looking at my phone.

But since December 2022 there is of course something else keeping me awake: our incredibly fearful and socially anxious Romanian rescue dog. From the time she arrived, she's been occupying a lot of my mental space – especially when I wake in the very early hours, I find my thoughts frequently returning to my worries about Sophie and this sets my mind racing and my anxieties spiralling. And now in mid-February, getting less sleep than ever, I decide that I need once again to seek expert input.

When I get in touch with Professor Espie, he's kind enough to give me some of his time and listens as I relate the latest problem to disrupt my night-time hours. And he has a solution, quite a novel one – to me anyway. He suggests that I deliberately focus on my Sophie-related worries at a time other than in the early hours: 'What's recommended is to set aside some specific scheduled time for worrying. So, you can worry as much as you like, as long as it's at the time that you've set aside for it . . . Even if you get to say 9 pm and you don't feel particularly worried, if that's your "worry time", you have to get on with it . . . It's a form of exposure therapy,' he concludes. I'm a little dubious about how effective this might be – somehow, setting aside a time to worry about Sophie seems a little daft.

Apart from anything else, my worries could rise to the surface at any time, night or day.

Over the next week, however, there are some lovely moments on the Sophie front. When I capture on video a moment when she allows me to stroke her – me, a male person! – the internet goes bonkers. The video has been viewed nearly half a million times on Twitter. Hundreds of joyous messages include this from the rower Matthew Pinsent, four-time Olympic gold medallist: 'This is so great. All your hard work and patience beginning to bear fruit.' It is really uplifting to receive such kind messages. But it is becoming clearer that we are still a long way from being able to walk Sophie the mile to Elaine the ballet teacher's house as we used to do with Cabbage – or even pack her into the car – on the weekend I go skiing.

But then on 17 February, just a fortnight before I am due to fly, our Dog Whisperer comes to the rescue. Si gets in touch to say he will fly down from Scotland to look after Sophie during the period that we are away. We are both so grateful and, particularly for me, this is a huge relief. For the next couple of weeks progress is still halting – one day Sophie is bounding around the garden, the next she is sulking behind her red leather sofa. But now without the pressure of a deadline, I am more relaxed about it.

Strangely though, it is when she does emerge and goes out into the garden that I am most tense, still worried she might escape. One morning I am watching her from the kitchen window and turn away for a few moments to make a cup of tea. When I turn back there is no sign of Sophie. No problem, I tell myself, she is probably behind the shed and will pop out in a minute. After five minutes, I am getting nervous. After ten, I am thinking she could be a mile away and I must sound the alarm. I rush out into the garden and there's a sudden scrabbling and a rustling sound from under a bush – and Sophie bursts out, looks at me in terror, and runs past me back into the house.

Plenty of kind people continue to send advice on social media. All of it is well-meant but I am uncertain whether I should try any of their approaches. Fortunately, Si is monitoring it all up in Scotland, playing the Sophie 'buzzword bingo' game with his partner Nina. He has been building an online community of his own and sometimes intercedes in various exchanges on our behalf. A week before he flies down to see us, he tweets this: 'I understand the well-meaning suggestions to try different things with #sophiefromromania, such as sitting on the floor. The reason we don't – we stay with things we know will be positive rather than things that may not be. It is going as it should and does.' This makes sense to me though I do vaguely wonder what 'going as it should' means.

But minutes after I read Si's tweet, we are celebrating what feels like a major step forward. Sophie, out by herself in the back garden, suddenly unleashes a sustained volley of barks – the most sound we have heard from her since her arrival. What on earth is going on? Diane and I rush to look out of the window, and there she is – standing peering at a garden table, which is folded up and propped against the wall. We quickly realise that she is reacting to what she sees in the round table's shiny top – another dog, namely herself – she's been barking at her own reflection! She seems delighted rather than angry, then she stretches out her front paws and lowers herself into a play bow, directed at this rather appealing stranger in the table.

And there are a couple more positive developments over the weekend. Firstly, she grabs a slipper of Diane's and takes it with her to her spot behind the sofa for safe-keeping – more evidence of normal playful doggy behaviour. Then on the Sunday there's a long spell when she repeatedly takes herself in and out the kitchen door to the back garden – and by now, she's confident enough to come and tap on the door to let us know when she wants to be let back in.

That evening Diane and I have a chat about where we are. I'm surprised when she has a rather depressing observation – she is generally far calmer and more patient than I am, and in particular when it comes to Sophie. She tells me that although our dog is now coming to terms with her environment, she is not making the same progress in terms of socialising with us. She doesn't come up and ask for treats or approach us in any way, even though she does just about tolerate the occasional stroke (especially from Diane).

That Friday, 3 March, Si is flying down from Inverness and we are full of nervous anticipation. On his brief visit back in January, he did not even get to see Sophie – so how will she react this time, when he is going to be staying until the middle of next week? A little before he arrives, there is a furious chorus of barking from Sophie when she hears the postman, which doesn't inspire me with confidence about how she'll react to another stranger who's actually going to be coming into her space. But Si settles himself calmly at our kitchen table, making no fuss. So while she is indeed a little wary at first, soon she is out walking back and forth and under the table – and by late afternoon she seems pretty comfortable in his presence.

I am not heading for the Alps until Sunday, so we have the whole of Saturday to see Si working with Sophie and understand more about his training technique. It soon becomes clear that it's all about food. Si comes back from a trip to the supermarket with supplies of cheese and sausage which he proceeds to chop up into tiny pieces. Then he sits for hours at the table, holding his hand out with a scrap of food, as Sophie quickly comes to realise that there are treats aplenty if she cosies up to this nice man. 'Money in the bank,' he explains as she comes back time and again.

I take the opportunity to have a chat with him about how we are doing. He says when I first sent him the video from Romania of Sophie leaping up enthusiastically at the vet's father, he had been optimistic that she wouldn't take long to settle with us. But on reflection he is not so sure: 'That video represented her being used to a very small number of people and a very small number of dogs,' he explains: 'And that means that if she hasn't had a lot of contact with strangers, unfamiliar people in that first twelve to sixteen weeks, she's going to find it a lot harder as an adult to cope with new people.'

But he still believes we've come a long way in the eleven weeks since she arrived: 'I think you've been doing a really great job of getting her to just recognise you as something positive in her life. I know it feels slow, painfully slow at times. And it may seem sometimes like you're going backwards – but actually, when you look at this process in its entirety, the steps she has taken are massive.' He then points to the way, in just a day, Sophie has got used to his presence: 'The distance you've travelled from that shutdown little dog in the doorway at three o'clock in the morning to one who's now actually coming out and investigating the stranger. And I know that she can be a little touch sensitive. But I think that'll peter out.'

Then I ask the question that has been occupying me when I lie awake at 4 am – just how long is this all going to take? 'There are various things that obviously we'd like her to do – go for a walk, be happy riding in the car – so that we take her on holiday with us in August.' Si says he can understand why we – and thousands on social media – want things to move faster, but he comes back once again to his own central mantra of dog training: 'The important thing is to go at their pace. Because it's about fear. This isn't about her choosing to be stubborn or difficult. It's about her being frightened of everything. If it was a human being who had just experienced a trauma or PTSD or any kind of mental health issue in their lives, and how long their recovery period would be – when you consider it like that, it's clear that dogs can adapt and recover really remarkably quickly.'

In the last few days I have slept particularly badly, worrying not just about Sophie but about how I will cope in the mountains. But that Saturday night, perhaps reassured by Si that we are on the right track, I get a solid six hours. At 6.30 am on the Sunday, with Sophie still snoozing behind her sofa, I climb in a taxi for Luton Airport. Both man and dog need to conquer their fears. And who knows – perhaps a week apart for the first time since we got acquainted will leave both of us in a better place?

Chapter Six

The Needy Boyfriend

How I became more anxious than my rescue dog

'The only thing you need to do right now is less!'

Si Wooler

It doesn't quite work out like that – well, for the man anyway. I return home from the Alps the following Sunday evening, weary after a four-hour delay to my flight, and dispirited to have to admit that in the battle between man and mountain, the mountain has won. Spending a week in a chalet with new friends and old, eating, drinking and laughing has been a wonderful experience. Skiing has not. I was expecting it to be a little harder than my first attempt at skiing with Parkinson's the previous year – when, despite getting tired by early afternoon, I had managed to get down the mountain in reasonable shape, keeping up with the less dedicated skiers in our party. I am all too aware that my symptoms have worsened a bit over the past year, with the weakness on my right side now more pronounced and compounded by a growing stiffness in my right hand. But I had still thought I would cope on the slopes.

By the end of the week it was clear that was not the case and that this was to be my last adventure on skis. The problem was a simple one – I could not turn effectively any more. Skiing is all about shifting your weight from one side to another to carve a turn and control your speed – but on anything but the gentlest of slopes, I found myself incapable of doing this. After more than thirty skiing holidays since my mid-twenties, I was back to week two in my original learning process, when anything with a gradient meant returning to a beginner's tortured snowplough stance to control my speed.

This was a sobering moment, a reminder that Parkinson's is a progressive disease and there were other things I might have to give up in the years to come. But I was not too downhearted – off the slopes I had enjoyed a relaxing week – as well as which there was some good news from home . . .

While on my trip, I become like the thousands of #sophiefromromania followers, eager to check in every morning for the latest update on our dog's progress. On Twitter, Diane (@dianecoyle1859) and Si (@sociabledog) do not disappoint. Early on Monday morning, with Diane already on the train to Cambridge, Si posts a picture of Sophie heading out into the garden with her tail up. Phew! I had worried that she might refuse to come out when she was alone with him. Later, he posts a picture of Sophie waiting patiently as he prepares treats, and publishes a piece on his own blog explaining why you shouldn't be cautious about doling out what he calls 'the good stuff' while 'teaching behaviours or putting emotional £s in the emotional bank'. We learn later that he has been out to Waitrose to buy blocks of Comté, meaning our dog will develop a taste for this delicious if pricey French cheese.

On Tuesday Si reports that Sophie has had 'a bit of a lie-in' (which I interpret as a bit of a sulk behind the sofa), but that she is now going purposefully into the garden. Later, he posts a photo of her lying curled up at his feet in the kitchen and says it's important to celebrate the little wins as well as the big ones. Si still has only a small Twitter following but it is growing fast, and he is much better than me at engaging with those who comment on his posts, and starting all sorts of conversations about dogs. In response to his asking for examples of happy firsts with fearful dogs, he gets hundreds of responses. All of them are heartwarming – from the rescue greyhound who learned to have fun on the beach, to Willow the Romanian rescue dog who took two-and-a-half years to get around to sitting on her owner's lap, to the dalmatian who no longer bedwets when left alone in the house, and the rescue dog who didn't know what a dog bed was. The stories are often accompanied by photos of the dogs now, looking relaxed and happy – and every single one gets a response from lovely Si.

Meanwhile, Diane is in Cambridge, going about her typical work as a professor – collaborating with colleagues on major research programmes; supervising PhD students; giving lectures – including one today about competition policy at a conference at King's College. But even in this rarefied environment, a certain dog intrudes. Accustomed as she now is to fielding questions about Sophie, and to appease any fans who may be in the assembled group, she ends her lecture with an image of our dog relaxing in the sunshine.

On Wednesday, his last day in sole charge of Sophie, Si checks in on social media to give an update, as is now his wont. He reports on her first experience of snow, albeit just a light dusting in our back garden, and in the attached photo, we see her heading outside to investigate, her tail held high – and clearly a more confident and playful dog than when our Dog Whisperer arrived a few days ago. In another tweet he reflects on what has been achieved, saying that Sophie has done some 'top stuff' with him, including eating from his palm and his fingers, not just from under the table but out in the open. She is also spending much less time behind the sofa, if still retreating to her safe place on a regular basis – but, as Si points out, 'We are on a journey!'

So in just a couple of days, Si has already managed to forge a relationship with Sophie – and perhaps an even closer one than Diane and I have managed to achieve in nearly three months. I am happy of course that we are making progress, although if I'm completely honest, I can't help feeling a little envious of his success. It may be just an ego thing – however I'm sure many other dog owners would feel the same in my position, if they'd be willing to admit it. With Si leaving to return to Scotland, for the next few days Diane is able to build on the progress he's made. Sophie looks relaxed in her presence, popping in and out of the garden with more confidence than ever. And one tweet from the Prof the following afternoon seems to suggest she is also acquiring some of the more annoying habits of a 'normal' dog: 'A certain dog is driving me nuts by repeatedly knocking at the kitchen door to come in and then saying, "maybe not" . . .'

That Sunday, as I sit at Geneva Airport waiting to board my flight home, I check in on Twitter again and am greeted by a new picture of Sophie in the garden, looking up expectantly at Diane as if eager to play. It's a heartening sight and I realise I've missed seeing our brave dog, and I'm all the more keen to get home and continue with the process of helping her move to the next stage of settling in. Needless to say, I've missed my wife too, of course! When I finally get through the door at 8 pm, there is no exuberant welcome from Sophie – not that I was really expecting such a thing, although it would have been nice and perhaps some irrational part of me had somehow held out hope. But I thought I'd at least see our dog out and about, whereas it seems she has taken up residence behind the red sofa again.

There is, however, an obvious explanation at least – it turns out that our grandchildren, aged four years and five months respectively, have been visiting Diane with their parents, and Sophie retreated in terror as soon as they arrived. Still, when it is just me and her on our own for our usual three days at the start of the following week, I am sure things will be different. Of course they will.

We are back in the normal routine on Monday. Diane's alarm goes off at 5.15 am and at 5.45 she is off to Cambridge with just a quick glance behind the sofa to say goodbye to Sophie. By 7.15 she is texting me to ask where the first photo of the day is, and I am straight back into the job of being Publicity Assistant for the country's most famous dog. In fact I have just shot and am about to post several pictures of a slightly wary dog scooting past me and out into the back garden. She still seems nervous around me – on one occasion when I follow her out into the garden she dives under some patio chairs, rather as she did on her first day with us when we tried to coax her to go for a walk. My hope that Si's visit last week has seen us turn a corner begins to fade.

Over the next couple of days Sophie and I are like an ill-matched couple on a first date – tense and slightly awkward with each other, not able to find an easy connection in our exchanges despite our best efforts – well, mine anyway. Meanwhile she is off her food, leaving her bowl untouched, and circles me warily when I am sitting at the kitchen table. When we're alone in the house together Sophie and I now have a new routine – a little dance of sorts, where the main theme is that I'm the one who has to make all the moves while Sophie plays hard to get. And the more I try to move towards her, the more she seems to retreat. Once I have come down for breakfast, I wait impatiently for Sophie to make an appearance. When she does eventually emerge, she waits hesitantly by the entrance to her den, then scuttles under the kitchen table while I call out, 'Sophie – garden!' She waits until the moment feels right for her and then gallops past me and out through the back door. Meanwhile, I fry some bacon and when it's ready, I call out to her once more, 'Sophie – bacon!'. Which she ignores. When she does come back in, I hold out a rasher of bacon to her, but she looks at it and turns away. It's truly exasperating – I know she wants it, but she just won't risk getting close enough to take it from my hand. I advance slowly towards her with the rasher, step by step, but she retreats further and further until she turns and heads back behind the sofa. I sigh deeply – another morning of rejection. I channel my frustration into making a video called, '#sophiefromromania and Bacon – a Story of Unrequited Love' – which I then post online.

But once more on the Wednesday evening, when Diane comes home, everything changes and the outlook brightens. Soon, Sophie has polished off the bacon which she'd left untouched in her bowl all day. And on Thursday her better mood continues, with her allowing both of us to feed her and stroke her, although she is still more comfortable with Diane than with me.

Back up in Scotland, Si has been looking at my video about Sophie, bacon and unrequited love. Sensing my frustration, he sends me a message sympathising but insisting I must resist the temptation to try and persuade Sophie to come to me. He explains that, while it may be our instinct as humans to do this with fearful animals, the fact is that the more we do it, the more cautious the pet becomes. 'You're going to have Sophie coming up and soliciting either food or attention from you very soon,' he promises. 'And so the only thing you need to do right now is less!' He then gives me quite a complex set of instructions on what to do next, which in a nutshell amount to: 'Slow down, shut up and let it happen.'

I concede to Si that I am anxious around Sophie, and that I know this probably communicates itself to her – whereas Diane has a much calmer, more assured approach with her. I explain that I can't help feeling a little disappointed in how things are panning out. What I was hoping by now would be a close bond between man and dog – with Sophie waiting for me at the foot of the stairs each morning, eager and getting excited as I put on the lead for our daily walk – is instead becoming a neurotic relationship. She still seems quite scared of me, recoiling if I make any sudden move and apparently unsure whether the treats I offer her are a trick. Meanwhile I am perpetually nervous about her, with an anxiety that can sometimes turn into irritation or even annoyance when – as I see it – she 'refuses' to get better. It's around this time that someone – it could have been Si or Diane, it could even have been me – comes up with the term 'needy boyfriend' to describe my relationship with Sophie.

Meanwhile I've been trying to work out why the dog is so much less relaxed with me than with Diane. Is it simply because I'm a man? Another possible explanation – which some of Sophie's fans have hinted at – is that she somehow senses my Parkinson's and that this might be making her feel uneasy around me. I wasn't particularly bothered that people were openly speculating about my condition in this way – fortunately I am fairly thick-skinned. When I speak to Si about this, he tells me he has been getting similar messages about whether my Parkinson's might be affecting my progress with Sophie. He asks me if I'd be ok for him to address it publicly and explain that it isn't a factor in his thinking.

I tell him that is fine with me – but that I really don't think it's a factor, except for my inability to easily get back up from the floor if, as so many have suggested, I get down to Sophie's level. Si agrees with me about my Parkinson's: 'The key point I want to make is that whether or not Sophie "senses" your condition or finds involuntary tremors unusual, it doesn't change what we do and therefore is irrelevant.' He adds that Sophie being more hesitant with me is far more likely to come down to the fact that I am a man rather than my Parkinson's.

Keen to get as much insight as possible into all this, I then ask Si if there is any solid science behind the idea that dogs prefer women to men. His first response is to scratch his head, sigh and warn me that we risk disappearing down a rabbit hole . . . Something incidentally that it would be fun to see Sophie do! 'The general consensus,' he then says, 'is that if a dog is fearful of strangers, that fear is likely to be more intense with a man than with a woman.' But he is not at all certain that anyone has done any serious research into this specific question and says he'll see what he can dig up on his side.

A few hours later Si comes back to me with a couple of finds. The first is a study which initially appears to be nothing to do with dogs. It involved an experiment where people (both men and women) were given very fuzzy images of humans walking and ended up deciding that the ones walking towards them were male, while those walking away were female. Apparently an experienced American behaviourist has seen this and somehow concluded that dogs must perceive men as always moving towards them in a threatening manner, while women are seen as retreating and therefore safe.*

* https://www.patriciamcconnell.com/theotherendoftheleash/why-dog-are-more-afraid-of-men

Next up is a paper Si has found on 'Dog-Human Coevolution'. Apparently, 15,000 years ago when humans started using dogs, women were more likely to treat these animals as part of the family, whereas men saw them in a purely functional way, as being useful on their hunting expeditions.* Given this historical background, it doesn't seem completely unlikely that over the centuries, dogs may have acquired an internal sense/instinct that women will be more nurturing and unthreatening, whereas men may be more of an unknown quantity.

In my search for stories of other Romanian rescue dogs, I meet Nicola and Dimitri, owners of Angus. They are another couple who have found that their fearful dog seems happier with the wife than the husband. No two experiences with Romanian rescue dogs are the same, of course, but what Nicola tells me she and Dimitri have been going through with their dog, Angus, seems to have a lot of parallels with our life with Sophie.

ANGUS FROM ROMANIA

Nicola, a British woman living in the Netherlands, says that before she met her husband Dimitri, she had never had any pets. And even though he had always wanted them to get a dog, for years she was against it: 'Dimitri has MS and I'm his carer, so [for a long time] I felt it was too much to have a dog too.'

* https://bioone.org/journals/journal-of-ethnobiology/volume-40/issue-4/0278-0771-40.4.414/Dog-Human-Coevolution-Cross-Cultural-Analysis-of-Multiple-Hypotheses/10.2993/0278-0771-40.4.414.full

Nicola changed her mind, however, after the couple moved to a more dog-friendly home, and decided it would be nice to have a canine companion on her daily walks after all. She found two orphaned four-month-old Romanian pups – a brother and sister – at a local Dutch shelter which regularly rescues dogs from Romania and other countries: 'The sister had more confidence, so obviously I thought the brother needed us more,' she recalls. So in early 2023 they brought him home and named him Angus.

Angus' initial time in his new home sounds very much like Sophie's: 'He spent the first four days hiding under our dining table and, as we discovered later, chewing through various cables . . . At first, any sudden movement or noise would send him back under the table.' If you swap 'sofa' for 'table', this sounds familiar. And Nicola and Dmitri somehow sensed that it was important for Angus to have this place of refuge: 'We never went near his safe space, as we felt it was very important that he had that – in fact, we still don't go anywhere near it to this day.'

Nicola took advice and spent hours sitting on the floor with her back to the puppy, throwing treats. In time, it worked and he began to venture out. She says it all seems a blur now, but she does remember how thrilled they were with every bit of progress – and, she adds, even now, there is still something new to celebrate each day: 'Today for example, he didn't bark at a visitor to the house until she was leaving . . . That's a first!'

Angus is now quite comfortable with Nicola, even allowing her to stroke his belly and so on – 'when he's in the mood!' But he's still adjusting to Dimitri. That also sounds similar to our own scenario with Sophie. Nicola feels that they have come a long way. Angus loves to play with her and run round the garden, and also enjoys recall training – if there are sausage treats on offer.

There is still progress to be made – 'The big hurdle now is getting a lead on Angus so that we can go for a walk. We've had advice from an expert at the shelter and have hired a private trainer.' Nicola admits that a very energetic puppy can be hard work, and that she and Dmitri were quite naive when they adopted Angus: 'Never having had a dog before, I have no comparison, but I realise that other dogs are probably easier.' They have lost two rugs after 'accidents' and lots of their stuff has been chewed to bits – something which the couple seem to be quite tolerant of: 'We both found the destruction funny . . . we might be bad parents! But the whole experience is amazing and he's wonderful. Every bit of progress is a joy . . . The key is clearly patience, patience, patience. But we have time and he's worth it. He makes me laugh every day and I'm happy that he's happy with us.'

Like us, Nicola and Dmitri have received a lot of well-meaning advice from other dog owners. Some of it was quite contradictory and confusing, and some of it just didn't sit right with either of them, as Nicola recounts: 'Just yesterday, someone advised me to get a choke collar! I'd rather never walk Angus than put him through that.' So eventually they decided to focus on following their own instincts about what felt right, based on Angus' behaviour and reactions: 'I constantly remind myself that the most important thing is that he's happy and comfortable. Patience, time and love seem to be effective.'

This sounds very much like Si's philosophy and after less than four months it seems to be working for Angus and his devoted owners. In March 2024, Nicola gets in touch to give me a quick update, telling me that things are continuing to progress with Angus and he's now going out for regular walks with them: 'Just this evening, while taking Angus for his wee night-time walk, I was thinking about how all the effort and patience has been worth it. Especially as, when we got home, he spent the evening climbing all over me for cuddles . . .'

On the Friday after my return from skiing, something happens which shows that my 'needy boyfriend' vigilance around Sophie can sometimes be a good thing. That day starts out with the three of us in a cheerful mood. Sophie really does seem more relaxed, sitting by the open back door basking in the spring sunshine, and even accepting pieces of sausage from me out in the open. When she starts playing with one of Diane's old shoes – more 'normal dog' behaviour and surely a positive sign – I decide to film her, intending to put together a little video for Si.

But as I review the footage, I notice something strange – Sophie keeps violently shaking her head from side to side as if trying to dispel a cloud of imaginary insects. I have seen her do this before outside in the garden but assumed that it was real insects she was chasing away. When I send the clip to Si, he too seems concerned. One of the many wonderful things about Si is that he belongs to a wide network of all sorts of animal healthcare professionals and related experts. So while he's not a vet himself, he has colleagues within this network who are, and who he can consult for an expert opinion if need be. 'I'm wondering if there's something irritating her . . . I rang a vet colleague of mine and she says it's most likely gastrointestinal. So, something irritating her gut. Sara, my colleague, suggests you should mention it to your vet, who will most likely advise monitoring and keeping track of toilet habits, etc. It could just be an upset tum. The other two typical reasons for these behaviours – "fly catching", yawning, neck stretching – are seizure and compulsive disorders. But if this is new, then GI is the most likely reason.'

Si then suggests that we could drop in to our vet and see if someone will take a look at the video for us. This sounds like a better option than immediately booking her in for an appointment. When Sophie first arrived, we registered her with a newish vet's practice which had opened just a few hundred yards from our front door. But as she has not yet ventured even into the front half of the house, let alone out onto the street, neither we nor our dog have had any dealings with the vet so far.

But as she doesn't seem to have a tummy bug, and 'seizure or compulsive disorders' don't sound good, I decide to drop into the practice that afternoon. There I show my video of Sophie shaking her head to a veterinary nurse, who promises to pass it on to the vet. A day or so later we get a message back – one of the vets has reviewed the footage and is suggesting that we should check Sophie's ears and possibly mouth, to see if there's anything stuck inside, which can be another common reason for a dog shaking its head in this way. However, the message continues, if it doesn't happen very often, we should just monitor the situation and then decide if we want to book her in for an examination: 'She might need some medication to help her to calm down, so that we can examine her properly. Depending on how she reacts, we will need to put a muzzle on her initially, and if she seems calm enough, then we will try to examine the mouth. Another option would be giving Sophie sedation and examining her while she's sleeping.'

This sets off a whole new chain of worries of course – and not just for Needy Boyfriend. Of course we rarely get close to Sophie, and certainly not close enough to look inside her ears or mouth. And getting her medicated enough to visit the vet where they will in any case want to muzzle her seems both daunting and likely to wipe out any progress we have made in winning her trust. But thankfully, there are no further signs of head shaking over the next few days, and we're gradually able to relax and put any thoughts of a visit to the vet to the back of our minds – for now, anyway.

While she is becoming an obsession, there is a lot going on in my life besides Sophie right now. I am just finishing the memoir I'm writing about my mother, based on the extraordinary collection of her letters I found after her death. At the heart of it is a pink box with a note inside, which says: 'For Rory to read and think about, in the hope that it will help him to understand how it really was.' The letters within tell the story of my mother's love affair with the father I only met as an adult. With a tentative title of *Ruskin Park* – the name of the council block where I spent my childhood – the first draft will soon be ready to send to the publisher. The writing process has been an incredibly challenging and emotionally intense experience for me, but a richly rewarding one too.

Meanwhile our Parkinson's support bubble has been making great strides with the idea of a podcast about living with the condition, largely thanks to the endless positivity and entrepreneurial drive of Nick 'the Judge' Mostyn, with me, as the only one with experience of podcasting, dragged along for the ride. Somehow, the supremely well-connected judge – he had, after all, previously been Britain's top divorce lawyer representing the likes of Paul McCartney – had managed to get us meetings with a series of luminaries from the podcasting world. However, it rapidly became clear that we would not be a good fit for a company that would want any new podcast to generate hundreds of episodes a year, whereas we were looking to start off with a cautious ten.

But we had struck lucky with a young man called Nick Hilton, who was a jobbing freelance journalist *and* had a one-man podcast production company. He introduced us to a few people and then we began to realise that he was just the man we needed to get *Movers and Shakers* – yes, the judge's idea for our name, which met with even Paxman's approval – off the ground. We decided that what we needed to reproduce was the conversations, the banter, the laughter and the moaning about our condition that happened every time we met in the pub.

And so one Monday afternoon in February 2023 we recorded a pilot episode, with the six of us gathered around a table in a cramped space at the back of Jeremy Paxman's local, the Ladbroke Arms in Notting Hill. We blathered on for nearly an hour which Nick Hilton expertly edited down to about thirty minutes, and when he sent this to us we couldn't help feeling that it was . . . not bad, not too bad at all. So over the rest of the month we recorded a couple more editions, quite an intense process but one which everyone enjoyed. We were all pleased with what we'd produced, and made the collective decision to launch the *Movers and Shakers* podcast in mid-March.

So it's finally D-day, Saturday, 18 March, and we press the button and *Movers and Shakers* goes live. Helped by a very positive review in the *Observer* – and undoubtedly by Paxman's fame and his gloriously gloomy presence – it is an instant hit. At one point it briefly tops the podcast charts – which is an amazing achievement, considering it consists of five old blokes and one middle-aged woman talking about what is still quite an obscure disease.

That Saturday I also appear live from our kitchen on *BBC*

Breakfast to promote the podcast, with Paul Mayhew-Archer up in the studio in Salford alongside the presenters on the red sofa. The broadcast goes well and of course the presenters of a programme which has already had two items about Sophie ask about her progress. To their delight and that of her many online fans, the Nation's Shyest Dog makes a brief appearance at the corner of her own red sofa, peeping out at me as if to ask what on earth I am doing.

The overwhelmingly positive response to *Movers and Shakers* is exhilarating but also means a lot more work for us all – especially for me and the judge, tasked with scheduling the recording of further episodes, booking guests and, in my case, trying to secure sponsorship to cover our quite modest costs. The six of us are doing this for nothing, and our producer Nick Hilton has to be repeatedly pressed to accept even a small fee for all his work.

So our Sophie is just one of the preoccupations I am juggling at this point. She continues to both delight and dismay me in this two steps forward, two steps back dance, and because I'm so attached to a happy outcome for our new dog, whatever is happening with her often risks crowding out everything else. But something I continue to find really heartening is the way her ever-larger community of online fans focus almost exclusively on Sophie's progress rather than the setbacks. When I post a clip of her performing a play bow while wagging her tail to Diane in the kitchen, we receive several hundred replies. Many are highly emotional, and even tearful. Around this time, several rather beautifully executed portraits of Sophie arrive at our house, the beginnings of what may well turn out to be a whole gallery. A present addressed simply to 'Mr Rory Cellan-Jones (Sophie's Dad), West Ealing, London' is somehow delivered safely to our door. It would be hard not to be cheered up by such lovely gestures and all the positive feedback on the part of Sophie's fanbase.

But life with Sophie continues to be a conundrum for me. The Thursday after her brief appearance on breakfast television starts well, with Sophie hanging out with Diane in the kitchen, performing a play bow once more, and even coming close to a nose bump. Then her favourite person disappears to go to a dentist appointment. When she returns, I am with Sophie in the kitchen. Taking up my phone, I decide I'll monitor our dog's reactions by filming her as Diane comes back into the house. When she hears the front door open, Sophie barks loudly then, tail wagging, she does a play bow when she realises who it is. But as Diane comes into the hall, Sophie appears to suddenly take fright and briefly dives back behind the sofa. So what, I wonder, is going on here – is her growing playfulness still being overshadowed by her underlying fearfulness?

A little later that day, I send the clip to Si and, responsive as ever, he comes back with his verdict: 'I've watched this a couple of times, Rory, and it's almost entirely playful. Barking at the sound of the door is normal "watchdog" barking. The gradually increasing tail wagging and the play bow and spin are fabulous. And then Sophie seems to get a bit overwhelmed and does her default sofa retreat. But the joy she clearly shows at Diane coming home and the fact that she then chooses to check in with you about the noise – all that is really good news . . . Apart from the monster,' Si concludes with a smile, 'which lurks beyond the force field of the living room threshold of course!'

Dear Si – he's always such a glass-half-full person, accentuating the positive, providing much-needed encouragement and downplaying any bumps in the road towards the emergence of a Sophie more like what I would regard as a 'normal' dog. Meanwhile, I'm uneasily aware that in recent years my natural cheerfulness has sometimes given way to a tendency to look for reasons to be gloomy. Just as every time I go to watch Brentford play, I expect them to lose – so anything else is a bonus – each time Sophie retreats behind the sofa, I wonder whether she will ever be the happy dog I need her to be.

Then again, when I am told that her behaviour is not out of the ordinary for a rescue dog and I need to be patient, I remember the '3-3-3 rule', the tried and tested yardstick when you adopt a rescue dog to get a sense of the various phases your new pet may go through in the period after they first arrive – the first three days, three weeks and three months of the settling-in period.

And so now, in mid-March – three full months since Sophie's arrival – I find myself deciding that it's worth checking in with the rule to get a sense of how she is really doing. After three months, so the accepted wisdom goes, our dog should be 'finally completely comfortable in her new home'. Also, according to the '3-3-3 rule', Sophie should by now be 'building trust and a new bond' with us her owners, and have 'gained a complete sense of security within her new family'.

Well, I reflect wryly, it could be said that Sophie is comfortable – behind the sofa, that is. Because apart from that, she is still very wary in her new home, and if there are loud noises or strange people (and unfortunately our cleaner Halina still comes into this category), she will retreat to her one safe space. What is more, aside from our kitchen-living room and the back garden, there are still many areas in our home where she has not yet been brave enough to venture – the hall, the front door, the front room, and the upper two floors of our house – as well of course as our front garden. In three months she has never put so much as a paw into this strange and forbidding territory which lies beyond the threshold of the door to the living room.

As for bonding and building trust, well, I suppose she trusts us to feed her – especially small morsels of cheese and bacon, if she happens to feel so inclined – and will grudgingly accept a little light stroking from Diane and even occasionally from me. But if we are building a relationship of trust, this is a project way behind schedule, with just a few bricks being added from time to time, often only to fall off the next day.

So even measured by this cautious yardstick for rescue dog owners, our progress has been painfully slow. And what about me – how is my health as I settle in with my new animal companion? When I examine the data on the Apple Health app I use to monitor my exercise regime it reveals that so far this year, I am doing far fewer daily steps than this time twelve months ago. I am now averaging 7,776 steps a day, compared with 9,342 in 2022, for most of which I did not even own a dog. So, just another reminder that things with Sophie are not panning out as I'd hoped.

If one of the reasons for getting a new dog was to help keep me fit and healthy, at this point she is falling down on the job. On Instagram, I post an image of my step count with a message saying: 'Now listen #sophiefromromania I need you to shape up and come walking soon if we're to hit our 2023 target.' When someone replies, commenting that they forced the issue with their dog, got a lead on and never looked back, it sets me thinking. Is the 'take it at her pace' strategy advocated by Si really working?

Some days later, in the process of working on this book, I look back at the notes I made in January about Sophie's progress – back then she had started going into the garden, accepting food from our hands sometimes and allowing the occasional stroke. Two months later, have we really moved on, I ask myself yet again. When I talk to Diane about this, she reminds me of all that's been achieved lately – the puppy pads are now gone and Sophie is just about house-trained, most mornings now emerging from behind the sofa within half an hour or so of my arrival downstairs to pop out into the garden and do what has to be done. She now spends much less time hiding in her safe space and, especially when the two of us are around, seems happy to hang out with us in the kitchen or in the back garden. She'll accept food from our hands, allow Diane to pet her and even actively demands strokes. Have I forgotten all the things Si achieved with Sophie during his stay? And what about that wonderful play bow out in the back garden in February – something she continues to do, now directed at actual people (Diane and Si) rather than just a ball?

The next day, Si is equally reassuring when I talk to him. After the by now usual joke about my needy boyfriend tendencies, he prompts me to remember more recent markers of progress. Such as how, just a few nights previously, Sophie approached the bed in the living room we bought for her before she arrived, until now unused. She circled it, pawed at it, and eventually seized a soft toy we had placed in it and took it away to tear it apart. I have to admit, watching her do what any normal dog would do with something chewable was strangely uplifting. 'And in no time, Sophie will be snuggling down into that bed,' Si tells me. And then he points out, gently as ever, how important it is in this process to acknowledge the small wins – and to take the time to celebrate them when they happen.

Part of me knows Si is right – but when you're a naturally impatient man who has always enjoyed looking to the future and planning next steps, it's not always easy to have such a Zen approach to everyday life. But maybe that's something Sophie is slowly teaching me. And as I think about the fact that she is starting to do some normal doggy things, I can't help hoping that maybe it is a sign that next month we will at last see her desert the sofa for a proper bed, learn to play without fear and wear a harness, in preparation for what I have begun to think of as The Big W – going for a walk. Although I may be getting ahead of myself again . . .

Chapter Seven

Dog Parents

Do we know what we're doing?

'She'd been rejected because she couldn't be made whole. I just thought, "We are all broken in some way – why should she be left behind?"'

Sadaf Maruf

April – the month of our wedding anniversary and a time we nearly always manage at least a weekend away in celebration – often to the Lakes, and every five years to Venice. This year, 2023, will be our thirty-third anniversary. We originally had nothing planned, but then Diane got invited to speak at an economics conference at a luxury hotel on Lake Como, so we decided I'd tag along as her plus one and we'd have an anniversary dinner while there. Once again, we wonder whether we will make enough progress over the coming three weeks to be able to leave Sophie with someone for a couple of nights.

But we begin this bright 1 April, a Saturday, with an assessment of where we have got to so far. After the usual Saturday busy start, with my weekly Pilates class followed by a piano lesson, we fire up a laptop and sit down at the kitchen table for a video call with Si up in the Aberdeenshire seaside village which is his home. Sophie has been reasonably sociable this morning, staying out in the living room while our piano teacher

Theo gives a lesson first to me, then to our daughter who makes a quick weekly visit for this and stays for lunch. As usual Theo, a dog lover, is desperate for a glimpse of Sophie but he knows by now that even peeking through the door to the living room will provoke an anxious bark and a scuttle behind the sofa.

I remain the gloomiest of the three of us about our progress, in particular the fact that Sophie won't approach us readily which means that targets such as getting her into a harness seem impossible. As ever, Si is deeply reassuring on our call, pointing to a couple of video clips I sent him, each showing Sophie having positive interactions with Diane as evidence that we are getting somewhere. Diane is also less pessimistic than me and much more patient.

But I bring the conversation back to short-term targets which, if we can achieve them, will give us a sense that life with this painfully nervous dog is getting easier. When will we get that harness on her, how will we be able to get away together to Lake Como and, crucially, will we be able to take her on holiday to Cardigan Bay in late July? Every year we rent a wonderful house overlooking the sea, and Cabbage and I used to love our early walks along the coastal path. But for Sophie it will mean a five-hour car ride to a strange environment where she will have to rub along with six of us, including our two young grandchildren. Will she really be ready for that in less than four months?

Si's answer surprises and delights me. 'That'll happen,' he says, then laughs when I tease him that I've recorded the call and will hold him to his promise. But as we end the call, I am in much better spirits. If we really can head off on holiday with a much more confident dog, then all the anxiety and hard work of the last three months will have been worth it.

We then have a typically up and down week. On Sunday Sophie, who has been moulting steadily, allows Diane to brush her for a full ten seconds which feels like a big breakthrough. Then from Monday to Wednesday she is back in grumpy 'my mistress is away' mood, skittish around me, eating very little and spending a lot of time behind the sofa. On Monday I am out all afternoon recording three more episodes of *Movers and Shakers* in the pub with my Parkinson's gang. We talk about dogs and when I mention my envy of Jeremy's rescue dog Derek, often found in the pub with him, he is characteristically blunt about Sophie's deficiencies. Which makes me feel strangely protective of her – how dare the Grand Inquisitor diss my dog?

On Wednesday a *BBC Breakfast* crew is coming to our house to shoot a follow-up piece on Sophie's progress since her first appearance on the programme in January. Knowing they are extremely unlikely to see her, I have been trying to get together some footage for them and this morning, before the reporter and cameraman arrive, I try something new. For weeks people on Twitter have been suggesting I 'get down to Sophie's level', sitting on the floor so I'm not such an intimidating presence. I have pointed out that getting down is one thing but getting my Parkinson's stiffened body back up again is quite another. But now I grab my phone, squat on the kitchen floor and see what happens.

Sophie seems wary, giving me sideway looks, as if she's thinking, 'What on earth is the old fool up to now?' She does keep approaching and then retreating and at one point even sniffs my socks. After I have heaved myself back up, I post a clip on YouTube, and there are kind comments about another breakthrough. I remain unconvinced – whether I'm standing up or sitting down, this dog is still extremely nervous around me and other humans. And sure enough, when the reporter and cameraman arrive, she retreats behind the sofa and stays there.

As ever, they do a very professional job, filming me peering over the sofa and having a Zoom call with Si about Sophie. I give them the footage I have shot, and they depart at lunchtime happy but I am curious as to what their report will say when it is broadcast next week. It is not until 4.30 that a nose appears from behind the sofa and then the rest of the dog emerges – and of course it is Diane's arrival home which has sparked the change of mood.

While I am mildly exasperated that all it takes is the sound of my wife's key in the door for the dog to perk up, both Sophie and I feel happier when Diane is home, and we have a relaxing evening together. But then a WhatsApp chat with Si takes a surprising turn:

> Si: If Sophie isn't ready to go to Pembrokeshire in August, I'll house and pet sit for you.
> Rory: 👍 That's so sweet of you but she'll be ready!!
> Si: I know. That's why I offered 😁🙂
> Rory: But if you fancy a holiday in London, you are very welcome!!
> Si: Genuine offer though. Hopefully it'll take the pressure off . . . just in case 😁 . . . ! Backup plan!

Just five days after assuring us that Sophie will be ready to come to Wales with us, Si appears to be a little less confident. Now, once again he is making an incredibly generous offer to come and help us out of a hole in the summer. And while I say confidently, 'She'll be ready', a nagging little voice inside me wonders whether that really will be the case.

While I meet plenty of people online going through similar experiences with Romanian rescue dogs, there is one person who is even more valuable to me because she lives nearby, we can meet face-to-face and what's more, she's a friend and former colleague. This is Sadaf, the person who told me about Friends Indeed, and who since then texts me every couple of weeks to ask how things are going. But one day we meet up, so that she can tell me more about her own Romanian rescue dog, Cookie.

COOKIE FROM ROMANIA

I meet Sadaf at her house, which is just a ten-minute walk away from where we live. While we sit chatting, Cookie slumbers by my feet under the kitchen table.

Sadaf tells me that for years she and her husband resisted the pressure from their children to get a dog. Then shortly after the family's pet hamster died, they finally relented. Initially they looked after friends' dogs when they were away, then in 2020 as the Covid pandemic got underway, Sadaf began the hunt for one of their own. From the outset she was clear about what she was looking for: 'I wanted to have a dog that was a rescue. I felt that that would be a good thing to do, rather than go to a breeder and get a puppy.'

Much like us, she signed up with a number of the major UK dog charities but had a similarly frustrating experience in the search for a suitable pet. She felt that the charities, which are all quite strict about who they let adopt a pet, were wary about her family because they had never owned a dog before. So Sadaf then turned to social media. She quickly found herself bombarded with pictures of rescue dogs, many from abroad, and came across an Anglo/Romanian charity called Shelter to Sofa. She liked the look of one dog on their books.

This was a dog called Pufa, a smallish, exuberant shaggy-looking Terrier in need of a haircut: 'She looked like a sheepdog in the photos – there were lots of action shots.' Which was ironic, given that Pufa turned out to be quite badly disabled, apparently after an encounter with a car which left her with a front left leg that was damaged in a few places.

Sadaf was then put in touch with a man called Dan at the shelter in Romania where Pufa was being cared for. Dan spoke little English but used Google Translate to tell her that because of Covid restrictions in transporting animals, he now had more than fifty dogs waiting at the shelter for homes in the UK. He said that another English lady had been interested in Pufa but had pulled out after paying for a number of scans, because it became apparent that the chances of her leg being restored to any kind of normal function were not great.

Given that, I ask Sadaf, why did she choose this dog? She replies without hesitation, 'Honestly I think it was partly because I thought she looked very cute without looking like a toy – and then very quickly, because she'd been rejected because she couldn't be made whole. I just thought, "We are all broken in some way – why should she be left behind?" '

But first, just like the UK rescue charities, Shelter to Sofa had to carry out certain due diligence checks on the family, as with all their potential adopters. Sadaf had to give a video tour of the house and garden to a British woman, who wanted to make sure it was a suitable environment for Pufa. Or rather Cookie, as she would be known from that point – the name Sadaf's twin teenage daughters had suggested because they couldn't imagine calling out 'Pufa!' in a London park.

Then, to arrange delivery of the dog, Dan told Sadaf she should speak to his partner in the shelter, a Romanian man who had been based in the UK for many years. Enter Adrian Tataru – at this time he was just in the process of setting up his new charity, Friends Indeed, which a few years later would deliver

Sophie to us. Dan also told Sadaf that if she ever decided she could not cope with Cookie, she should not give her away, but contact Adrian who would take her back.

Sadaf then had a ninety-minute call with Adrian and came away much happier about the whole set-up. It was in May 2020, just as the first Covid lockdown eased, that the van carrying Cookie arrived outside their front door – in the middle of the day rather than Sophie's dead-of-night slot for delivery. As Sadaf relates, 'The driver had a mask on and he pulled out this very bedraggled-looking, quite large dog – I thought she was going to be smaller. She was very, very hairy – she had almost dreadlocks in fact. He carried her from the van and then handed her to me.'

It seems that this dog, too, was traumatised by her trip across Europe: 'For the first week she was basically hiding – the thing that I remember most is how much she was shaking; she was just shaking with fear . . .' Before her arrival the family had prepared a safe space for Cookie – a cage with an open door and a blanket over it. But as Sadaf recalls, 'She stank to high heaven,' so they took her into the garden to give her a bath in a big tub, thinking that would be less scary than hauling her up to the bathroom.

They had been told not to take Cookie for a walk straight away. And in fact, Sadaf tells me, they did not take her out for a whole week and even then, only round the block. She finds and now shows me the video of Cookie they shot on the day in question: 'She's kind of struggling . . . Kind of going, "What are you doing? Where am I? Why am I going out of the house?"' As I watch the footage, I can't help thinking to myself that getting a nervous animal out of the house within a week sounds like a triumph to the owner of a certain dog . . .

While Cookie was soon going further afield, it was not all

plain sailing. To date she has run off twice – on one occasion, racing out of the park where Sadaf had inadvertently dropped her lead, and dashing across a busy main road before being found hiding under a parked car, quivering with terror.

Meanwhile at home, any noise would spook Cookie at first and, Sadaf tells me, she still hates the sound of the vacuum cleaner and is distraught during fireworks season. She is not at all keen on men – so if a plumber or electrician comes to the house she has to be shepherded away. And she can't really be left alone, either.

But Sadaf and her family have persisted in taking Cookie for walks, even straight after the incident when she ran out of the park: 'I just thought we have got to do it, otherwise we will never leave the house.' And there is another issue with going for walks which is very particular to Cookie. Her lame front leg means she shuffles rather than walks – although she can move quite fast until she tires. But it seems that some passers-by, seeing her gait, can get into their heads that she is being mistreated. As Sadaf relates, 'You can't go down the road for more than five minutes without someone tutting or going, "Oh, poor thing!"'

But now, three years after Cookie arrived, she is clearly a much-loved member of the family. Sadaf takes her everywhere – even on the five-hour train journey to Edinburgh where one of the twins has started university. And while the family may have rescued this little dog, it has definitely been a two-way street, Sadaf tells me, since Cookie arrived at a time when they were confronting some serious issues: 'She's done a lot for all of us, kept us going and kept us sane.'

Meanwhile I've been thinking about Si's offer to come and stay with Sophie if need be in July while we are on holiday. While it is such a generous suggestion, I am struck by the change of heart it seems to indicate – a few days previously he had after all assured us she would have made enough progress by then to be able to travel with us. It occurs to me that some of the more critical voices on social media might be undermining his confidence – as indeed they have been on occasion undermining ours over the months. The next time I'm in touch with Si, I put this to him and he confides that, while he continues to believe wholeheartedly in his methods and the path we've been taking, he is feeling the strain a little when it comes to the naysayers on social media.

From the early days there has been an undercurrent of comment on Twitter/X suggesting we are taking the wrong course with Sophie and need to change our approach. These naysayers are massively outnumbered and indeed shouted down by those who support what we are doing, but they persist. Some of them seem perfectly genuine in wanting to help, even if we do not think they have the right answers. The best of them do not shout the odds on social media but get in touch privately to offer help. An organisation called Dogs 4 Rescue was involved in the first *BBC Breakfast* broadcast, with a representative and a rescue dog in the Salford studio to offer advice. Their approach involves housing nervous rescue dogs with more confident animals and after the broadcast they emailed the *BBC Breakfast* producer, asking her to pass on a message offering a solution for Sophie.

This is what they said: 'We could lend a well-rounded rehabbed street dog who could provide a perfect example of how to behave as a UK dog, and motivate and help her move forward. This in turn gives our dog a much-loved home life while they wait to be adopted rather than them being here when they don't need to be.' They emphasised that this arrangement could be for a short or long period depending on Sophie's progress, and that while it might seem like a strange suggestion, it was something that had worked wonders many times before.

The email went on to suggest alternatives, including an offer to take Sophie into 'rehab' at the Dogs 4 Rescue centre near Manchester with the eventual aim of getting her on a lead and then out for a walk: 'How long she may take to get to the walking stage is very much an unknown, but we would know very quickly if it is going to work . . . We have taught dogs to walk on lead that could not even be touched by people but are now rehomed happily, and you would never know they'd ever been so afraid.'

To us, however, after just a few weeks with Sophie, introducing another dog as a tutor and sending her away for rehabilitation seemed like very radical measures that we weren't prepared to take at that point. We asked the producer to pass back a message, saying we were very grateful for this generous offer but that, on the advice of our dog behaviourist, we were taking things nice and slowly and were having some success.

From the very beginning the idea of introducing Sophie to other dogs has been a constantly recurring theme amongst the many online commenters offering suggestions to help her 'normalise'. But Si has always been sceptical, pointing out that it can be a risky approach. It might work – however, allowing another creature into the only safe space that Sophie now has could terrify her and undo all the good work that's been done. But as the months pass and the 'nice and slow' approach advocated by Si appears to be yielding few results, I do sometimes wonder what would have happened if we had accepted the offer from Dogs 4 Rescue after all.

But while the Dogs 4 Rescue suggestion was indeed a

generous and well-meaning offer, we have been less than impressed with some of the suggestions about what we should or shouldn't do with Sophie. And now, in early April, even Si – surely one of the most gentle, upbeat and patient people I've ever met – is beginning to find this difficult at times.

Concerned, as I am, that Si is feeling under such pressure, Diane takes a look at what has been happening on his Twitter account, after which she gets cross herself. It seems that someone she knew as an acquaintance from work circles many years ago, and now long retired, has been responding to Si's updates with a persistence even a saint would find irksome. In fact, the same person got in touch a few months back when the story about Sophie first emerged, advising Diane blithely and in the most familiar of terms that she should give up her Professorship at Cambridge and acclaimed work in public policy in order to devote herself to Sophie on a full-time basis. And now it seems this person has turned the spotlight of his scrutiny onto our dog behaviourist.

Si has posted a thread about how well Diane, Sophie and I are doing: 'They're making excellent progress. Sometimes it's tempting to try alternative approaches because progress feels so glacially slow . . . But things are going as they do with fearful dogs. Sometimes quickly and sometimes slowly. Desensitisation and counterconditioning is an evidence-based, science-led approach that is proven to be the most efficient in resolving fear-based issues . . . With Sophie we're playing the long game because slow and steady is the shortest route to the goal. I thank everyone for their support and continued enthusiasm for Sophie's journey. She'll get there.'

This post invites a back and forth from various naysayers. Fairly soon after Sophie's arrival, a dog trainer with a very vocal group of supporters began commenting regularly, advocating a much more hard-headed interventionist approach to Sophie, which would show her exactly who was boss. When this advice was ignored, one of this trainer's most vocal acolytes tweeted after I posted a photo of me frying bacon for the dog that what he described as 'the most boring life ever' with no walk in months wouldn't bring the dog round. The tweet wanted to know where I was getting advice, accused me of being 'pig-headed' in refusing free offers of help, told me my approach wasn't working and I was failing Sophie.

It turns out that the trainer in question, Jamie Penrith, is the UK's leading advocate of what are known as 'shock collars' – a controversial means of training or disciplining an unruly dog. These collars, which deliver a shock of between 100 and 6,000 volts, have been condemned by many animal welfare organisations, which regard their use as a return to cruel and outdated approaches to dog training based on punishment. There have been promises from the government to bring in a law to ban what their defenders call 'e-collars'. In 2018 Michael Gove, then the environment secretary, stated that these cause unacceptable 'harm and suffering', and urged dog owners to use 'positive reward training methods' instead. But five years on, no law has been introduced and these 'pro-shock-collar' groups continue to promote them as a viable approach to training on their well-subscribed YouTube channels and via Twitter/X.

A couple of people have suggested that in sharing Sophie's story on social media, I have made our dog and our family public figures and as such fair game for criticism – that is a position I must accept. So, why have I done that? I suppose because on Twitter it has been my style for a long time to develop a more relaxed persona than the rather buttoned-up role of BBC correspondent had allowed me. Over time, I had gradually supplemented tweets about technology stories with more personal

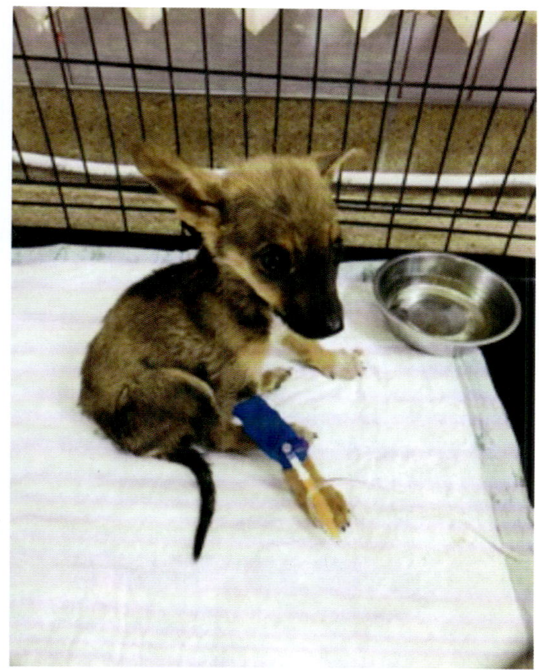

At the beginning of 2022,
frail newborn Sophie is rescued by
a vet after being found dumped by the roadside

Sophie arrives, 2.45 am, 17 December 2022

We put a lead on her the morning after she arrives but she digs in her heels and refuses to budge

Sophie in her safe space – behind the sofa – where she will spend most of her time until July

For the first seven months, Sophie will only emerge from behind the sofa with extreme caution

After her first month, in January,
Sophie begins to come out from behind the sofa to explore the garden

By April she is starting to spend more time enjoying the sun

Six months after arriving, a trembling Sophie rides in the car on the way to the vet for the first time

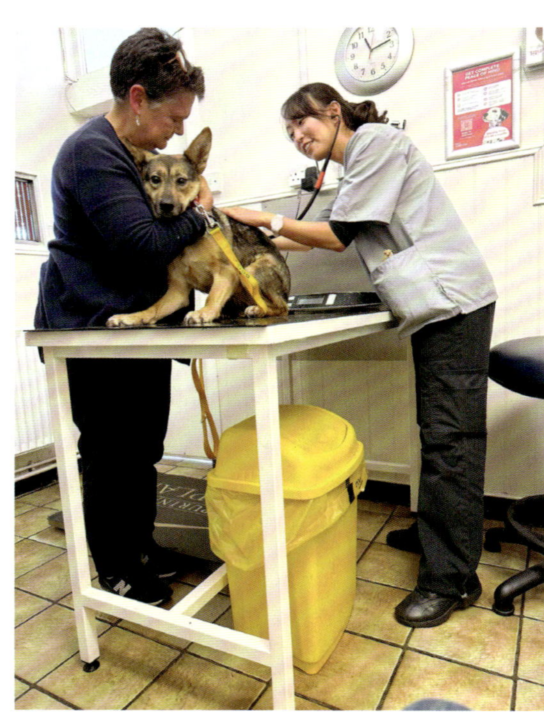

Sophie's first check-up with the vet on 2 June

In July, Si manages to get Sophie to accept her bed

The kitchen becomes her new favourite place

Finally, in August, Sophie starts to show her playful side, deconstructing our shoes and arranging them near her bed

Si and Sophie become best of friends

In September, no longer hiding behind the sofa, she is taking an interest in household activities

Sophie is ready to play and seems to say, 'Look at me, not the television!'

After my fall, it is more difficult for Sophie and me to connect, but by December we are making progress again

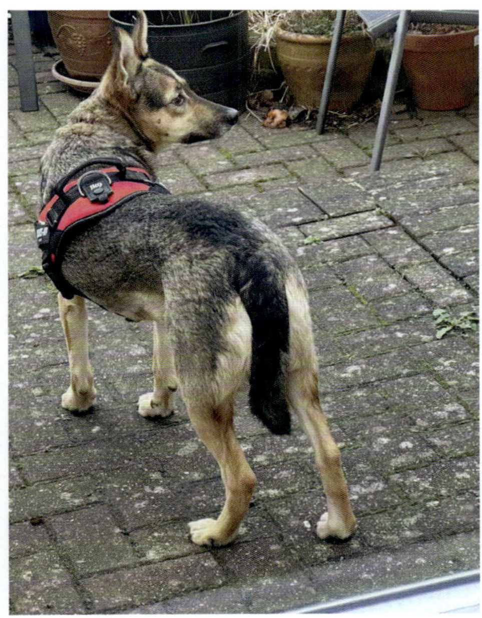

In February, she starts getting comfortable with the harness . . .

. . . and is ready to venture out beyond the front door

Finally, after fourteen months, on 25 February 2024,
I'm out on a walk with Sophie!

matters – my passion for sourdough baking, the fortunes of my football club, and my walks with Cabbage. It worked, bringing me a sizeable audience, and I admit I got a kick out of seeing my follower numbers grow and interacting with them in a way which had never happened when I was just a TV reporter watched by the indifferent millions who tuned into the *Six O'Clock News*.

So sharing Sophie's story was nothing new, but it has become a far more complex and emotional tale than I had expected. Perhaps I should have been more cautious but it now feels too late to change course. And for every critic who brings my mood down, there are a thousand enthusiasts telling us how well we are doing and restoring our faith that we are on the right path. Around this time, one such person sends me a direct message on Twitter. Bennett Cohen tells me not to let what he calls 'the slings and arrows' of my critics stop me from sharing my journey with our dog:

> 'It is brave to embrace a rescue with all the unknowns involved. Braver still to share the journey with others – which I understand is tied to your own journey with Parkinson's. Which again is braver still.' And he ends: 'It's a joy to follow you here. For the tech. For the politics. For the health information. And for Sophie.'

Over the Easter weekend there are some more positive signs on the Sophie front, as she spends much of Saturday afternoon and Sunday morning roaming the kitchen and garden in what seems an amiable mood. Though when our four-year-old granddaughter arrives at lunchtime on Sunday to spend the night with us,

Sophie disappears behind the sofa and doesn't show her face again, even when the granddaughter is safely tucked up in bed. Early on Monday morning I go downstairs and try to persuade the dog to come out while everyone is still asleep. But she's not having any of it – and it is not until the child has been picked up by my son and his wife that Sophie finally emerges, after twenty-two hours in isolation. In one sense this is fine – if a four-year-old and a very nervous dog were both out playing on the living room carpet, Diane and I would probably have been constantly on edge in case something went wrong. But at some stage Sophie is going to have to learn to live alongside people other than the two of us.

On Wednesday the *BBC Breakfast* report filmed last week is broadcast and the nation is given a hopeful message about the progress Sophie has made over the last four months. Mind you, the reporter John Moloney teases out of me a few quotes where you can sense my growing frustration – such as my comment that Sophie is 'like a moody teenager', and my admission that, unlike me, Diane is 'the ultimately patient person', whose attitude on the issue of going for a walk is, 'Just let it happen.'

The following day Si arrives in London early, having taken the sleeper train from Scotland, though this time he's not on a dog-sitting mission. He is on his way to Cambridge tomorrow to attend the annual conference of Diane's Bennett Institute for Public Policy – he's become so fascinated by her work that she's invited him along. But he'll be staying overnight with me and Sophie first, and is happy to look after Sophie while I go off to my regular checkup at Moorfields Hospital, where they want to see how the malignant melanoma behind my left eye is doing.

By the time I leave home at noon for my appointment, neither I nor Si, who arrived before 9 am, have seen so much as a whisker of Sophie, which is immensely frustrating. Today is a day when I should be focused on my health – every time I get an appointment letter from Moorfields, that dread word 'oncology' leaps out at me – but instead I'm worrying about a dog. When I arrive at the hospital there's a ping from WhatsApp and I see that Si has sent a picture showing that the moody teenager is finally up and about.

And there's good news for me on the health front too – the doctors tell me that the melanoma is continuing to respond well to the proton beam treatment I had a few years back. I am, I feel, doubly exploiting Si, as I'll be having a night out in town later with some former BBC colleagues, but I return home briefly to see how things are going. Sophie is out and about, though not overly friendly, but as ever Si is very encouraging in his assessment: 'She's doing really well.'

After this is a period when Diane is away a lot – not just in Cambridge as usual but also on a three-day trip to California for a high-powered conference about AI. When she is briefly at home Sophie perks up, then we both get a bit gloomy when she goes again, as my diary reflects. The Sunday of the weekend Diane is in California starts well, with Sophie emerging fairly quickly from behind the sofa and hanging out with me until I go out for my regular fitness training session with Wendy (who has long since given up on the idea of meeting Sophie). But things seem to go downhill from there, as my diary entry shows: 'Get back at 12.30 – she's behind sofa and stays there for the rest of the day! Very irritated and even depressed by this.'

That word, 'depressed', cropping up again . . . So am I feeling seriously down or am I overdramatising my feelings? After all, as I said earlier, I had suffered from depression for a year or more around the time of my Parkinson's diagnosis – so I know what it is like. But this feels different somehow – not as if there's a permanent black cloud over my life but still something that has me lying awake at night and in the early morning hours, worrying and ruminating. And a lot of this thinking seems focused on Sophie. I have grown to love our little rescue, but this makes me all the more sad and frustrated that she is not right now the dog I need her to be. I dream of the day she'll become my constant companion on walks, a pet that my grandchildren can stroke. And, much as I hate to admit it, I also need Sophie to be the kind of dog that is happy to travel in a car and to stay in other homes – otherwise I will be trapped at home with her all year round.

Fortunately I was able to share at least some of this with Si during his recent overnight visit. Once again he was trying to reassure me, by stressing that Sophie's slow progress is nothing out of the ordinary – to which I replied that while this might be the case, waiting two years for a walk can't be part of my plan at this stage in my life: 'Because, don't forget, this has a material effect on our lives. I'm of an age where I'd like to be making the most of my life right now.' I didn't say the word Parkinson's, but I know Si understood my meaning. Like anyone with an incurable degenerative disease, I am only heading in one direction – downhill. I think I have coped pretty well in the first three years since my diagnosis, still walking confidently and determined to do all the things I've always done. But every now and then I catch a glimpse of myself in a mirror or, as has happened a few times recently, I am filmed for a TV report and I think, 'Who's that doddery old man shuffling along?' Who knows – five years from now I could be in a wheelchair.

What I also don't tell Si is that in truth, I'm wrung out and exhausted by all the worry that comes with trying to help Sophie. At times I feel something close to despair when I look at the calendar and realise she has now been with us for four months and is still spending the majority of her time behind the sofa.

Luckily, I'm about to get the perfect antidote to that emotional exhaustion the following weekend. That Friday, leaving our daughter in charge of Sophie, we jet off to Lake Como for Diane's conference at the luxury hotel. This is one of the many times it is great to be Mr Diane Coyle – eating fine meals, doing a little light tourism while the professor is in a conference session, and meeting some fascinating people – and yes, even here at a meeting about developments in intellectual property law, there are those who want to know how Sophie is doing.

We're both feeling the benefit of this intensely relaxing environment, but we're keen to check in from time to time on what is happening at home. Our daughter is a private person and one of those rare young people who doesn't 'do' social media, but she's happy to keep us updated on Sophie over the weekend – albeit not quite in the same diligent way Si would. We'd left home at 5.15 on Friday morning and then had to wait until after 5 pm before getting a rather fuzzy picture of Sophie, finally out from behind the sofa. Another terrible photo arrives at some point on Saturday – to our great relief – and on Sunday as we fly home, we get a message to the effect that she has 'made a second garden trip'. So that sounds positive – Sophie has been out on all three days, and not staged a sit-down (or stay-behind-the-sofa) strike as we had feared. And when we get home, she even seems moderately pleased to see us.

For the last week of April Sophie remains skittish and shy around me – however, she has some great moments with Diane, when she leaps up at her as if to say 'hello' and allows the longest cuddles yet. These interactions are a reminder that deep inside our little rescue dog there is a loving and playful pet waiting to come out once she has shed the fear that is paralysing her.

With the summer coming, and our big holiday in Wales on the horizon, it feels as though it is time to take stock – and it seems our advisor is of a similar mind. Si sends us a long note on WhatsApp. He says that under normal circumstances he would see things as going along nicely, with Sophie more relaxed and comfortable, and if it weren't for other considerations such as our holiday he'd be inclined to leave things as they are. He is very much aware of our deadline and the need to take preparatory steps now: 'We don't want to be in a place where we have no choice but to bundle Sophie up and put her in the car, if that is going to scare her.' He's clear that his offer to dog-sit still stands, but says it isn't the best option at this point. He then lays out what he calls a more structured plan to 'optimise' Sophie's rate of progress. This is music to my ears of course.

Next Si wants to know how much time we will have for the intensive work he's envisaging. When, as he rightly suspected, it becomes clear that we won't have the necessary free time for the 'desensitisation and counter-conditioning' of our scared dog, he has a proposal: 'I'm planning a trip down south in May to visit my Mum. I could make a trip to you too and have some days with Sophie to see how far I can progress with getting a harness on her if I do nothing but focus on that. Given the rate she came on with me last time, I'm hopeful that it may go well.'

'Excellent,' I think to myself. At last we have a plan. Things are looking up.

A few days after this conversation, I bump into Sadaf and Cookie on one of the streets near us. Once again, I'm charmed by the obvious bond between the two of them, and the spirit of this brave little dog who has responded so well to the love she's been given and lives life to the full in spite of her lame front leg. Afterwards I remember Sadaf's inspiring words: 'I just thought,

"We are all broken in some way – why should she be left behind?"' It occurs to me that Sophie too is broken because of her excessive fearfulness – and in my own way, so am I because of my Parkinson's. But that doesn't mean there isn't hope for both of us and the possibility for us to live our lives to the utmost for as long as we can . . .

Chapter Eight

Sad Dog

When tender loving care isn't enough

'Take time to celebrate the small wins.'

Si Wooler

It's early May and the Coronation weekend has arrived. On the day after King Charles III and Queen Camilla are crowned, the residents of our road in West London hold a street party. Over the thirty years we've lived here, soaring house prices have seen more affluent people arrive, including executives from overseas companies who only stay for a couple of years for the easy access to Heathrow. But it remains a sociable neighbourly street with a couple of really energetic residents who make events like today's party happen. The previous weekend, I'd dug out and watched a video I made of the street party we held in 2012 to mark the Queen's Diamond Jubilee and the first thing I noticed was Cabbage sitting serenely in the middle of the road watching the world go by. Oh, how I wish we could replicate that scene with our new dog today. But then Diane reminds me that by then Cabbage had been with us for a full five years, whereas for Sophie it's only been a little over five months.

Back then nobody made any fuss of Cabbage but today, as we munch on sausages from the barbecue outside, grilled vegetables from the new young couple at the other end of the street, and the homemade focaccia that is our contribution, one name and one question is on everybody's lips: 'Where's Sophie?' says just about anyone we run into. Even our MP – who has popped by on her tour of street parties in her constituency – wants to talk about our dog, speculating that Sophie has shunned the event because she is a republican. The truth is, of course, that a dog who hasn't yet even ventured down our hall to the front door was never going to go out in the big wide world and mingle with dozens of terrifying strangers – no matter how momentous the occasion being celebrated on this day might be. But as I try to explain this to one neighbour after another, I see the puzzlement spread across their faces, which means that inwardly, I ask myself what has by now become a perennial question: should it really be like this?

As if to underline this, on the Bank Holiday Monday we meet a dog who is the opposite of Sophie. When we visit our son Adam and daughter-in-law Franny, our granddaughter is playing with a dog called Katie and it is hard to know who is more excited – the four-year-old or the bouncy little Spaniel. The dog belonged to Franny's grandmother who died recently and has been taken on by her parents. Seeking a bit of respite from a quite demanding dog, they have handed Katie over to Adam and Franny for a couple of days. We all head off to the pub with the grandchildren and Katie, and although she is a touch annoying, climbing all over me, trying to get at the beers on the table, I think wistfully how great it would be if Sophie was a bit more like this. But again, perhaps these constant comparisons, where Sophie always seems to end up falling short, aren't helpful for anyone.

And the truth is that progress on the Sophie front is continuing to happen, sometimes in tiny almost imperceptible steps, but sometimes in more significant ways also. One sunny afternoon shortly after the June Bank Holiday, Diane and I are both sitting on the bench in the garden when Sophie comes out to join us and starts mooching around – previously she has not been inclined to share this space with humans. We send a video clip to Si, who is most excited and then takes the opportunity to run through some of the complex training procedures we need to follow to help build Sophie's trust and get her more comfortable with being around us.

Si wants me to work on a routine whereby Sophie comes up close to me and I deliver her a treat. If she's hesitant, I can put it on the floor and let her take it. Apparently I have to keep doing this until she's approaching me at least a dozen times a day for these small morsels of food. Once this routine has been established, and only then, I can focus on getting her used to being petted and stroked by me. I have to start by moving my left hand slowly to the side of her head before I hand over the treat. If she gets spooked, I must go only part of the way with my left hand. Gradually, ever so slowly and methodically, I'm to move my hand closer, Si tells me, 'until you can gently and briefly touch the side of her neck'.

This is beginning to sound like a full-time job, and both Diane and I are already being pulled in so many directions. But Si urges us to ignore those siren voices online telling us there is a faster way: 'Contrary to the advice of those who have only anecdote to support their thinking, there are no shortcuts to this process or "other" things to try. The most efficient system is tried, tested and repeatable.' His method may take time but, he assures me, if it's followed to the letter, it works: 'Go with the tried and tested plan, and pretty soon you will notice Sophie making contact with you to alert you to her presence – and physical contact from you can follow from there. The goal is to have the harness on, go for a walk and get her through "driving school" by the end of July.'

Well, at that, I sit up and take notice! Si is clearly saying that Sophie will be able to come with us to Wales. This is just the kind of 'can do' talk I like to hear.

The following day, Tuesday, 9 May, Si arrives around teatime after spending the day on the train down from Inverness. He has promised to stay for as long as it takes – with a couple of days out to see his mother – to move Sophie forward. I cook the two of us a nice steak each for dinner – Sophie gets a good chunk from both of our plates. We then sit and watch some football, but she remains resolutely behind the sofa as if to say, '"Move me forward"? We'll see about that.' It's not a promising start, but tomorrow is another day . . .

Thankfully, Sophie does emerge the next morning after breakfast, which is fortunate because for much of the next few days she and Si are going to be alone together. I'm off to Exeter for the day to investigate some new technology connected with the treatment of Parkinson's for the newsletter I write. Then in the evening I'm at the launch of a book about the art of political interviewing written by Rob Burley, a former BBC colleague who has recently announced he has Parkinson's. But at a party packed with Westminster's finest, everyone I meet seems to want to talk about Sophie – 'I'm obsessed with her,' Beth Rigby, Sky's Political Editor tells me.

The following lunchtime – Day Three of Si's visit – after a brief stroke with Sophie which cheers me up no end, I head to the airport. I have a whirlwind trip to Sweden to do some media training with a major multinational company. It is strangely relaxing not having to think about the ever-changing moods of our dog for twenty-four hours.

Over the weekend I'm back from Sweden and Diane has returned from Cambridge, so we can all regroup and see how Si and Sophie have been getting on. She is certainly comfortable in his presence, especially when he is handing out tiny cubes of Comté cheese. On Sunday I cook everyone – including Sophie – a big breakfast, ignoring those social media grumblers who seem to think a rasher of bacon once a week could prove fatal to our dog. She is in a sociable mood, hanging around under the table while we eat, and later following Diane and Si into the garden. But when I return at 4.30 pm from watching a football match, she is behind the sofa, where she remains for the rest of the day. That evening, our regular Sunday evening get-together with neighbours is in our front room, and Si joins us for a glass or two of wine. Our friends ask how things are with Sophie, and Diane and Si tell them it's all going really well. I'm not sure I quite agree – but I decide to keep my mouth shut.

The following morning, Day Six of Si's stay, Diane heads off to Cambridge, and Si and I sit down for a kind of five-month review of Sophie's progress. 'My view is that you've come a very long way in truth, although five months can feel like a long time, I realise,' he starts. 'It's difficult to know with dogs from her background, who've gone through the kind of journey that she has, how long it's going to take for them to familiarise themselves with their new environment and new people . . . It could be significantly less than five months – or it could be significantly more.'

Si must have noticed the glum expression on my face as I take in this last statement, because he quickly adds, 'Before you get too despondent, the progress you're making with her is really encouraging. And the progress that I've seen just in the last five or six days is also huge.' I point out that she's still spending 90 per cent of her time behind the sofa, but he reckons it's much less than that. He says he wants me to stop looking at things in what he calls my 'Yes, but' way – as in, 'Yes, but she was going in the garden and eating food from our hands back in February' – and actively choose to keep my focus on any small steps forward.

Perhaps it is age but I seem to have turned into a 'glass-half-empty person', always seeing the worst of things, when throughout most of my life I have been an optimist. I try to explain to Si that with Diane away in Cambridge for the first three days of the week, I am the one who has to deal with Sophie most of the time – and that it can be hard: 'We have this up-and-down, rollercoaster relationship. I'm the constant presence and sometimes Sophie is pleased with me – but sometimes she's not, and I find that difficult. What I also find dispiriting is how scared she still is with me. I come in, and she's wary and that is kind of sad to me.'

But Si coaxes me back into a good mood. One of our big worries has been about getting a collar back on her. But Si does not think that will be a problem – 'Diane is millimetres away from doing that,' he reassures me.

With a couple of days away in the middle seeing his mother, our dog behaviourist ends up staying ten days with us. There are some highs – Sophie seems to be spending more time with us, both in the house and the garden – but also some lows. Diane does not manage to get the collar on her, with her one attempt seeing the dog leaping away and hiding behind the sofa. And on his last night with us, Si finally makes it clear that Sophie is extremely unlikely to join us on our holiday in Wales in a couple of months. He also raises the possibility that we might have to get her on some kind of anti-depressant drug. As he heads off to catch the train home that Saturday morning in late May, I am feeling pretty depressed myself and once more, seriously questioning the path we've been taking.

But the next day, Sunday, everything changes and we make a decision that will set us on a different course. It all begins when I am at the garden centre and Diane sends me a photo of Sophie. I look at it, a perfectly standard shot of the dog in our kitchen and wonder what the big deal is – then I notice she is wearing her collar! I rush home to find out how this miracle has been achieved and Diane explains nonchalantly that she just leaned over the back of the sofa where Sophie was resting and slipped the collar on with no fuss.

When we let Si know this, it seems to spur him into action. He tells us I need to call the vet on Monday and arrange a visit to get Sophie on drugs. He then sends me a note explaining what I should say: 'What you should tell them is that we're five months into a desensitisation and counter-conditioning protocol with Sophie, which has been going well. She's much more comfortable with both of you, having formed a particularly strong attachment to Diane. Despite this, she is continuing to exhibit signs of underlying fears and anxieties that are slowing progress. It is my feeling that Sophie would benefit enormously from anti-anxiety meds such as the selective serotonin reuptake inhibitor, fluoxetine. And please tell the vet that we would all greatly value their input and advice on what the right medication might be for her and how we need to proceed in terms of evaluating her medical needs.'

So now at last we have a plan, and I'm keen to push ahead

with it. I read up on fluoxetine and discover to my surprise that it is listed on the NHS website as a medicine for humans: 'It's often used to treat depression and sometimes obsessive-compulsive disorder and bulimia. It works by increasing the levels of serotonin in the brain.'

Then I notice, in brackets next to the listing of 'Fluoxetine', the word 'Prozac'. Si wants our dog to be put on Prozac! At first this sounds bizarre but Diane, who has read more widely on this subject than me, assures me that this is quite common because dogs experience anxiety and depression in the same way as humans. And when I consult Dr Google, I quickly find an article quoting Dr Stefanie Schwartz, an American vet and behaviourist, in which she makes this very point: 'The part of the brain that controls emotions in dogs – called the "limbic system" – is very similar to that of humans. Because of this, scientists generally accept that dogs experience all the basic emotions that we do, including joy, fear, anger, disgust, love, aggression, anxiety and depression.'*

So that is why the drugs used to treat anxiety and depression in humans can also be used to treat dogs. The more I think about it, the more I appreciate how lucky we are to be advised by Si Wooler, who clearly knows his stuff – unlike some of the flaky 'experts' who have been critiquing his methods on social media. But then I realise that I need to prepare for another ordeal – an appointment at the vet, which will mean forcing Sophie to leave our house for the first time and to meet a stranger.

On the Monday morning, I call the vet's surgery two streets away, where we registered her in December – and hit the first snag. The practice has hit a problem with a lack of staff and has suspended all its business. The call is actually taken by another

* https://www.thedodo.com/dodowell/do-dogs-have-feelings

surgery a mile away which has taken over all their customers. Fortunately this is the same vet's practice which looked after Cabbage; unfortunately, it will mean a car journey instead of just picking up Sophie and taking her down the road. And worse, the receptionist tells me that she won't be able to give us an appointment until the senior vet returns from holiday on the Thursday of that week.

Now we have made the decision, I just want to get on with it. Over the next few days, there are some of the usual Sophie ups and downs. On Wednesday, she emerges first thing, goes into the garden and even allows me to give her a brief tickle – which of course I'm delighted about. Not long after that, however, she goes back behind the sofa – and remains there for the rest of the day, refusing to emerge even when Diane comes home in the late afternoon. I channel my exasperation into that day's diary entry – and there are a lot of exclamation marks.

Perhaps I'm feeling under pressure because I am tense about the call I am expecting from the vet the following morning, Thursday. This is another quiet day for Sophie, and I find waiting for my phone to ring very trying. Eventually, at 1.30 pm, unable to bear it any longer, I call the surgery. When we spoke on Monday, the receptionist told me there was a chance I'd be able to pick up some temporary calming medication before the appointment to help make our forthcoming visit less stressful. Today, however, I learn that this will not be possible. What is more, I am warned that Sophie will probably have to be muzzled for our visit, which has now been confirmed for Friday, 2 June – that is, a week tomorrow. This of course will mean getting a lead on her – for the first time since my doomed attempt to get her to come for a walk the morning she arrived in December . . .

Over the weekend, Sophie warms up a little, spending time

in the kitchen with Diane while she is cooking. This seems encouraging and on Sunday, Diane takes the opportunity to try to clip a lead onto her collar. But it all goes wrong. On WhatsApp later that day she tells Si what happened: 'I clipped it on while she had come to me for a stroke and she panicked at once. I let go and she scooted behind the sofa. I reached to unclip it and now she's sitting on it. Sorry for rushing – I was thinking ahead to having to go to the vet on Friday . . .'

The message from Scotland is, as ever, 'keep calm and carry on'. Si then has a couple of suggestions we can try to get Sophie accustomed to the lead: one of these involves luxury treats: 'Get something "high value" (lamb or Comté), show her the lead over the back of the sofa and then drop her a lamb morsel. Rinse and repeat as above. Make sure the treat is some distance from her initially, then wait for a short time to create a sense of anticipation before you move it slightly closer to her. Once it's within her reach, lean over the back of the sofa, open the clip then "pay" [deliver the treat]. Go really slowly – it's her safe space and you need to be uber-cautious.'

I read these exacting instructions a few times and begin to feel a bit wound up. All this seems both complex and time-consuming and I cannot see us getting very far by Friday. It suddenly strikes me that Sophie's community of social media followers need to know just how hard this all is. I take a picture of Diane sitting on the red sofa with the lead draped over a corner, and post a tweet: 'Sometimes I think we give too rosy an impression of life with #sophiefromromania, which can be an emotional rollercoaster. Today for instance the Prof tried to put on her lead, because she seemed in such a friendly mood – but she took fright, hid behind the sofa and has stayed there since.'

This gets some wonderful responses, a reminder of how much love there is out there for our dog and for us: 'Must be so hard sometimes when the progress feels so painfully slow, just have to remember how far she has come and the quality of life you are providing'; 'You shouldn't underestimate the importance of the love and patience you're giving her'; 'You are doing so well making her feel safe. This is going to be a long journey for Sophie but I think she has found the family to stick with her.'

Until now Diane has been the calmest member of the household, but that Sunday, she has a very bad night's sleep – unsettled by what she feels has been her mistake in rushing Sophie into having her lead put on. Having told me not to worry about Friday, she now admits to being anxious herself about the appointment at the vet. The next day is a Bank Holiday Monday, so we are both at home. We sit together at the kitchen table and for a couple of hours, things go well. Sophie nudges me from under the table, and I give her a treat – today it's that Comté cheese; yesterday it was morsels of chipolata sausage. This is just the kind of interaction Si has been encouraging us to try, and we've got used to having boxes of treats ready on the table. But by 11 am Sophie has had enough of us. She retreats behind the sofa and yet again we do not see her for the rest of the day. I start brooding yet again about everything Sophie-related.

As if he has been inside my head, that evening Si gets in touch with an extraordinarily kind offer – he is proposing to fly down on Thursday evening and then come with us to the vet on Friday. I feel the relief coursing through my veins and some of the tension evaporating. Thank goodness for that – when the moment comes and we have to put a lead on a terrified animal, pick her up and carry her into the car, we will have an expert in dog psychology with us.

I then ask Si how we should prepare Sophie for Friday. To my surprise, he says we should do nothing: we'll just spring it on her that morning. Perhaps he has realised that we are finding it quite onerous, trying to follow the complex programme of desensitisation to the lead that he has been advocating. But he keeps up the encouraging messages the next day, as we update him on how Sophie is now getting accustomed to nudging us for treats. 'Sophie "working the room" on a Wednesday morning – excellent!' he says enthusiastically. But my diary entry for that day is considerably less upbeat: 'She's still ridiculously nervous. We really haven't moved far since February.'

Our dog behaviourist and now good friend arrives at 7 pm on Thursday and we all have a relatively relaxed evening, with Sophie hanging around under the table, nudging each of us. But I cannot help feeling apprehensive about the next day. Just how are we going to get Sophie into the car, put on the muzzle which Diane has bought, and bring her inside the vet's surgery – a place where even the most well-balanced dog feels ill-at-ease? Isn't it likely that in one morning, we may wipe out any progress we have made since December?

With such gloomy thoughts swirling in my head, I have a worse night than normal, getting even less than my usual four hours' sleep. By 7.30 on Friday morning however, the three of us are all sitting around the breakfast table, eating the poached eggs on mashed avocado Diane serves on important occasions and trying to pretend this is just another normal day. At 8.30, Si leans over the back of the sofa, removes Sophie's collar, adjusts it a little, and then replaces it – without any fuss. We are conscious that a terrified dog might wriggle out of a collar if it is too loose and escape, so it is a relief that Si has managed to tighten it, and without any drama. By now I have realised – with some relief – that our dog behaviourist will be in charge and I am just going to be an anxious onlooker.

At 9.30, Diane goes and sits in the back seat of our car, which is parked right outside our house – I've been jealously guarding this space for days. Meanwhile, deciding to spare Si my eagle-eyed scrutiny of his efforts in the living room, I stand outside the open front door, waiting for him to carry Sophie out. After a brief silence I hear a scrabbling, which sounds like Sophie's long claws scraping along our wooden floor. Then silence. I wait for ten seconds. Then thirty. Then a minute – still nothing. What disaster has happened – has Si given up? Then suddenly I see him – walking purposefully out of the front door, clasping a terrified Sophie to his chest. I rush to open the back door of the car and he gently places her on the seat next to Diane.

Later, he explains what had happened. Putting the lead on her behind the sofa had worked fine but when he tried to pull her out, she refused to budge. Then when he started to move the sofa out, she panicked and ran into the kitchen: 'I tried not to put pressure on her: I just tried to follow her until she stopped. And then she allowed me to comfort her and eventually pick her up.'

I have the least demanding job – doing the driving – and as I head slowly down the suburban streets, I can see the journey is proving very stressful for Sophie but is also piquing her curiosity about the new world outside the car. She allows Diane to stroke her, even resting her head on her knee at times, while turning from side to side as if to try to grasp what she is seeing through the windows. We arrive twenty minutes early and I manage to find a parking space right outside the surgery. We sit for a while, and I reflect that the last journey we made here was to have Cabbage put to sleep.

I go in and speak to the nurse, who had been rather brusque on the phone, but is extremely sympathetic in person. She suggests that the vet, Esther, might pop out to the car and assess whether Sophie needs to be fitted with the muzzle we have brought with us but never used before. Getting the trembling dog out to see Esther proves a bit of a trial – she attempts to squeeze herself under the front seat and Si has to extricate her. To our great relief, the kindly vet decides Sophie does not need to be muzzled.

Eventually, Si scoops her up and we all troop into the vet's surgery and the treatment room. Diane squats on the floor stroking Sophie, who is huddled in a corner, and we discuss her history. When it comes to the idea that she needs to be on anti-depressants, we let Si do the talking – which he does with immense tact, wearing his expertise lightly and making it clear that the vet is the one in charge of making the decision.

But first Sophie has to be weighed and examined. Diane and Si manoeuvre her onto the scales, and then up onto the examination table. Diane cuddles our trembling pet while Esther the vet has a quick listen with her stethoscope, accepting that she won't be able to do much more than that this time. She then talks us through the two drugs she is thinking of prescribing. The first is fluoxetine, the Prozac equivalent Si has been advocating. This is designed to lower our dog's anxiety levels, but it will take between four and six weeks to have a discernible effect – and once Sophie has started it, she is likely to stay on it for life. The second drug is trazodone, another medication which is given to both humans and dogs. It is also an anti-depressant but one typically used to give short-term relief to help dogs get through one-off traumatic events such as Guy Fawkes night or a visit to the vet. Si does not seem so keen on this – however, having been presented with the idea that drugs may be the answer to Sophie's problems, I am eager to give anything a go.

We agree to the vet's plan, and I pay for the first round of both drugs, while Si brings Sophie back to the car. As I drive us home, I feel some of the tension leaving my body. The morning has been a difficult experience but not quite as bad as I'd feared – our dog has not bitten anybody, neither has she managed to squirm out of our grasp and escape. And the good news continues once I get us all home, and Si carries Sophie into the house and puts her down in the kitchen.

Given that her natural reaction to any apparently traumatic event – the doorbell ringing, someone turning over the page of a newspaper too forcefully – is usually to dash behind the sofa, we had fully expected her to go into hiding there for the rest of the day or indeed the rest of the weekend. But no, instead she appears remarkably placid, strolling around the kitchen and then following Diane and Si into the garden. After lunch our dog behaviourist departs to catch his flight home to Scotland, taking with him our immense gratitude for shepherding us through what could have been a far more traumatic day without his help. Si warns us that Sophie could still suffer a delayed reaction to the vet's appointment, but we brush this aside, convinced that we are now on the right path.

Now all we have to do is wait for the drugs to work.

Chapter Nine

Waiting for a Miracle

'Fear is the easiest thing to instill, but the hardest thing to get rid of.'

Jean Donaldson

The first few days of June 2023 are warm and bright; by the end of the month, we'll learn that it has been the hottest June on record across the UK for many decades. Like many people in this part of the world, I'm always buoyed up at this time of the year, because of the long hours of daylight and the knowledge that three full months of summer still lie ahead. In Sophie-land, however, both Diane and I know that we'll need to hang on in and be patient – the fluoxetine, which I'm now calling 'Puppy Prozac', will not kick in for four to six weeks.

So, once more, it's a case of playing the long game with our painfully nervous rescue dog. Nevertheless, as we start to conceal each daily blue pill in a cube of paté, we can't help being just a little hopeful. After all, Sophie returned from her recent visit to the vet in a much better state than we had feared, so perhaps she might be quicker off the mark in responding to the drugs too . . .

Over that weekend, she shows some signs of coming out of her shell, suddenly appearing in the living room while I am watching the FA Cup Final, and apparently taking an interest in what is happening on the pitch as Manchester City clear the next hurdle in their pursuit of the treble. Let's just hope she doesn't turn out to be a City fan. And when on Sunday I prepare our regular scrambled eggs and bacon breakfast, with a mini version in her bowl, it is met with enthusiastic approval.

On the Monday, both Diane and I have early starts – she is, as usual, off to Cambridge by 5.45 am, and I have to head into London soon after 7 am for one of my consulting jobs. So I come downstairs at 6 am to give myself an hour to get Sophie up and about, give her the pill in some paté and make sure she visits the garden. But by 7 there has been absolutely no sign, even of her nose peeping out from behind the sofa. It is incredibly exasperating. I check the train times and realise I can wait no longer. Cursing under my breath, I rush out, leaving a plate of treats – including the Prozac in paté – just outside the entrance to Her Majesty's boudoir.

When I return at 3 pm, the plate is untouched and there is no sign that Sophie has been out. This is already shaping up to be an epic sulk, I think darkly, and push the treats nearer to the back of the sofa. Half an hour later when I check, I see that just one of these items has been eaten – luckily it's the paté with the pill. I remember how cunning Cabbage was in finding ways of avoiding taking her medication and think to myself that most likely Sophie has spat hers out under the sofa. But until she comes out there is no way of checking. As evening arrives, she still hasn't budged and is shunning the rest of the titbits on the plate.

In an attempt to distract myself, I decide to check in on Twitter and Instagram – something I do multiple times a day, and more so since Sophie's following skyrocketed. Perhaps there will be some tech development to absorb my interest, or I'll find some supportive new comments from Sophie's loyal Twitter community which always boost my mood, reminding me of all the positives of having her in our lives. It can be really cheering to feel the tangible sense of support and goodwill from Sophie's fans – and often just when we need it most.

But unfortunately today is not one of those times. When I check my DMs on Twitter, I find a message which only intensifies my gloomy mood. It is from a long-term critic whose repeated DMs I have chosen to ignore. She tells me that I need a 'loving, outgoing dog' who cares for me just as I care for it. She mentions my 'illness' and says I can't afford to wait for years for what may still be an unsatisfactory outcome – I need a 'doggy friend' now.

The reason this hits me so hard is that part of me thinks it is true. My Parkinson's is definitely getting a little worse. I am starting to experience more of the slowness and stiffness of movement which is a very common symptom. I'm finding it harder to walk long distances, and of course I have now lost six months when I should have been out and about with a dog. And even though I told myself at the beginning of this year that I would continue the daily early morning walk, dog or no dog, I haven't followed this through in a regular way. The truth is that I've got out of the habit and am finding it hard to get back into it without the motivation of having a dog who needs to be walked.

By that evening, with still no sign of Sophie emerging from behind the sofa, I'm feeling thoroughly fed up. It's not just down to the antics on Twitter – along with that DM, there have been a number of other unhelpful comments from one of our regular naysayers – it's also because I seem to be brooding more than ever on how little progress we've made in all the months since January. At the same time, I recognise that I am being ridiculous. It will be weeks until the fluoxetine starts working so I know I need to calm down – apart from anything else because Sophie may well sense my stress and be even less inclined to come out of hiding and spend time with me.

I realise that another reason that I've been dwelling so much on the lack of positive developments is that I've just begun work on this book about Sophie. And maybe part of this gloom is also down to the fact that, as a writer, I'm aware that something is missing in the story I'm trying to relate. And although Sophie is a beautiful dog whose sweet face and brown eyes tug at my heartstrings, I find myself leaning over the back of the famous red sofa and saying, 'Now listen, love – "Day 342: Sophie still behind the sofa" just does not work. I need some huge change, some character development!' But then I remind myself that's not how real life always works and that Si's mantra 'Slow and steady wins the race' is probably the best mindset after all.

Before calling it a night, I check in with Twitter and am relieved to see it's all calmed down again. And then, when I take a final look at my DMs, I find a message from Tricia Baines which gives me a much-needed lift:

> 'Hello Rory! I just want to let you know, as I imagine so many others have, how much joy Sophie brings me. I'm having a bit of a rubbish time with my health as well and little Soph is just the antidote. Her progress and all of your collective love and gentleness is a light in this sometimes very dark world. Thank you for sharing her with us 💖'

June continues to be an up and down month – Sophie morose and hiding at the beginning of the week when Diane is away but livelier and more eager for contact with both of us when she is back. There's a weekend early in the month when Diane disappears to Glasgow from Friday until Sunday for a conference, and Sophie makes her displeasure clear. On that Friday she stays behind her sofa for much of the day, and I'm feeling dispirited again – and not a little angry. But I try not to show this to Sophie. Diane sends me encouraging texts from her conference in Glasgow urging me to stay calm.

But over the weekend the sun comes out, and so does Sophie on what is the hottest day of the year so far. I relax a bit and so does she. Diane comes home, the heatwave continues and over the next week we see a little more of the dog, and I even get an occasional stroke and ear scratch in. Yes, perhaps I really am beginning to win her trust, although there are still times when she seems to have an innate fear of me, and backs away as I approach.

So as far as our relationship with Sophie goes, June continues in a holding pattern of sorts with the usual two steps forward, two steps back, as we wait for her new medication to begin to take effect, and I get increasingly impatient for any signs of improvement. In other areas of our lives, however, some wonderful things are happening.

On a warm Friday evening in mid-June our son and his wife and our two grandchildren are in the garden with us – Sophie is indoors safely behind the sofa – and we can finally tell them we have some news that we have known about for a few weeks. In her usual low-key way Diane allows me to be the one to do it: 'So, later tonight, when the King's Birthday Honours are announced, Mum is going to be on the list – she is being made a dame, for services to economics.'

Cue huge excitement – lots of hugs and mock curtseys, and an explanation to granddaughter that a dame is rather like one of the princesses in her storybooks. The four-year-old is of course thrilled with this development. And while it is in the DNA of our family to make a joke of such matters, I find I have a lump in my throat, so proud am I of my wife's achievements. By now it is past the children's bedtime and their parents take them home, while Diane and I stay in the garden, quietly savouring the moment over another glass or two of wine.

'Who'd have thought it – me, just a girl from Ramsbottom!' she says with a smile.

As a sweltering June gasps its way to the finishing line, I'm keenly aware that it has now been four weeks since Sophie began the new medication with no discernible signs of change in her demeanour or behaviour. Meanwhile the first week in July will bring a change in routine for both me and Diane, with each of us embarking on trips abroad. I am off to Barcelona on a long-planned trip to the World Parkinson's Congress – a jamboree which brings together drug companies, researchers and plenty of 'Parkies' like me to each add our own unique insights, expertise and knowledge to wide-ranging discussions about every aspect of the world's fastest-growing neurological condition. Diane will be heading off to an economics conference in Washington all about the impact of artificial intelligence, one of her great interests.

What all this means of course is that there will be several nights when neither I nor Diane will be at home with Sophie. But once again the wonderful Si steps into the breach, offering to come and stay with her during this time. As well as helping us out of a tight spot, he is hoping to make enough progress with Sophie so that we can take her away on holiday to Wales towards the end of the month. I have long since written this off, but I am hoping that at the very least Si will be able to coax out of her a few signs that the Puppy Prozac is working.

I head to the airport the next morning, still worrying about Sophie-related matters. However the next three days are totally absorbing, as I get the chance to talk to some fascinating scientists working on a cure for Parkinson's, learn about how the right diet can help, and most of all get to meet dozens of inspirational people who form a community to which I now belong. One of the most remarkable among them is the indomitable Matt Eagles, now in his fifties but first diagnosed with Parkinson's aged just seven. After we have recorded an interview for the special edition of the *Movers and Shakers* podcast I am making with two of my fellow movers Gillian Lacey-Solymar and Paul Mayhew-Archer, Matt presents me with a gift. It's a T-shirt with the slogan, 'I'm not pissed, I've got Parkys', which he insists I wear all day.

I do check in twice a day to see how Sophie and Si are getting on. Moderately well, it seems – he even gets a tail wag once – though she still gets spooked by sudden movements. On the Friday I arrive home, it does indeed feel as though progress has been made. Sophie seems happy to hang out with the two of us, although she still retreats behind the sofa as is her wont when Halina arrives.

Diane is due to arrive home from Washington in the morning, so for now it's just Si and me. Diane and I get on very well with Si and he with us – 'like a house on fire', is how he puts it himself – and by this time we're all relaxed in each other's company. It wouldn't be possible from anyone's standpoint for him to stay for extended periods if things were otherwise! Nor, as Si points out, would it be possible to 'let it all hang out' as he has to for his work with Sophie – for example, rolling around on the living room carpet with the dog in a pair of colourful socks from his vast collection, or even barefoot – if we weren't all very comfortable with each other.

On evenings when it's a 'boys' night' because Diane is away, Si and I will sometimes order a takeaway and keep Sophie company in the living room, putting our feet up, cracking open a few beers and watching the football – or an episode or two of *Detectorists*. Since I introduced him to the gentle, wistful comedy, he and I have binge-watched our way through the whole saga of two middle-aged men obsessed with a pastime that brings them sudden moments of great joy interspersed with long periods when nothing happens. I wonder why it speaks to both of us . . . In terms of working with Sophie, however, when he comes to stay, Si is never truly off duty – even during such evenings as this, he's always keeping an eye on her and remaining alert to opportunities to help her bond with us. Part of his expertise is being able to pick up cues from his canine charges as to when they are open to engaging with their human(s), which will be a chance for them to learn something (both dog and human, that is).

The next day, Diane arrives back from her trip, tired and a little jetlagged, but upbeat after a stimulating time hanging out with some AI big thinkers in Washington.

A few weeks back, I'd arranged a trip for the next day, Sunday – I'd be driving to the home of Adrian and Maria Tataru who run Friends Indeed, the charity which brought Sophie to us. I want to find out more about Sophie's background and about how the whole business of importing Romanian dogs works. But now on the Saturday morning, in a WhatsApp chat with Adrian to check out what time they want me to be at theirs, he casually drops a bombshell.

'By the way, Sophie's sister – Bella – arrived last Friday night from Romania to her new home in the UK,' he texts. He has attached a couple of video clips to this message. These show a dog which looks quite like Sophie, apart from her floppy ears, behaving, well, just like a normal dog – accepting treats from her owner, wagging her tail and enjoying a belly rub. I am transfixed as I watch this, and then confused and even angry – how come this dog is acting in such a normal way so soon after a traumatic trip, when her sister Sophie is still basically a recluse more than six months after her arrival? Diane meanwhile is dubious about whether Bella and Sophie really are sisters, pointing out how different their ears are, for example – however, Adrian insists they are from the same mother, and the same litter. Once more I'm thrown into a quandary about whether we have been following the right path all this time with our dog.

The next day, Sunday, as I get into the car and set off, I'm still mulling over the revelation about Bella. I'm more anxious than ever to learn more about Sophie's history from the people who brought her here, as well as the wider picture of the Romanian dogs who end up in the UK. In a village just outside Peterborough I find the home of Adrian and Maria from Friends Indeed. The house is next to a yard housing massive drilling machines – both house and yard are owned by the company which offered Adrian work as a drilling engineer back in 2007 – the reason the family came to the UK in the first place. In the years since, Adrian has moved on to other jobs which often take him to North Sea rigs but he and Maria still rent the home provided by his original employer. It's from here that they run their Romanian rescue dog charity.

When Adrian welcomes me at his front door, I am also greeted by six enthusiastic dogs, several of which he soon has to shut in another room so that we can hear ourselves speak. It immediately becomes clear that this couple are passionate about dogs – the ones I've just met are their pets, not animals destined for other homes – and are definitely not in this business for the money. The couple, both in their late fifties, speak excellent English after sixteen years in the UK, but Adrian does most of the talking, the words pouring out of him as if he fears that this is his one and only chance to tell their story. For some years before they came to the UK they had been funding a rescue centre in Romania. Then a while after they had settled in their current home, they decided to offer Romanian dogs for sale here, first of all placing adverts on Gumtree. Their charity Friends Indeed, an attempt to do this on a more professional basis, was set up in 2020. As Maria prepares a huge roast lunch, Adrian runs me through the economics of importing dogs – £70 to get each animal neutered in Romania, £260 per dog to pay the company which transports it to the UK, various other costs such as getting them vaccinated, and so on. And now he tells me, looking stressed, vets in the UK are lobbying for all imported dogs to have a brucellosis test – another expensive business . . .

After a hearty lunch of roast chicken, Yorkshire pudding and all the trimmings, followed by a huge slice of Maria's home-made gateau, I am suddenly whisked off in Adrian's car to a village a couple of miles away, to be shown something else that weighs heavily on the charity's balance sheet. We arrive at a scruffy-looking bungalow where we find a Romanian man who speaks no English looking after seven dogs – they are playing in a garden that looks like it has been the site of a First World War battle. Adrian explains that they rent this place and pay the Romanian guy to look after dogs which are either on their way to new owners or have been returned by people who have been unable to cope with them. Bella, Sophie's sister, Adrian tells me, is sadly in the latter category.

And there – amongst the dogs racing in and out of the door

between the sitting room and the wasteland that is the garden – is Bella. She seems a lively, friendly dog, apparently unscathed by being rejected, and at first sight it's hard to imagine why her first UK owners have sent her back to Adrian. But, as he explains, it seems that after she suffered an attack of diarrhoea and barked all night, the new owners decided that this was not what they had signed up for and drove her to the bungalow.

Adrian tells me that this has only happened with a dozen or so of the 200 dogs they have imported so far. I gently suggest that the adverts they place – 'Betty, a very affectionate Girl, looking for a loving Home', or, 'Brody, a lovely shy Boy hoping for a forever Family' – may need to be a little more realistic about the challenges of taking on a Romanian rescue dog . . .

It's been good to meet Adrian in person at last and learn more about the operation he and Maria run. I really like this hospitable couple and there can be no doubting their passionate commitment to the welfare of dogs. As I drive home, though, I can't help feeling that I've been left with more questions than answers. Especially about Bella. For the rest of my journey and for a long time afterwards, I continue to wonder why her personality seems so different from her sister's, when their life experiences have been virtually identical.

The following week, the sixth since we started Sophie on fluoxetine, she seems a little more sociable without any radical change in her behaviour. On Tuesday, a woman called Jo, who has paid £500 for a sketch of Sophie in a charity auction, drops by to visit. Extremely generously she has decided we should have the picture to add to the growing gallery of Sophie portraits. As a dog lover and a fan of Sophie, she wants of course to see the animal which has inspired so many artists – unfortunately on this occasion, our temperamental diva is not to be lured out from behind her sofa. That evening, I am at a House of Lords reception about Parkinson's when the Lord Speaker Lord McFall interrupts his speech to ask me how Sophie is doing, having spotted me in the crowd. Not for the first time, I think to myself she could have a great career in public life if only she would loosen up a bit. Be a little more Bella.

During this time, I've been continuing to read over my Sophie diary entries from the last few months for the purposes of starting work on this book. I conclude that maybe I am just too close to the daily process of what's happening with our dog to be able to clearly see what progress there has been. At my most recent review with Si after his visit a couple of weeks ago, it's obvious that he sees progress where I don't. This is probably partly because, given the long periods of time away from Sophie which he gets, it's easier for him to spot changes.

But, I realise, it's also because he and I still diverge about what progress means. And looming over the whole discussion is the fact that we are now well into the four- to six-week window of Sophie starting the course of fluoxetine – when the vet told us we could expect something to click into place in Sophie's brain, with possibly a related step-change in her confidence – and we are seeing no sign of that yet.

And yet, small positive things continue to happen. Around this time a friend comes to stay the night and, although he is barked at furiously when he first comes down for breakfast, he is then cautiously sniffed as he sits eating his toast and there is no further barking. The next day, Sophie somehow manages to chew off the collar we put on her back in the spring – which is annoying as it means we face the task of getting another one on her – but it's also another encouragingly 'normal dog' thing for her to do. A day or so later, when I open the back door at 7 am, she walks straight out into the garden, then spends a couple of hours in the kitchen with me. But then she is behind the sofa once more, and there she stays for the rest of the day, even when I try to lure her out with pieces of sausage. Yet the Friday of that week is much better, with our little recluse out and about and fairly sociable all day, while Diane manages to get a new collar on her without too much trouble.

But that evening I am looking at the new website Friends Indeed have just launched and, seeing a tab titled 'Success Stories', I click on it straight away. Right at the top of the page is a picture of our dog with an article headlined, 'Sophie from Romania – the rescue dog who stole the nation's hearts'. It's the piece that Diane wrote for the Cambridge University website back in March. 'Success story,' I think angrily. Nearly seven months since she arrived and six weeks after we put her on Puppy Prozac, and we have a dog still too terrified to go into the front half of our house, let alone out for a walk – and you call that a success?!

But the next day, everything changes.

Chapter Ten

Breakthrough

Adjusting to Puppy Prozac

'Play is the way in . . . Everything flows from a playing start.'

Si Wooler

It is a Saturday morning in mid-July, six weeks and one day since we put Sophie on fluoxetine, and a week before we set off for our fortnight's holiday in West Wales, where this year my son and his young family will be joining us. Diane is in the hall sorting out some empty boxes to take to the recycling bin in the front garden. She opens the front door and then turns round to get the shock of her life. There – standing in the hall looking curious about the world beyond the doorstep – is Sophie.

It is hard to explain what a startling but thrilling moment this is for us. Ever since she arrived that Saturday before Christmas, and sat trembling and peeing on the carpet in our hall, this area of the house has been forbidden territory in Sophie's mind. Apart from the one occasion when Si scooped her up and carried her out to the car for her trip to the vet, she has not been through the doorway from the kitchen-living room to venture into the hall or the rest of the front half of the house. Sometimes we have left the door open and tried to coax her through, but it is as if there is an invisible forcefield on the threshold which she is unable or unwilling to cross.

Now Diane realises the front door is open and Sophie could escape, something we worried about a lot when she first arrived, although much less once we realised how terrified she was of leaving her safe space. Diane closes the door and Her Majesty wanders casually back into the living room. So was that a one-off, a brief moment of courage which will quickly evaporate, never to return? We soon get our answer. It is as if someone has put a sledgehammer through that invisible barrier and Sophie now happily trots back and forth through the door to the hall.

Then our brave explorer discovers more new territory – the front room. This is where the piano lives and my Saturday morning lessons with Theo take place but, apart from when we have people round for tea or drinks, we don't spend a lot of time here. Now Sophie wanders round sniffing everything, checking out the lie of the land. The next day, Sunday, her explorations continue and I try to capture them on camera, positioning myself first halfway up the stairs to be able to catch her coming out of the living room into the hall, and then into the front room. Once there she is wary at first, as if unsure she is allowed to enter this room which is 'my' territory but gradually she gets bolder. At one point she even puts her paws on the white sofa so that she can peer through the net curtains to the outside world.

I edit together a few bits of footage and put the video online, linking to it from Twitter with the caption, 'It's been a really good day for #sophiefromromania – exploring parts of the house she hasn't seen since her arrival in December.' This is the first cautious hint I have given Sophie's army of fans that there has been a major breakthrough. Meanwhile Si, using his @sociabledog account, is more explicit in his comments: '#sophiefromromania regularly takes some big steps forward on her journey. This must be the biggest yet and bodes well for getting her out into the world and broadening her horizons further still.' He then takes the opportunity to frame this as a teachable moment: 'The thing always to remember with fearful dogs like #sophiefromromania is that recovery is a process. A process the speed of which is dictated by them. If you stay true to that, you'll be rewarded with days like this one.'

The reaction to the video is immediate and heartwarming: 'If you have been following #sophiefromromania's story, this will 100% be the best video you have seen all week'; 'Wonderful. Lovely that she looks inquisitive not scared as she explores. Feels like such a big step forward.' And that too is what we are daring to hope – that this will prove to be a new beginning. There are countless more such comments and being able to share this positive news with so many Sophie fans, who are as excited as we are, adds to our own delight.

Meanwhile our Diane–Si–Rory WhatsApp group is red hot. Si of course immediately sees what a significant moment this is but picks me up on a Tweet where I indicate that only now are we seeing major progress: 'Seven months after she arrived, it finally feels like we're making progress.' He responds with: 'Oh boy, you're a hard man to please Rory,' and a wink, then gives a Si take on the process so far: 'My version: we've made so much progress in seven months. We've seen this frightened little dog go outside the house for the first time, wag her tail for the first time, run around the garden, play with a plant pot, play bow us, ask for a cuddle, take food from our hands. Every moment a huge step forward from fearful to safe. All in just seven months . . . And all of it, including the spectacular wins of the last couple days, is down to the patience and perseverance the two of you have shown . . . Just sayin'.' This weekend I am very happy to let Si celebrate the vindication of his approach after all the carping from the tiny yet very persistent group of online know-it-alls.

Our holiday in West Wales is just a week away now, and Si will be arriving on Friday to dog-sit for a fortnight, so this breakthrough has come too late for us to change our plans – even if Si does joke about cancelling his flights after seeing the video of Sophie exploring the front room. In any case, we can't be sure that the events of the last few days signal a lasting change in our dog's behaviour. We know that the start of the week will give us a better sense of that and if, with Diane away in Cambridge, Sophie's mood will dip as it usually does and she'll revert to her old reclusive ways.

That Monday, as it happens, Diane is spending most of the day at home before leaving at teatime, so when Sophie hangs out with us in the kitchen in a companionable way for the morning and a lot of the afternoon, I tell myself this could be down to the usual 'Diane effect'. But on Tuesday, from the moment Sophie emerges during my breakfast that morning, I sense something has changed between us. Soon she is out in the garden, popping back in to scoff her pill in paté, then happy to hang out with me while I work at the kitchen table.

We have a new game where I head to the front door and she follows me, cautiously and then with increasing confidence. I open the door just a crack – still wary of Sophie escaping though she shows no sign of wanting to barge past me – then we turn around and explore the front room. Sometimes I sit at the piano and play a few notes – some researchers say classical music can be effective in calming dogs. For now though, she appears unappreciative of my musical talents and sees this as a cue to head back to the original safe space of the kitchen-living room. Admittedly this may be more to do with my less-than-perfect rendition of the piece and Sophie's finely tuned sense of hearing than a sign that her fearfulness has returned . . .

Meanwhile Si is on WhatsApp again, and increasingly confident about what he will be able to achieve when he comes to stay: '72 hours ago I would have said 60:40 against getting her out on a walk this next fortnight. Now I'm feeling very differently about it. T minus 3 days to mission walk.' Wow, I say to myself, wouldn't that be great? But secretly – and rather guiltily – I find myself hoping that 'mission walk' does not reach its triumphant conclusion while we are away in Wales. I'd very much like to be the one holding the lead when that momentous day comes . . .

By Wednesday evening when Diane returns home, we can look back with some satisfaction on three weekdays which have consolidated the gains of the weekend. While Sophie still retreats to her safe place if something scary happens – tonight, it was a noisy delivery man – she has spent more time out apparently enjoying our company over the last few days than I can remember over the previous seven months.

And the following morning there is another positive development. Every day, when I come downstairs to make a cup of tea for me and Diane, Sophie normally stays resolutely behind the sofa. We know she will only make her first appearance later when we come down for breakfast and even then, she may keep us waiting for ages – and sometimes she is a complete no-show. But this Thursday she is out the moment I put the kettle on, sniffing around me as if she is actually happy to see me and eager to know what the day holds. After such a great start, the three of us have another very sociable day, although Sophie decides at 5 pm that it is time for bed and retires behind the sofa for the night. Maybe she knows that tomorrow is a Big Day. Si will be arriving for a handover of a couple of days before we leave him in charge for two weeks while we holiday in a beautiful Airbnb home overlooking Cardigan Bay.

Let's pause there for a moment and talk about dogs and anti-depressants.

I must admit I was a bit embarrassed when we put Sophie on fluoxetine. It seemed such a London middle-class, 'overheard-in-Waitrose' thing to do: 'Oh yes, our lurcher Benedict's been on it for months and his therapist says he's doing awfully well' – and I hadn't yet mentioned it on social media. (And in fact, it will be many months before we decide to do so.)

But with my usual journalistic approach, I decided to do some further research about the use of anti-depressants in treating fearful dogs. I asked around to see if anyone knew of an expert in the field. While Si was of course our go-to expert on all behaviour-related matters, he has always been clear from the outset that it was not in his remit to prescribe medication for any of the animals he works with – in the same way that clinical psychologists for humans cannot prescribe drugs for their patients. Hence he was able to suggest that fluoxetine might be helpful for Sophie and he was happy to facilitate that conversation with our vet, but was insistent that the vet would need to do their own assessment and make the call as to the best drug to prescribe. In my search for a clinical expert, Si and a few other people suggested Daniel Mills, Professor of Veterinary Behavioural Medicine at the University of Lincoln. So I set up a call with Professor Mills without delay.

We're able to have a chat one weekend shortly after Sophie has begun the course of fluoxetine. Although we have a crackly phone line to contend with, Daniel Mills' passion for dogs and the depths of his knowledge are immediately obvious. He tells me he had initially trained as a vet and practised for four years from 1990, then in 1994 flung himself full-time into research into animal behaviour. 'My dad said to me, "Find a field no one knows and you soon become the world's expert." I wouldn't say I'm the world expert by any means. But it's a field so few people are working in – and there is so much to learn.'

What I want to learn, I tell him, is: when did vets start giving dogs Prozac and why did they think a drug meant to treat depressed humans would be suitable for helping anxious dogs? The professor says it began in the early 1990s and makes the obvious point that the drug had been tested on dogs anyway in the process of clearing it for human use – so it was already known to be effective for them.

He goes on to explain that in many ways the same things happen inside the heads of dogs as in human brains: 'The key structures underlying the emotions are common across vertebrates. You've got the basic process of hard-wiring, which is very much in early life. And you've got the learned associations.' In other words certain things are hard-wired in the brain: sudden noises, for example, make us jump, provoking fight-or-flight impulses. Meanwhile other associations are learned by experience – so we learn to expect that, for example, a bright streak of light in the sky will usually be followed by a scary rumbling noise.

These basic workings of the brain exist in both humans and dogs but, Daniel tells me, one big difference between our brains is that we humans have a prefrontal cortex – 'the big bit at the front of your brain that allows us to do a lot of abstract association'. So we can imagine all kinds of things happening, projecting ourselves into the future, envisaging all sorts of things to be anxious about. Knowing I am writing this book, the professor gives me a rather pointed example: 'You're waiting for the first review of this book that you're writing, and you're already thinking, "Oh my God, are they going to hate it or love it?"'

The sort of things dogs worry about are completely different, he then explains: 'They might worry because they thought you were coming home and you don't come home at that particular time. They might worry when a bit of food falls out of their bowl and they can't get to it . . . They are living very much more in the present – much more Zen, if you like – whereas we can project ourselves in time, we'll worry about very abstract things.'

Yet however different Sophie's worries might be from mine, it seems Prozac can work equally well for her as for a human. So what, I wonder, is the mechanism behind the drug? The classic explanation is that anti-depressants like Prozac keep the levels of serotonin high in the brain – serotonin is a neurotransmitter that regulates mood and it is known to be at low levels in people with depression.

But Professor Mills is not so sure: 'The reality is that the science doesn't totally stack up,' he says, going on to explain that if the drug works by boosting serotonin levels, you would expect it to have an effect pretty quickly rather than taking several weeks or more. He starts to tell me about another theory involving epigenetics – in simple terms, the study of how our experience and the environment can affect the way our genes function, switching them on or off. Drugs like fluoxetine can have an epigenetic effect, he says, in that they 'switch on inhibitory circuits in our prefrontal cortex'.

By now my head is spinning! But the bottom line is that while scientists seem divided on what Prozac is doing inside the brains of dogs and humans, they do seem to agree it does work in reducing anxiety in both. So I move on to my next question – is it true, as the vet indicated, that Sophie might now have to be on fluoxetine for life? In reply, Professor Mills stresses that first and foremost, his own philosophy when it comes to drugs is that they should be about improving the dog's wellbeing rather than just changing behaviour that a human finds annoying. But he holds out the prospect that Sophie may not always have to swallow a pill every morning: 'Depending on your circumstances and your skills in behaviour modification, I would say it may not be necessary for your dog to remain on it for life. But better your dog remains on it for life, than she lives a miserable life.'

We continue our conversation with a fascinating discussion about dog behaviour and the changing approaches to dog training since the days when obedience was everything.

During my chat with Professor Mills about Puppy Prozac, he made the point clearly more than once that, just as with humans, individual dogs can react very differently to anti-depressants, and that such drugs are not absolutely guaranteed to be effective, or make a noticeable difference, in every case. Our next Romanian rescue story is a salutary reminder of this, and that even when you get the dog on anti-depressants, there is not always a happy ending.

PAULINE FROM ROMANIA

Chris and his husband had found Pauline in a UK shelter after she and her siblings had been brought over from Romania: 'We adopted her when she was roughly one. She'd never lived in a home before. She was essentially wild when she arrived in the UK and they worked to get her comfortable with people, etc.

When we got her home, she was very subdued and scared but slowly with the help of behaviourists we made progress (and we had her on Prozac for the first year). We soon learned that her initial fear was masking a lot of the behaviours that were to come.

'We also realised quickly that Pauline was not happy having visitors in the house. She bit our cleaner and my mum. We had to have her on a lead when anyone came round, and we soon avoided having people in the house at all as it was too stressful. She was very triggered by noises and movements in and around the house.

'Pauline liked walking and learned to have her harness put on quite quickly – but this was only possible inside the house. Any other contact was impossible – brushing her, cleaning her feet, wiping her eyes or anything like that. Vet visits [were] similarly nightmarish. But she was comfortable in the car and hopped in and out happily. There were a lot of contradictions like this in her behaviour – some things she'd readily accept, others you never stood a chance.

'A couple of nightmare incidents . . . I dropped her lead once and couldn't then reach her to get her back – cue 36 hours in Epping Forest trying to catch her. This happened multiple times on a smaller scale too. She would never let you close enough to touch her so if you lost hold of her in public, it was game over. Many many hours [would be] spent sitting on the floor waiting for her to come close enough to catch, knowing you only had one chance . . .

'She became very comfortable with my husband and they developed a strong bond, but she never fully accepted me. She barked when I moved, barked when I came home (and not a happy, 'welcome home' bark). She'd growl at me when I entered a room or stood up to leave a room. It was pretty soul-destroying.

'We had multiple behaviourists who were very helpful, but my mental health was taking a battering. It was just a very stressful way of living and we decided we couldn't do it any more. So in January this year, after two years, we brought Pauline back to the rescue we got her from. It was totally devastating.'

Chris said there was a lot of nonsense online about dog behaviour, adding, 'There is also an unhelpful narrative about "not giving up" which I understand but at the same time, every situation is different and we just couldn't go on as we were. I think people are very quick to judge – but my husband and I really did try everything and ultimately Pauline wasn't happy here either.' Chris ended this account of a very difficult and indeed sad experience with an apology: 'I'm sorry if this has been an extremely depressing read!'

Chris is right, this is indeed a disheartening story and it was clearly a very challenging time for all involved. But ultimately, he and his husband had to make the right decision for themselves – and likely for Pauline too – at the time. I would certainly never be someone to judge the call they made – especially now that I've had personal experience of the kinds of issues involved and how difficult they can be to manage.

However, although I recognise some of the same worrying traits in Sophie as in Pauline – her reluctance to be touched, the stress she causes when visitors come to the house – our dog has never shown any signs of aggression which is a comfort. Although Friends Indeed had always made it clear that if things got too hard with Sophie we could hand her back, we weren't going to do that – were we? Fortunately, this doesn't feel like a possibility we need to consider at the moment, given how Sophie seems to be beginning to respond to her new medication and the positive steps forward she's been making, especially very recently.

But let's get back now to our anxious rescue dog and see if her fears are continuing to subside.

Si arrives on the Friday evening before our Sunday departure for Wales. He knows what to expect because en route from Aberdeenshire, he has seen a picture posted by Diane on Twitter which seems to encapsulate the progress we have made. It shows Sophie in an elegant pose in our front room with her front paws on the white sofa, peering curiously out at the world. Diane has captioned it: 'Yes #sophiefromromania, that is the big wide world out there and you'll soon be there too.' Underneath, the comments reflect this sense of excitement and hope – 'Wow! What incredible progress. She looks interested rather than fearful.' And someone else has a prediction: 'She has made such great advances in the last couple of weeks, I'm starting to believe she soon will be going out for a walk . . .'

On the one hand we're reluctant to leave Sophie just when this transformation is beginning to happen, but on the other we are very happy that Si will be able to have two weeks of intensive work with her, building on what we have achieved over the last week. And on Saturday morning there is further progress. Sophie barks nervously at my lovely piano teacher, Theo, when he arrives – but at least she does not retreat behind the sofa as usual. Then, as I am clumsily picking my way through a few bars of a Bach piece, a little face with pointy ears peers around the living room door, as if to ask, 'What on earth do you call *that*?'

On Saturday afternoon Si and I sit down for one of our regular sessions exploring where we have got to and where we are heading. I tell him we think that Sophie has suddenly made rapid progress and ask what his first impression was when he arrived. 'I think she's made rapid progress too,' he says. 'But it's not something I'm entirely surprised by and I wouldn't characterise it as sudden, although these sorts of steps feel that way because they're quite dramatic. But they are the result of seven months of patient work by you and Diane, as well as to some extent the medication.'

The drugs, he goes on to say, have merely accelerated the process. If we had not put what he calls 'emotional money in the bank', the medication would not have had the effect we are seeing now. And he too is finally being rewarded for his many hours of work with Sophie: 'In the kitchen earlier was the first time I've stroked her when she actually came up and asked for it.'

So, I ask, what is his plan while we are away? 'The main objective is going to be to try and get that lead on and get her happy walking – whether that is with the harness or with the collar. I'll give her a few days to settle back into me being here, and see just see how she responds to stuff.' He will start work in the kitchen, where she is most comfortable, and then try the living room – but he warns that getting a lead on Sophie will take time. 'She's probably never had a lead on her so she just won't understand what's going on with it – which means we need to build up her acceptance of that.' Not for the first time it strikes me that this is vital information we should have had upfront when choosing her from Friends Indeed – if we had known that she had never had a lead put on her, we might have thought more carefully about taking on such a potentially challenging case.

Si and I then talk about the assumption on social media – well intended of course – that Sophie must have been badly mistreated in Romania and how that is probably not true. But it does look as though when she was kept in a barn by the vet's father, she had met few other dogs or people, and Si says he can see the consequences of that: 'Although she most likely hasn't been mistreated, she's hugely undersocialised. So as a result she has no means of processing the experience of seeing new things, meeting new people or encountering new situations.'

We conclude by discussing the small but noisy minority on social media who continue to question the patient approach he has adopted towards Sophie. He says that after first being eager to know what his critics were saying, he has started muting some of them because it got too demoralising and at times verged on abusive: 'I remember one exchange where I was told that you and Diane deserve better than me.' How outrageously unfair, and nasty – it would be impossible to imagine anyone more generous with his time and energy, or more thoughtful than Si throughout this whole process. As well as which, it's now clear that his methods are paying off.

The following morning we load two cars with luggage, install our grandchildren in their child seats in our car, to head off down the M4 to Wales. As I'm getting into the driving seat, I look at our VW Golf – packed to the gills with luggage, and now with two young children in the back – and wonder why I ever thought a dog traumatised by her one previous long road journey was ever going to be joining us on this trip.

Six hours later, after a stop at our friend's house in Cardiff, we are drawing up at our destination, an Airbnb rental in the seaside village of Tresaith on Cardigan Bay. We found this place five years ago and fell in love with it. From the front it looks like an unremarkable bungalow but at the back there is a deck over a steep slope down to the sea, and the walls have been cut away and replaced with glass so that the interior space is filled with light and there are stunning views over the bay.

Last year, with Cabbage gone, I did the daily morning walk – along the coastal path, down to the beach and back up for breakfast – on my own, and I had been looking forward to canine company this year. But as we unpack and our four-year-old granddaughter and baby grandson – now at the crawling stage – rampage around the quite compact home, I realise that I am quite relieved that Sophie is not with us. Even if she had been able to make the trip, having a still very anxious dog share an unfamiliar living space with four adults and two children would have been far from relaxing.

It feels good to settle in for two weeks of doing not much but cooking, strolling down to the beach between rain showers and getting plenty of reading done without having to worry about the dog. And what makes it even better is that there is soon some very good news from home. Si, who is a keen and skilled photographer and video cameraman, has brought a lot of kit with him. He has set it up in our kitchen at home and will be using our WhatsApp group to show us what he has been doing. Just before 9 am on Monday he sends us a short clip with the message: 'Just a little bit of this morning's one hour and 20 minutes' footage. The rest is on the big camera so I'll go through that later.'

The video shows Sophie with her two front paws on his leg looking up adoringly at him, as he scratches her behind the ears, strokes her and gives her a playful hug. 'That's amazing!', I message him – after all it was only two days ago that she first gave a positive welcome to any physical contact from him. Si knows that part of his job is to also keep Sophie's vast army of social media fans supplied with news while we are away.

His @sociabledog Twitter account has acquired thousands of followers since he began talking about his work with us, and on that Monday evening he posts a tweet which is by far his most popular yet: 'Just a little two-minute clip of some of the things that #sophiefromromania and I got up to today,' it says – and when we click, wonders unfold before our eyes. A locked-off camera set up in our kitchen shows Si rolling a tennis ball across the tiled floor while Sophie watches with interest – that in itself is remarkable because any previous attempts to get her to play with a ball have seen her run away. But Si uses the opportunity to start scratching her behind the ears, and then she lies on her back and, for the first time ever, invites a belly rub. The video, cut to music, ends with Si sitting on a stool while Sophie stands resting her chin on his knee as he strokes her, and those famous ears twitch with pleasure.

The internet goes bonkers – the video gets 1.5 million views and tens of thousands of likes. 'Amazing!' say dozens of commenters, 'At last, we get a glimpse of playful Sophie'. And it also looks like Si has picked up another customer: 'Wow, what progress! Can I hire you to visit California to train my dog? He is a Basenji and so shy! Learning from you! Thank you.'

The following evening Si posts a photo in our WhatsApp group showing another major breakthrough. Until now, Sophie has simply ignored the cosy blue bed we bought before her arrival, spending every night and much of the day behind the sofa, except for a few days in February when she slept on the kitchen tiles. But now Si's photo taken at 10.50 pm shows her snuggled in her bed which has been placed in front of the oven. My old Wales rugby shirt, for a long time behind the sofa, is tucked around her as a blanket. The question is – will she stay there overnight?

We have quickly got into a holiday routine where I'm up

before 6 am – no hardship because my insomnia means I rarely sleep beyond 5 am – ready for our baby grandson to wake and loudly demand his porridge. Our granddaughter wakes soon after, Diane gets up and we allow our son and his wife a lie-in. So I'm first on the floor, so to speak, and am quick to check in on the Sophie front. At home it seems Si too is up early because by 7.15 am there is a new photo of Sophie, in the blue bed, with the caption: 'Sophie's been out, had her meds and gone back to bed'. Then he jokes that all he has to do now is find a new place for the cooker, in front of which the dog bed is stationed. I'm delighted by this development and so are the others when I tell them later over breakfast. It's another huge first for our Sophie.

We spend our day picnicking on a beautiful but chilly beach, and watching our hardy daughter-in-law rushing into the sea with the grandchildren. By the time we get back to the holiday home at teatime, Si has posted another picture of Sophie sitting on the bed, which is still on the tiled floor but has been edged away from the cooker. She has her head held high, and is looking rather regal. 'Lovely,' Diane responds. 'Has she spent the day there?' 'Yep,' comes Si's reply. 'Yep! I went to the shop and when I got back to the house, I walked into the kitchen, emptied the contents of the bag into the fridge, made a cup of tea and she didn't budge at all. I've got estate agents coming to value Behind-the-Sofa.'

For us, this feels in many ways like the biggest leap forward of all. If Sophie is going to abandon the back of the sofa for her bed, then she will be spending most of her time in our company and the process of socialising her can accelerate. Soon, Si is posting a picture of Sophie in the bed in the living room – he has managed to shift it away from the kitchen. Diane tells him there is another bed in the loft – a great big fluffy doughnut given us by Julie, the lovely French woman Cabbage and I used to encounter with her dog Luna on our regular park walks. And a few hours later Si posts a picture of Her Majesty relaxing in this bed too! So she now has a choice of sleeping accommodation, all of it out in the open.

Meanwhile it is not only her ever-vigilant social media fans who have noticed that, after a long wait, there has been a breakthrough in the story of the dog behind the sofa. Radio 4's *Today* programme call to ask if I would join them on Thursday morning from our holiday home to talk about Sophie. I agree – but then lie awake worrying on Wednesday night. So far, we have not revealed that the vet has prescribed her fluoxetine and this is at least part of the reason our dog is making this recent progress.

I call Si first thing for advice – should I reveal the role the drug played? As usual, he's very helpful: 'If you do, make it clear that this isn't just about the drugs. They help in the process but it's not a case of "put your dog on drugs and the job is done". There's an important message here: that meds aren't a last resort but can play a really useful frontline part in helping anxious dogs. But they're not a panacea; they're an adjunct to behaviour modification.'

In the event, as so often happens in radio broadcasting, a breaking news story means that my Thursday slot is first moved, then ditched. But that does not mean the *Today* programme has given up on the Sophie story – on the contrary, they now want to interview both me and Si on Friday morning. This time it's our dog behaviourist who feels nervous after he gets a call from a researcher asking what exactly has changed, and he sends me a WhatsApp to that effect: 'That call unsettled me – because that's going to be the question they ask me on air. As we've discussed, I do believe that anti-anxiety meds at appropriate doses have an important part to play in improving the prospects of profoundly fearful dogs, by acting to reduce the underlying anxiety enough to make the work easier. So, if I'm asked the question directly, I'm not going to lie or I'll look like a fraud when it comes to disclosing it in another forum.'

Part of Si's concern is about his duty of care to us as his clients: 'I don't think it's for me to discuss Sophie's medical needs in a live broadcast without first consulting both of you – but it puts me in a potentially awkward position, so I would appreciate your thoughts.' I ring to offer reassurance – and say to him that if he is asked what exactly is behind the change in Sophie, of course he should mention the medication – and the same goes for me.

But when our slot arrives there are no questions about what might be behind Sophie's newfound confidence. The whole item is presented by Martha Kearney as a simple good-news story. I begin by outlining the big leap forward the weekend before the holiday, and then Si explains what he has been doing in our absence:

'We've been engaging in the kitchen, Sophie's been playing with me, she's been investigating items I offer her. She's been standing up at the kitchen units and, most importantly, inviting attention from me.' He says she now spends most of her time in her bed and – we are conducting the interview via a Zoom video conference – he tilts the camera down to show Sophie snuggled up.

'Oh wow!' says Martha Kearney, 'I can see her now. That's lovely.' I have a great big grin on my face too as this is the first time I have seen this live.

Later, the *Today* social media team post this clip on various platforms, generating a huge reaction, certainly compared with the clips of politicians which are their usual fare. It seems Sophie may have even won a new audience for the programme, with one tweeter saying they had tuned in to Radio 4 for the very first time just to hear the interview about Sophie. Not everyone is impressed though. Diane is a member of a WhatsApp group of current and former senior figures in public service broadcasting – and one of them fulminates about BBC news values, 'when they spend 5 minutes on their former technology correspondent's dog wagging her tail'.

During the second week of our holiday Si seems to perform miracles almost every day. His pictures and videos – first shown to us on our WhatsApp group, then on social media – tell the story of a dog transformed. We observe Sophie snoozing contentedly in her fluffy new bed; we see her blue bed moved successfully from the kitchen and now cluttered with her soft toys; we watch as she waits for Si to open the door to the garden, her tail wagging enthusiastically. We have had the occasional tail wag over the past few months but mostly Sophie keeps it tucked in between her legs – now with Si it seems her default mode is happy.

Most impressive of all is a video using a locked-off shot which captures Si and Sophie in the kitchen. She brings him a series of soft toys, things we got her months ago and she has never shown an interest in until now. They end up playing a game of tug-of-war with one of them, squeaky Phil the Pheasant, and Sophie appears to be having tremendous fun. It's this new playfulness which is the biggest change in her character and something we will have to encourage when we get back home.

As our holiday nears its end, there is a certain nervousness in the air – having had such an intense two weeks with Si, how will Sophie react to our return? And it is not just us wondering how things will pan out. As we set off for London I check in on Twitter and see this tweet from @micky_kilburn: 'Anyone else keep checking for updates on the #sophiefromromania and @ruskin147 reunion? Just me?'

In the event, things work out fine. We aren't expecting a lot of excited leaping up and down from Sophie as we come through the front door – and we don't get it. She's a bit wary at first about these people she has not seen for two weeks, but then within an hour we're back to normal – or at least where we were when we left for Wales, if not quite the Si new normal. It is so good to see Sophie hanging out in the kitchen with the three of us or lying in one of her two beds. That evening Diane sits stroking her in the big fluffy bed and we get a full debrief from Si on how he has worked such miracles.

The biggest lesson during this intensive time with Sophie, Si tells us and is keen for us to take on board, is that there is one thing that is now even more important for her as a motivator than food – and that's play: 'Play is the thing for her, is absolutely the thing. Play is the way in.' And with play came an awful lot of cuddles, belly rubs and scratching behind the ears.

We should now try to go with the harness instead, which he has started to work on with Sophie. This is because for the time being anyway, the lead has been tainted for her – something she shies away from. But he warns us not to expect to be out walking with Sophie in a hurry: 'I know that it's got such significance for you, Rory, for very real and important reasons, to have her going for a walk with you. But contrary to the way that people on social media view these things, if she doesn't want to go out on a walk, she doesn't have to go out on a walk, and it's not detrimental to her wellbeing.'

So as Si packs up his camera kit and prepares to head home to Scotland, I am both excited about the transformation he has wrought in Sophie and just a bit sad about what he has said about the prospect of a walk. Missing out on a morning stroll to the park may not affect her wellbeing but it certainly harms mine, both physical and emotional. Still, I decide not to let my disappointment on this score to overshadow all the incredible progress Sophie has made, with Si's help. The three of us, including Sophie, gather at the door to see him off. 'Don't forget, play's the thing,' he says as he departs with a cheery wave, trundling his giant suitcase down the path to the front gate.

So let's see if we can now play nicely on our own with our brave little dog . . .

Chapter Eleven

A New Sophie

'Take time to enjoy the big wins.'

Si Wooler

Shortly after we get back from our holiday in Wales, a message pops up for me from Ana-Maria – the Romanian vet who had rescued Sophie and half a dozen other puppies after they were dumped by the roadside. Attached to the message is a photo – of a tiny dog, whose head seems out of all proportion to the rest of her body, with huge sad eyes and big pointy ears. This forlorn-looking puppy is sitting on an absorbent pad in a cage with a bowl of water next to her; on one of her legs there's a bandage with what looks like a drip attached to it.

There is a caption with the photo, which reads, 'Sophie after 1 week she was found'. I decode this as meaning that this is Sophie a week after she was found – presumably she was kept for a while at the vet's surgery before Ana-Maria handed her over to her father, along with some of the other puppies. Our little rescue then spent several months in a barn with very limited contact with other humans or dogs. When I show the picture to Diane, I can see her getting a bit emotional, which doesn't surprise me – Diane has always had a deep, instinctive love for dogs. She had such a strong bond with Cabbage and by now, she's very attached to Sophie too – as indeed am I. And there's something very poignant about this photo of our new dog as a tiny pup, looking so lost and vulnerable.

Later that day, I seek out another old photo, a very familiar one this time – the one taken on that fateful night last December, which shows me standing on our doorstep with, in my arms, Sophie, looking terrified after the long trip across Europe in a van. And now, back at home after a fortnight's holiday and settling back into our daily routines, I know I'm looking at a very different dog. Here she is – relaxing in her blue bed surrounded by her toys; in the kitchen with us, wagging her tail as she watches us prepare food; bounding energetically into the back garden to do some zoomies or chase some pigeons. It feels as though we have a whole new Sophie.

Over the next few days, the tension I often feel while looking after Sophie – and which, Diane is convinced, communicates itself to the dog – seems to melt away. When the two of us are around, Sophie stays out with us all day, rather than retreating behind the sofa. She will accept cuddles at any time and is beginning to learn to play with us, showing us glimpses of a mischievous side we've never seen before. And having watched Si at work, we now talk to her all the time: 'Hey Sophie, good morning – it's Dad here! Did you have a good night?'; 'Sophie sweetheart, do you want the garden?'; 'Hey Beautiful, come and get your breakfast, it's ready now!' Sometimes, when Diane and I are in separate rooms, we get confused, each of us thinking the other person is talking to them. Cue laughter – 'Ah, thank *you*, Beautiful – that breakfast looks delicious, but hold the kibble!'

Of course we still need to remain vigilant on certain fronts. In the first days after Si's departure, I find I have a problem. He's told us that he feels we need to keep Sophie and Halina apart for a while until the former is a little less scared of the latter – but on the day of Halina's next visit, it turns out I need to be at a meeting in town just around the time she is due to turn up. I come up with a plan, however. Half an hour before I am due to set off, I go and sit in the front room and Sophie follows me there. After a while I go to fetch her blue bed and her water bowl, place them in the room and then close the door, shutting her in. Four hours later, I return from my meeting and everything is calm – although Halina is a little sad that she is not allowed to hang out with the dog.

There's another hiccup in our progress a few nights later, when I am pulling out a freezer drawer and it makes a loud, screeching noise which spooks Sophie. She leaps out of her blue bed, runs around in panic, then heads behind the sofa – still clearly her place of refuge in moments of emergency. We assume she will soon be out, but there is no sign of her as we head for bed. When I come down in the morning, all is quiet – she has spent the night back in her safe space. But later when Diane comes down, Sophie does emerge and soon we are back in her good books. She graciously accepts our cuddles and we are once more in the new normal, although I am thereafter very cautious every time I open the freezer.

So we have come a long way. There is still a lot of work to be done with our nervous dog of course. Sophie is confident about roaming the ground floor of our house but has not yet been upstairs or – under her own steam – out of the front door. She is comfortable with three humans – Si, Diane and me, in that order – but she is still extremely nervous around anyone else, whether they're regular, occasional or one-off callers to our house. As for getting her to go for a walk, that still feels a long way off – something I've been working hard to resign myself to – for now, anyway. Still, we have three fairly quiet weeks of

August ahead of us now before a hugely busy autumn, so maybe we can make some big steps forward.

After talking to lots of Romanian rescue dog owners, I am struck by two things – how the job of training them is never really done, but how special the bond between these dogs and their owners is.

CHOCCO FROM ROMANIA

Lucy Evans got Chocco in 2017 when he was around nine months old. She found him via a local organisation which rehomes Romanian street dogs. As she tells me about the early days with Chocco, there's a lot that sounds familiar to me . . .

'Chocco was incredibly scared when he first arrived and it took quite some time to earn his trust. We'd been told he was a confident dog who loved belly rubs. But I can only guess the journey and being away from other dogs for the first time must have affected him, as he was definitely *not* confident. He bolted from the rescuer's arms into the corner of our hallway – and ended up staying there for several days! For about the first week we were throwing bits of chicken to him, and sometimes he would come and get them but quickly retreat again to the hallway.'

Lucy recounts that one of the most challenging things with Chocco initially was the issue of toilet training: 'We ended up surrounding him with puppy pads as there was no way we were going to be able to get him into the garden for toileting. I did try one night early on – I carried him out into the garden – but what a mistake! He bolted under some boxes in our greenhouse and it took a long time to "capture" him again – in the dark. Bolting can be a big thing for Rommies to start off with! Toilet training then had to wait until he was more confident. So we had to keep our kitchen floor covered with puppy pads, and it took a while to sort things out. We also had to spend a lot of time adjusting Chocco's diet so he didn't have tummy upsets – luckily though members of the rescue organisation were on hand to be called for advice at all times to help guide us through this adjustment period.'

Lucy's comments made me realise that our approach of letting Sophie go at her own pace worked well on this front – by simply opening the back door and allowing her to find her way into the garden when she wanted, our experience with toilet training her had been a lot less stressful. Even in the first few weeks she was disciplined about using the puppy pads and once she started regularly going into the garden instead, by mid-January our problems were over (though for our lawn they were just beginning!).

In terms of getting Chocco out of the house and going for a walk, Lucy fears she tried to do this too early, but it does seem to have worked out quite well at the start: 'After a few weeks I'd carry him up the road and let him walk back. He did it ok. We progressed to driving him to the local park and walking him there – he seemed to like meeting other dogs: he'd be all over them.' A few months in, though, disaster struck when, out walking with Lucy in some fields on a nearby farm, Chocco took fright badly after they came across some brightly coloured bird scarers newly installed by the farmer. The result was a huge setback for dog and owner: 'He became scared of walks and we spent many weeks having to drive him further afield, doing really short walks to rebuild his confidence.'

This backward step for Chocco had a big impact on Lucy, she recalls: 'This was without doubt the hardest part of the journey for me – I got very down . . . I did feel really out of my depth many times, as I'd never had a dog before – let alone a rescue dog – let alone a Romanian rescue dog!' But she and her family persisted with Chocco on other fronts and decided to take him to some puppy training classes. After another rocky start – 'he was so scared he shook . . . he didn't leave his bed for the first two sessions and the trainer discussed us giving up the classes because he wasn't ready' – he was luckily able to cope quite well with the classes.

However, with Chocco's increasing confidence came a new difficulty: 'He developed a reactivity to other dogs – he hadn't been like this in the earlier days . . . So we did several one-to-one sessions with the same behaviourist who'd done the puppy training classes, and she was so helpful – she explained that he'd simply gone from appeasement behaviour when younger to a more robust approach as he'd gained confidence.' Fortunately the work with the behaviourist – intensive training sessions involving Chocco being given high-value treats when encountering another dog – paid off: 'He is much less reactive now . . . if still a bit nervous with some other dogs.'

Lucy sums up her account of the early days with her Romanian rescue with these words: 'I would say it took several months for him to settle properly – with many ups and downs along the way.' Helping Chocco to continue to progress and become a secure and contented dog is clearly still a work-in-progress, but his owner is determined to see some of the upsides of helping him to manage his fears: 'Chocco is still nervous of lots of people and other dogs, so I have to drive him to nearby fields to walk him – but that means I get to enjoy the countryside each day.'

There is so much that I can relate to in Lucy's account of the early days of life with Chocco, especially the emotional aspect of seeing through the many ups and downs along the way. And while I am of course sorry that Lucy has had times of feeling low when progress was stalled or even wiped out, as I have with Sophie, it is comforting to realise that I'm not alone in this. I now understand that this is something a lot of people with Romanian rescue dogs go through.

Although Lucy's might seem like quite a turbulent journey, I am heartened to hear that within just a few months, she and her rescue dog have been through the worst and come out the other side. And the final thoughts she leaves me with are inspiring and hopeful: 'I've learned to be a more patient person . . . There were times at the start when I wondered if getting a regular puppy would have been easier – but that would have meant not having Chocco – and that, frankly, is unthinkable! In the home he is the daftest, most loving, intelligent, wonderful family dog and we manage his quirks pretty well.'

The chat with Lucy sets me thinking about Sophie again – she is certainly a loveable dog and if we can just help her become more confident, she too will become a wonderful part of our family. I reflect on some of the fantastic wins we have had in the past months – not just the big ones we've seen so recently, but the smaller ones too – like the day she stood in the kitchen allowing me to give her a tickle and scratch behind those lovely ears, and turning her head every time I stopped to encourage me to carry on. And of course there are wins on my side too. Slowly, surely, Sophie is teaching me the value of patience.

There's something else too – I realise that, a few weeks into life with the new Sophie, I'm feeling upbeat. It feels like my connection with her has moved on to a whole new level. I am still behind Diane in the pecking order, of course – but it's clear that she is far more willing to trust me: to remain close rather than bolt when I make the slightest move; to not even flinch when I reach out to touch her. I start to think about all the clichés about a dog being man's best friend and find myself wondering if there is any real science behind the idea that there is a unique bond between man and dog – or if that is just a load of sentimental twaddle? I want to find out more and decide to do so in the way I often do – by speaking to an expert.

So I get in touch with Gordon Harold, the Professor in Psychology from Cambridge University Diane talked to back in the spring for the piece she wrote about Sophie. Gordon is my favourite kind of academic – deeply knowledgeable, eager to communicate with the outside world but careful not to overstate his expertise. He's happy to talk to me, but is keen to stress that dog/human interactions are not specifically his field, as he specialises in the dynamics of (human) family relationships. But with a broad knowledge of where the research is heading, he is able to give me some helpful pointers.

According to Professor Harold, most of what we were being told about how dogs relate with humans as recently as a decade ago was pretty much low-grade pop psychology, but it is now a growing area of serious academic research. He points me towards some important work being done now on the role played by oxytocin in relations between humans and dogs. After I admit, rather shamefaced, that I don't know what oxytocin is, he explains that it is a hormone that makes us feel happy: 'Oxytocin allows you to feel connected and warm and positive towards someone ... It's only activated through personal interaction – such as looking at somebody, speaking to somebody and physical contact like having a hug.'

But new evidence shows that levels of oxytocin rise during interactions between dogs and their owners, and in both the human and the animal. Apparently, it's when dog and owner gaze into each other's eyes that this so-called 'love drug' – or in Professor Harold's words, 'serotonin on amphetamines' – is released. It's the same kind of effect that happens when mothers and babies gaze at each other, and – sorry, cat-lovers – it appears that dogs are the only domestic animals to enjoy this connection with humans.

As I listen to Gordon, it occurs to me this is the kind of bond I am beginning to have with Sophie at last. She is now happy to be stroked by me, have her tummy rubbed or those very distinctive ears scratched – and sometimes as it happens, we gaze into each other's eyes. So I'm sure the oxytocin is flowing and is a big reason why we are both feeling more cheerful about life.

Professor Harold then points me to other research which shows how intense the relationship between dog and owner can be. One such study looked at whether people were more distressed by dog or human suffering by comparing the responses in a group of 256 students at an American university to fictitious news stories about brutal beatings of adults and children, as well as of adult dogs and puppies.*

After being given these stories, the students were asked questions designed to measure the degree of empathy they felt for each category of victim. What this revealed was that, predictably enough, people had the highest levels of empathy for both the children and the puppies – however, when it came to adults of each species, their empathy for the dogs was substantially greater than for the human adults, who ranked lowest of all. I find this latter outcome shocking, if not particularly

* https://www.researchgate.net/publication/316478802_Are_People_More_Disturbed_by_Dog_or_Human_Suffering_Influence_of_Victim's_Species_and_Age

surprising. I love dogs but certainly don't regard them as being more important than humans. But the study's authors reckoned that many people regard their pet dogs as young or more vulnerable members of the family. Hence the term 'fur-baby', which is increasingly common when referring to the family pet, however old the dog is – with the clear implication that it is more vulnerable than an adult human.

The professor then talks to me about a concept in human psychology called 'empathic accuracy', where if you can at least understand what your partner is feeling, even a troubled relationship can have a chance of surviving. He speculates that many pet owners might feel greater empathic accuracy with a dog than with a human: 'We find it much easier, for example, to understand how trauma can affect an animal – particularly a dog – and be sensitive to how unfair and sad and distressing this is, to a greater extent than when considering an instance of an adult human being exposed to the same level of trauma.' So it seems that we think – mostly wrongly – that the human is more resilient and can just 'pull themselves together', while the dog is more or less defenceless.

But this greater capacity for empathy with a dog can have negative effects on us, Gordon points out: 'Because the empathy that we generate is actually higher and sharper, we become more and more connected emotionally to that animal.' And so, unsurprisingly, if the dog does not quickly recover from the trauma, its owner can suffer too. 'The animal is not showing an improvement . . . As a result of that you then begin to experience symptoms, which can be anxiety, depression and behavioural difficulties of your own.'

This last point is of course something I've been only too aware of since Sophie has been with us and which I've tried to give a sense of in this book. But now, with so much recent progress having been made, I decide to keep my focus on the feel-good factor being generated by the raised oxytocin levels in both man and dog . . .

As well as harness training, which we'll come to a little later, there are two other key areas we're keen to work on with Sophie throughout the rest of August: getting her used to being around other humans and introducing her to other dogs. In terms of the first, the people we need her to feel more at ease with as a priority are the regular callers to our house – our family members, close friends, Halina of course, Theo, and so on. We realise that getting her to be comfortable with occasional callers – delivery men, postmen, plumbers and of course anyone media-related who may want to talk about or take pictures of our star – may take quite a lot more time.

When she first came to us Sophie was a silent dog, apart from the occasional whimper. Now she that has at last found her voice, it is loud – particularly in her self-appointed role of defender of the front door. The weekend after we return from our holiday in Wales provides a series of opportunities for us to help her get used to having other people in the house, without immediately launching into a frenzy of barking. The first comes with the arrival of Theo. For the last eight months, he has been eager to meet Sophie properly – having been another of Cabbage's admirers. But of course, she has never been in the front room, where the piano lives, when Theo has been there, and has skedaddled any time he has come into the living room. When he arrives today, he is greeted this time not with a rapid retreat, but a fusillade of barking. Luckily, being used to dogs, Theo keeps his cool and edges his way cautiously to the piano stool, not trying to talk to Sophie or make any kind of fuss – which is exactly how Si told us we should ask visitors to behave. Sophie has a brief peer around the door as I am clumsily playing a short Mozart passage and then she's away again. But on his departure, Theo is rewarded with an approach and a prolonged sniff – which counts as success. And later that day, the new Sophie fetches a pair of Diane's sandals from the hall, brings them into the living room and starts chewing them – a real sign, then, that she is beginning to feel at home . . .

But on Sunday comes a bigger and more important test. Adam, Franny and the two grandchildren come by for coffee. A few months ago this would have been relatively relaxed because we wouldn't have seen Sophie. Now, as the front door opens, there is a standoff with Sophie barking furiously at the visitors, who stop in their tracks. Our granddaughter looks terrified and tearful, and our grandson, in his father's arms, looks quizzically at the strange creature who is even noisier than him. Gradually, we all retreat in a convoy to the kitchen, install the children at the table, and wait to see what happens. By now Sophie has wedged herself, trembling and silent, into a corner by the dishwasher. Once we have got everyone coffee, milk and cookies, we all sit down and try to ignore her.

And it works! After a while she stops trembling but keeps a close eye on us. Then, cautiously, she approaches the table and begins to sniff at its occupants. I utter a silent hurrah – this feels like another breakthrough. If Sophie is ever to become the family dog we wanted, she has to learn to love – or at least tolerate – our grandchildren.

Meanwhile we're trying to make progress on the second front – getting Sophie more used to other dogs. Bringing another dog into the house has been a suggestion repeatedly mooted by #sophiefromromania followers since her arrival. Si has always been very cautious about this, warning of the dangers of making her feel under threat, even in her safe space. So rather than having another dog come into our house to meet Sophie, I have a cunning plan. During his recent long stay, Si has installed a very useful child gate on our doorstep, outside the front door. We can close it and safely let Sophie come and peer at the outside world. And what if another dog was to turn up there one day?

We invite my old friend Sadaf to pop round to our house – she has often told me how keen she is to meet our internet star, but I've had to keep telling her that it wouldn't work yet. Now, however, I've asked her to bring Cookie up our front path and wait a few feet from the child gate.

At first Sophie is wary and growls – as much, I suspect, at the human visitor as the canine one. But it's not long before she appears curious and advances to the child gate, looks through at Cookie – who herself looks pretty nervous, sheltering behind her owner – and retreats again. Sophie does this a couple of times, with Diane telling me to stop calling out words of encouragement: 'Si told us not to do that, remember!' So while there's no dramatic breakthrough, it's a mildly positive start. But when I post a clip of the encounter on social media, the reaction is overwhelming, with hundreds of people posting excited comments about the interaction between Sophie and Cookie:

> 'This is wonderful to see and I am LOVING watching Sophie's progress with all your patience, love and support.' @JoanFis28230281

> 'That's amazing! She seems pretty interested. Hopefully one day they'll be friends.' @PurpleChocobo

> 'Aww . . . that interested face, the calm demeanour, the cute (and curious) visitor. Wonderful!' @RayBox23

The countless positive messages are very encouraging, but I recognise the dangers of succumbing to the dopamine rush that a chorus of approval from social media can bring. A more sober view is that Sophie has not, as predicted by some of her fans, leapt with delight at the sight of another dog and suggested a game of chase. Still, mild grumpy curiosity is better than the terror she might have shown just a few weeks ago.

The following week we set up another dog encounter for our shy girl. Rex from two doors down is an enthusiastic Jack Russell about the same age as she is. Our neighbours, Stella and Alan and their two teenage daughters, got him as a young puppy and he was a bit of a handful at first, though he has calmed down a lot. He is often out in the garden in the late afternoon, barking loudly, so I reckon Sophie must be familiar with his voice.

But the video I post that evening on WhatsApp shows a cagey meeting. Stella approaches the front door with Rex, and Sophie seems a little curious about him at first but then she barks and retreats to her new safe space, the front room. She's in and out of it a few times, grumbling at Rex all the while – it seems clear that they are not going to be best buddies just yet. When we ask Si for his take, he says this is what he would expect from Sophie: 'She's a dog with "neophobia" – anxiety about anything new. That's definitely improving but when it comes to other dogs, she's going to need plenty of exposure where nothing bad happens and she has the option to investigate (or not) freely.'

But the biggest task ahead of us with Sophie for the rest of August is harness training. Si believes that if we can get her to accept the harness, then clipping a lead onto that rather than her collar will not provoke an adverse reaction and we will be on our way to The Big W, Sophie's first walk. Not long after his return to Scotland, as promised, Si sent us a video – starring himself and his trusty cockapoo Ripley – demonstrating a long and quite involved process which will eventually get a dog accustomed to a harness.

Diane and I watch the video several times to get our heads around Si's method before beginning any work with Sophie . . . You begin by laying the harness on the floor, putting a treat in the middle of it and waiting for the dog to come and take it. If she does, then you start lifting the harness off the floor, so she has to duck her head through the harness to get to the piece of meat or cheese. Next you hold the treat in one hand beneath the harness and gradually the dog has to venture further and further to win the prize. Later, the reward can be a cuddle rather than a treat so that the harness is associated with the dog's preferred good experiences.

The only thing about the instructional video, we discover, is that Ripley is the very model of a well-behaved dog. This gentle, obedient animal responds perfectly to his instructions, moving seamlessly from stage to stage without problems. Once we start putting things into practice with Sophie, it is very different. Faced with this new ritual, she still instinctively does not trust us, fearing there is some kind of trick behind it all. Yes, she is interested in that piece of ham, but why can't we just give it to her instead of messing around with this rather sinister-looking harness? This is going to be a long, slow journey.

Over the next few weeks we take it in turns, with Diane making progress in the second half of the week and the weekend, while from Monday to Wednesday, I try – with limited success – to keep the momentum going in her absence. Meanwhile Si is unflagging as ever as the third member of the harness team, watching our every move from his home on the Aberdeenshire coast and providing constant encouragement. We are continually uploading video clips, describing what we're doing and seeking advice on WhatsApp. He responds each time with very detailed instructions.

Looking on, it feels as though getting the harness over Sophie's great big pointy ears could be a crucial stage. If we get it wrong, we could put her right off the whole idea. So we continue, slowly, steadily and with huge amounts of patience. And Si remains as attentive as ever as he monitors our progress. At one point, he even volunteers to come down again to help us keep up the momentum – even though he is just recovering from a bad bout of CRPS – Complex Regional Pain Syndrome – an as yet poorly-understood condition which he has suffered from for the last seven years. In Si's case, flare-ups, which can happen on an intermittent basis with varying degrees of severity, mean that his feet swell up and become incredibly painful – at times, this pain can be debilitating.

We decide not to take Si up on his very generous offer, not least because we're aware that he needs to rest up and take care of himself right now. He's been talking to us a lot since our return from holiday about how important it is to keep engaging Sophie in play. He has various suggestions for more ways to engage her in games and tells us not to underestimate the importance of introducing an element of fun into any of our dealings with her: 'This is your route in. Everything flows from a playing start.'

There are some days when we don't make much progress, and Sophie is resistant to further harness work – but Si tells us it's key not to push things too hard at such times and that it's not a problem to take the occasional day off: 'Sometimes that's how it goes and often an indicator that you need to take a step back with it.' But it's on a day that starts out like this that Diane is able to achieve some of our best progress yet – that evening, I send Si a video to show him what's been happening. In it we see Diane sitting on our wooden floor holding the harness in her right hand and a treat in her left, and then for ten whole seconds Sophie has her head right through the harness while Diane feeds her.

There are times when Si's ever-more detailed instructions can be a little overwhelming and it feels like the whole business of harness training has become an increasingly complex dance with the dog in which we're the choreographers. But the progress continues bit by bit until one evening in late August when I am able to send Si a video I've made of Diane and Sophie at work with some very pleasing final frames. Sophie begins by trying her recently acquired trick of ducking down beneath the harness to get directly to the treats, but very soon she accepts that she and her ears must head right through the harness to win the prize – today, cubes of Red Leicester cheese. Afterwards she backs out of the harness again, but with no signs of hurry or panic. Down the line from Aberdeenshire comes a round of applause from our stalwart dog whisperer: 'You're doing fabulously! And she's looking much more relaxed in the way she backs out. Amazing progress – congrats to all three of you!'

It is not just with the harness that we feel we are really making headway with Sophie. One evening towards the very end of August, as we sit on the sofa which is no longer her hiding place, she stands close by, gazing at us with interest. Then as Diane indicates, by patting the sofa, that there's a Sophie-shaped gap between us, she advances slowly, gives us each a good sniff and looks for a moment as if she is ready to jump up and cosy up to us as Cabbage once did. But then she thinks better of it and retreats to a safe distance. When a little later I post some footage of this latest Sophie 'moment' on social media, the supportive comments come flooding in, echoing our own thoughts: 'So close!'; 'Nearly there'; 'Next time'. It does indeed feel as though we are poised to make more big breakthroughs with a dog who is becoming increasingly confident that she can trust us. Perhaps The Big W is not so far away after all.

Mind you, these three August weeks since we returned from our holiday have been relatively quiet – especially for me – allowing us to give a lot of attention to Sophie. September by contrast is going to be manically busy for both me and Diane. So, please be patient with us, little dog, we may be a bit distracted . . .

Chapter Twelve

Slow Going September

'I'm optimistic . . . but of course I've been optimistic before.'

Si Wooler

'I thought you were retired?' That is the response I often get when I reel off the list of things that have been keeping me busy since I left the BBC in November 2021. There are two podcasts – one about Parkinson's, the other for Cambridge University – a subscription-based newsletter about technology and health – and four days a month advising two PR companies. I've also just finished one book and am writing another – this one – oh, and to fill my spare time there's the odd bit of freelance journalism.

Meanwhile, after a long career which has spanned the Treasury, economic journalism, consultancy and public service roles including membership of the BBC's governing body where she rose as far as acting Chairman, Diane is not slowing down either. Her work involves leading groundbreaking research on subjects such as the value of data and the regulation of the tech giants, teaching and fundraising for a new and increasingly influential institute, The Bennett Institute. It also means increasing amounts of foreign travel to speak at major economics conferences or to meet with other academics and policy makers. Just in the next few weeks of this month – September – she is making two trips to Germany, one to Brussels and will then have a short stay in California.

All of which is to say that, while many thousands of people on social media now see us as Sophie's 'mum' and 'dad', we are working parents often having to juggle our responsibilities to the dog with our professional commitments.

I have two major projects coming to fruition in September which promise to limit the time I have to focus on Sophie. Over the summer, the *Movers and Shakers* podcast about Parkinson's has really taken off and we've been thinking of where it goes next. The most energetic of us is the judge, Sir Nicholas Mostyn, who often rings me early in the morning with a whole lot of ideas. I am quick to tell him that most of them are daft – do the podcast from his golf course?! And just when some people have been saying we are a bit elitist and out of touch with the concerns of most Parkinson's patients? He swiftly accepts the logic of what I say.

But there's one of Nick's ideas that I do really like – even though it will do nothing to dispel the idea that we are privileged. He wants us to hold the first ever *Movers and Shakers* live performance in the Middle Temple Hall in the Inns of Court in London. As a judge and a member of Middle Temple, Nick is sure that he can get access to the historic hall where the first performance of Shakespeare's *Twelfth Night* took place. Once the idea is agreed we move fast and I undertake the boring practical task of setting up the ticketing site. All 300 tickets for the event on the evening of 6 September sell out within a day. I am going to be the moderator for the event, and start worrying about scripts, guests and technical matters which are going to have to be planned carefully if we are to pull this off. *Movers and Shakers* continues to be a somewhat chaotic venture, with nobody quite sure who amongst our anarchic collective is in charge of anything. But it's worked up until now, so I'm sure we'll be fine.

But a much bigger focus for me will be what happens the following day – Wednesday, 7 September is the publication date of my memoir, *Ruskin Park*. I have poured huge amounts of work into this book which is based on the thousands of letters and documents I found when I cleared out my mum's flat after her death in 1996. It has also been an emotional journey for me, finding out much more about the love affair my mum had with the father I did not meet until I was twenty-three.

Getting publicity for any book is a huge challenge, especially when your excellent but tiny publisher has a very limited marketing budget, so I am determined to do what I can to get people talking about *Ruskin Park*. That means accepting every invitation to book festivals, TV and radio interviews and podcasts. It all really gets underway on the first weekend of September and the Saturday before my Thursday book launch, when I am appearing at the Queen's Park book festival.

In fact, that Saturday turns out to be a hugely hectic day. I start with my weekly Pilates class, rush off to the festival in Queen's Park at lunchtime, jump in an Uber to go to see my football team Brentford playing at home, and end the day with a party given by old friends over in Camberwell. And there is one common theme at all these very different events – Sophie.

'How's the famous dog then? I see she's out from behind the sofa,' asks a cousin of Diane's who I sometimes run into at Pilates. Then early that afternoon, as we sit down in the marquee at Queen's Park, my old friend and former BBC colleague Hugh Pym, who is to interview me, asks if I mind if he throws in a question about the dog. I smile and say that is fine, and it rapidly becomes clear that many of the people who have come to hear me talk about my book about my mother are there because they are fans of Sophie.

Later at Brentford, I arrive twenty-five minutes into the first half with my team already 1–0 up against Bournemouth. As I climb the steps to my seat in the West Stand behind the goal, a woman comes rushing down to meet me. Does she want to share her analysis of Matthias Jensen's goal? Or maybe congratulate me on my book? Neither. 'Can I just say I so admire what you are doing with Sophie,' she says. Then that evening at my friends' party, I am keen to spread the word about *Ruskin Park* – but people keep returning to the real star of our household.

The next day, Sunday, I have organised a reunion in the afternoon of my mother's side of the family – the Parishes – to celebrate *Ruskin Park*, which documents how big a role my aunts, uncles and cousins, mainly based in the Midlands, played in my upbringing. Normally we would have hosted them in our house and garden but Sophie's presence means that's impossible – we know she would be terrified of so many strange faces and might well end up back behind the sofa for an extended stay. So I have hired a room in our local pub and laid on afternoon tea and half a dozen bottles of Prosecco. Still, despite not being there Sophie remains a presence at the party, with everybody eager to know how she is doing and see the most recent photos of her. It is a wonderful afternoon catching up with relatives I haven't seen for years and meeting some members of the Parish family for the very first time.

But our socialising on this action-packed weekend does not stop there. After my relatives have gone, Diane and I are due to host the regular Sunday evening drinks with neighbourhood friends. Luckily, it is a beautiful late summer's evening and we can all sit in the garden. When our half-dozen guests arrive, there is a fusillade of barking from Sophie, despite the fact that she has met them many times before. But later she stands at the French windows, peering out quite inquisitively at what is going on in the garden, almost as if she would like to join us. This again feels like progress. We do not want our house to become a no-go area, either because the dog deters visitors from coming, or because, unable to face the fuss, we simply avoid inviting people round. This highlights once again how important it is that we find a way of reducing Sophie's anxiety in the face of strangers.

Then begins a week which promises to be really exciting, but will not allow us much time to devote to our dog. Still, Monday starts well with Sophie apparently eager to play when we open the front door and, with the child gate shut, show her what is going on in the outside world. She keeps advancing a few steps, doing a play bow and then retreating, her tail wagging furiously throughout. Sadly, however, we cannot spend much time playing with her. Diane is off to Hamburg for a conference for a few days and I'm spending most of the day in Hampshire delivering some media training sessions for a major company.

I have been dreading the next day, Tuesday, because some plumbers are coming to fit a new radiator upstairs and it is also the day when Halina will be here. In the event, there is some loud barking at the plumbers until they head upstairs, and a low growl at Halina – but on both counts this feels much more manageable than I had expected. Meanwhile, at lunchtime, I do a long, live interview about my book down the line from the kitchen table, with Adrian Chiles on BBC Radio Five live. As expected, Adrian, who I know to be a big fan of Sophie, throws in a few questions about her near the end. 'She's more famous than Lassie,' he says at one point, which seems hyperbolic but may possibly be true.

Wednesday brings the week's first major hurdle – the Movers and Shakers live at Middle Temple Hall. Over the last few weeks we have had meetings with the hall's technical team, who have assured us livestreaming the event will be a doddle, and I have prepared a rough structure and scripts. There are those among us who think the whole thing will work better if it's completely unscripted, and just allowed to flow. I am not one of them. It may be a good approach when we are recording the podcast and our skilful producer can edit out the stumbles and the boring bits, but performing in front of a live audience is a whole new ballgame for us and we need some clear signposts to keep us on track.

Earlier in the big day, I have lunch in town with an old friend who happens to have Parkinson's. It would be logical to stay in the West End and then head to Middle Temple around teatime. But Sophie is already spending much of the day alone, so I pop back for a couple of hours to give her some company. When I arrive at Middle Temple shortly after 5 pm, I find the judge and Mark Mardell already there, and the excitement beginning to build. People have come from far and wide, and are now gathering outside in the late summer sunshine, an hour before they're going to be allowed in. Gradually, the other Movers and Shakers turn up. Jeremy Paxman is last to arrive and brings with him his dog, the delightful Springer Spaniel, Derek. The two of them sit quietly together in the back of the hall for a while, surrounded by their admirers who all want a picture. Derek seems more relaxed about all the attention than Jeremy, and I look on enviously, thinking again that I wish Sophie could be more like this.

The hall's technical team are there initially and show us the seven microphones – six lapel mics and one roaming mic for audience contributions – assuring us that they are all switched on and there will be no problem. Somewhat to my concern they then go home, leaving us with a number to ring if anything goes wrong. My anxiety levels have been rising for a while and I keep trying to suggest that it would be a good idea to have a sound check before we get going. Somehow that never happens.

At 7.45, we climb onto the stage to huge applause, five of us having clipped on lapel mics while I have grabbed the roaming microphone, sensing it may be more robust. Then it all goes wrong. It rapidly becomes clear that most of the microphones just do not work – not only can the people at the back simply not hear us, but the lack of reliable audio is also making the live-stream useless. Having commandeered the only microphone that seems to be working, I end up having to roam the stage, pushing it in front of my colleague's mouths to try and get some semblance of a show underway.

When it comes to taking questions from a distinguished audience, I climb off the stage and wield my precious working microphone. Somehow, we get to the end and those who have stayed are immensely complimentary about what we've done – but we all know that it has been a disaster. At least one family, who had travelled down from Scotland for the show, leave half an hour in, disgusted that they cannot hear anything. Worst of all, the recording is so bad that it is unusable and so we do not have an edition of the podcast, which was one of the principal reasons for doing the whole event.

I head home, asking myself how we could have made such a Horlicks of what should have been a great event, and kicking myself for not insisting on a soundcheck. Sophie looks at me rather morosely as I arrive back through the door at 11 pm. 'You dirty stop out,' she seems to be saying with those big sad eyes, 'Was it worth it, leaving me alone all this time?'

That night I sleep terribly, tossing and turning throughout a suffocatingly hot night, as I keep reviewing the events of the evening. But by the next morning I have moved on – after all, today is publication day for my memoir, *Ruskin Park*, and a hugely exciting and emotional moment as a project more than twenty-five years in the making comes to fruition. The book has already had a very positive reception with excellent reviews and healthy numbers of pre-orders. It is also becoming ever clearer that I have a powerful new marketing agent for *Ruskin Park* – none other than our Sophie.

The first review had come unexpectedly early, ten days before the publication date. I was staying overnight at a friend's house in Cardiff prior to being interviewed for the BBC's *Saturday Live* radio programme the next morning. As is often the case, my insomnia was even worse in a strange bed than at home. I woke at 3 am, my mind racing, reached for my phone and started scrolling through that morning's edition of *The Times*. Suddenly a familiar black-and-white photograph leaped out at me from the page.

This showed my mother and half-brother Stephen sitting on a beach with a smiling toddler – me – between them; it was being used alongside a review of *Ruskin Park*. I skimmed the article with growing delight and disbelief – it was hugely enthusiastic about what it described as, 'a touching social history in microcosm'. Then I fell asleep again and woke at 7 am, thinking what a great dream I'd had, as well as how unlikely it was that *The Times* would have reviewed my book. But when I looked at my phone, there was the review and this time I realised just how big a role Sophie had played in getting my memoir into the books section of the UK's newspaper of record. The reviewer, Ysenda Maxtone Graham, says I have become 'a much-loved figure', not just because I have been forced to retire by Parkinson's [hmm – not strictly true] but because I am the owner of Sophie from Romania, 'whose anxious face and weekend cooked breakfasts I gaze at on social media along with 300,000 other followers'.

And now on publication day, I once again exploit Sophie's fame, managing to contrive a photo featuring both her and the book for a tweet marking the moment *Ruskin Park* goes on sale. As luck would have it, today is also the day of an appointment with my Parkinson's consultant. So, after a brief celebratory video call with my publisher and agent, it is off to Charing Cross Hospital with a signed copy of my book for the doctor. He has something for me too – yet another tweak to my medication. This can be the problem with the long gaps between appointments with your neurologist – every time you see them, they make you walk up and down the corridor, ask you, 'How's it been?' and, depending on your answer, they'll propose a change to your medication. But they might have seen you on a day when you were feeling better or worse than normal – then you get new or stronger medication and, unless you are a very confident patient who doesn't mind 'bothering the doctor', you end up waiting another year for your next appointment before getting the chance to explain that you have never felt quite right on those new pills.

Afterwards I rush home again to spend a couple of hours with Sophie before heading off to my next engagement. I am to be on the *BBC Breakfast* sofa on Friday morning talking about *Ruskin Park* and that means travelling up to Salford where the programme is based. I feel guilty leaving Sophie again – am I imagining it or was that a baleful stare she gave me as I closed the front door? But at least Diane will be arriving home from Hamburg tonight.

Early the next morning I stroll over to the BBC studios from the hotel where I have spent the night. I immediately form a bond with the make-up lady who is making me look presentable, as it turns out that she too owns a Romanian rescue dog. Two-and-a-half years after joining the family, the dog is still very nervous – just what I don't want to hear of course – but the positive news is that she is very good with children. 'Our nine-year-old got her on a lead and out on a walk long before my husband,' the make-up artist explains. As I've said, one of our big worries is that Sophie and our grandchildren are terrified of each other, but now that our dog is gaining confidence, we'll continue to work with her to sort that out.

The interview on the sofa goes really well. I get plenty of time to talk about my book and then right at the end the presenter, Charlie Stayt, asks me how Sophie is doing – after all, *Breakfast* has already featured her story at least twice and viewers will be eager to know the latest.

At Manchester Piccadilly station I pick up a *Daily Mail* because I know it has a review of *Ruskin Park*, then sit on the train to London marvelling at the fact that Britain's bestselling newspaper has made my memoir Book of the Week.

The weekend comes and finally we can focus on Sophie again. Fortunately she does not appear to have been affected by our neglect of recent days. On the Saturday morning, looking pretty relaxed, she wanders into the front room where I'm having my piano lesson. She seems to be getting used to Theo, who has learned not to react when she barks; eventually she comes over and gives him an approving sniff. Then, on Sunday, she is in a hugely playful mood, zooming in and out of the garden in a manner that we could not have imagined even a month ago.

I know that I must concentrate on Sophie because we have a big week ahead of us for her. She is booked in for her second visit to the vet on Thursday, this time to get her vaccinations up to date. Then, next weekend, our grandchildren are coming to spend the night and we'll find out whether the new Sophie rubs along with them better during an extended visit than when they came for lunch. Having picked up the concern in our voices as we discussed with him the upcoming appointment with the vet, Si has volunteered to come down and help us once again. He is due to arrive on Tuesday and will stay through the weekend.

I get home on Tuesday evening after a meeting in town to find Si has arrived and is gently reintroducing himself to Sophie. She is a bit shy at first but really warms up as we prepare dinner. The next morning they seem to have got back to the point they'd reached in early August while we were away: lots of play, lots of cuddles and even a bit of harness work – an area where I've not had a chance to make much progress lately.

That Wednesday evening all of us – except Sophie – head into the West End, for my book launch party at a bookshop on Piccadilly. It is a lovely heartwarming occasion, a chance to celebrate with friends something that has been a big part of my life for so long. Afterwards, we take Si to dinner at a ritzy restaurant in the city centre. But even over dinner, my thoughts are turning to tomorrow morning and the visit to the vet.

I have a typically fitful night's sleep and wake up early because we need to give Sophie a trazadone, the short-term anti-anxiety pill prescribed by the vet. I wonder briefly whether I should have one too, so great is my anxiety about what is going to happen in the next couple of hours. But in the end, it all passes off with much less drama than last time.

Half an hour before our appointment Si scoops up Sophie, I clip the lead on her, and he deposits her on the backseat of the car, next to Diane. She is frightened, but this time much more eager to snuggle up to Diane on the journey. Again, she's trembling as Si carries her into the surgery, but she then settles down and eventually even takes a treat offered by the vet. We had thought of asking for her very long claws to be clipped, but once the shots have been administered, we decide to cut our losses while things are going okay. When we return home, we allow Sophie a little wander around the front garden – she is curious if rather nervous, and quickly heads through the front door to safety.

When I ask our dog expert to sum up his take on his protégée's latest progress, it's quite heartening: 'Sophie's much, much better. She's showing signs of more confidence.' He mentions our new routine of opening the front door and letting her look out: 'That's the right thing to do because she can choose to go and investigate. So she knows she can decide to be at a distance from it, but she's showing much more curiosity. Still very ambivalent about certain things like people, noises and changes, but in the house she's way more confident, way more outgoing, much more playful, and there's a lot more tail wagging.'

We decide that over the next few days, we'll try to progress with getting the harness on. 'Well, that's the plan,' Si says. 'I'm optimistic about that too – but of course I've been optimistic before!'

Ah, but first we have to get through the weekend and the visit of the grandchildren. Saturday morning brings a procession of visitors to our door, most a source of great anxiety to Sophie – which these days she expresses through very loud barking. The weekly supermarket delivery arrives, followed by our granddaughter who is dropped off by her other grandmother. Then there's the postman, followed by Theo. Finally, our baby grandson arrives in the arms of Diane who has collected him from his parents before they set off for a quiet, child-free night away.

After a while, Sophie's almost constant barking – which is sparked off by each new caller at our front door and never really stops in between – becomes very trying for us all. But for our four-year-old granddaughter, who loves dogs and used to chase a patient Cabbage around the living room, it is worse than that. She is now truly frightened of Sophie, and no amount of explaining that the dog is actually scared of her makes things any better. Still, at least when we all sit down at the kitchen table for a bit of lunch, Sophie retreats to a corner of the kitchen, grumbling rather than barking, and we can all calm down a bit. Soon after lunch, Sophie makes off to her new safe space in the front room and stays there all afternoon and then all night. But I can't help reflecting that life was a lot easier when her reaction to anyone coming into the house was just to retreat behind the sofa and not utter a peep – and although no one says this out loud, I'm fairly sure it has occurred to the others too.

The next day, Sunday, I come downstairs at 6 am and am able to lure the dog out of the front room before the children are up and about – I know that otherwise she will stay there all day. When first our perky little grandson is carried down to the kitchen for breakfast, quickly followed by his sister, Sophie is scared but at least she does not bark which feels like more progress. But by the time the children are collected by their parents at lunchtime, she is back in her new safe space in the front room. And what we have not done over the weekend is any work with the harness. What is more, poor Si's CRPS problem is flaring up again, making it increasingly painful for him to walk – so even if it were a possibility, an excursion with a dog is out of the question anyway. Very much aware that although he is putting a brave face on it, Si is in a lot of pain, Diane and I encourage him to put his feet up and try to rest.

By Sunday evening we are all feeling tired and a little down.

And when I check in on social media, I face a reprimand from one of Sophie's regular followers who doesn't approve of one of my earlier posts. I'd put a picture on Instagram of our baby grandson with Sophie in the background, adding what was intended as a humorous caption – 'Oh no, #sophiefromromania, what fearsome creature is this?' But one follower is clearly not amused that I have stooped so low as to make fun of the fears of a dog who has 'made you a star'. Well, that is me told. Forty years in broadcasting count for nothing – my life now is being PR to my dog, and I had better show more respect to my employer!

Si will be heading home the next day, Monday, having yet again helped us through a difficult moment and in spite of the agony of the fresh CRPS flare-up – just another measure of how devoted he is to his job and to helping Sophie. Meanwhile this week Diane and I will be resuming our whirlwind of activity. At different points over the coming days, we will both be spending nights abroad separately on work-related trips. And when I am not travelling, I'll be disappearing into London for more media interviews about my book. The result is that Sophie will be home alone for many hours this week and there won't be much time to pursue Si's training programme. I feel more than a little guilty about this, but resolve to do my utmost for the youngest member of our household with the time I do have.

I realise I need a better understanding of our trainer's approach to dealing with a frightened dog. From the outset of his work with us, Si has often talked about Jean Donaldson, the American dog trainer whose academy he attended and who he regards as his mentor and guru. Very early on, he gave me Jean's contact details, suggesting that it would be worth talking to her if I want to understand more about his methods and where they come from.

So now I have taken up Si's suggestion and set up a call with Jean in California where she is based. As we begin to talk, I am very quickly charmed by her obvious love of dogs and what feels like a common-sense approach to dealing with fear in these animals. One thing I want to know straight away is whether Jean's current methods, which put the dog's interests first and do not attempt to establish the human as the leader of the pack, represent a radical departure from the received wisdom in the profession back in the early 1990s when her career began.

'When I first started, it was considered very "fringe" to not show the dog who's boss, to not be very heavy-handed,' she tells me. 'The thinking behind using these very harsh methods was this adversarial notion about dogs – that somehow the animal was staying up at night cooking up ways to become the leader of your pack . . .'

She goes on to explain that her kinder, gentler approach, moving more at the dog's pace, has now become mainstream around the world – although there are still places in the US hanging on to the old ways: 'It's legal in this country to do anything, virtually anything, to dogs in the name of training – including making them far worse, injuring them and even killing them.' In Jean's view, though, harsh methods not only involve an element of cruelty, but they're also often not very effective – they may solve a relatively minor problem, like a dog pulling on a lead, in a very short-term way but at a cost: 'It's hit or miss. Maybe you'll solve that problem, maybe you won't but the side-effect you're going to get more often than not is to make the dog fearful. And as you very well know, fear is not a fast-moving problem; it's not an easy thing to fix.'

It's clear that Si has talked to his mentor about the fearfulness that we are trying to tackle in Sophie: 'It's the easiest thing to instill but the hardest thing to get rid of,' Jean says, going on to explain it in terms of evolution: 'If you fail to be fearful of stuff that's dangerous, you'll be wiped out of the gene pool.' The only way to get rid of it is the 'positive reinforcement method', something which Si talks about a lot with us. In Sophie's case, this involves finding things that she particularly likes – whether that be fine French cheese or belly rubs – and creating an association between these and things that she fears. Si often explains it as setting up an expectation that: A – a scary thing such as a stranger coming to the house – will predict B – something the dog likes, such as favourite treats or cuddles. 'We want to leverage that and let the dog earn those things for behaviour that we like.' Jean contrasts her approach which does not involve instilling fear in your pet with the old-fashioned methods which involve disciplining the dog: 'So instead of fear, you're going to get the opposite: a dog who's more confident, more comfortable, who thinks the world is a safe and happy place – which is what we want.'

This all sounds great but I realise that for me staying calm and never raising my voice at Sophie is going to be tough. What happens when she barks furiously at our granddaughter, making her cry? Am I supposed to just say, 'Good girl Sophie, here's a tasty treat'? I decide I'll need to talk further to Si about this and how to handle such situations – maybe it's a case of making sure Sophie gets 'some of the good stuff', as Si calls it, as soon as our granddaughter arrives, or even very slightly before?

I've enjoyed talking with Jean and feel reassured by her take on things and what Si has been doing with us all this time. As we conclude our chat, she takes the opportunity to stress once again that with profoundly fearful dogs like Sophie it's unrealistic for owners to expect to see overnight results from her methods: 'In those dogs we usually measure progress in terms of months and years. We don't tend to talk in terms of days and weeks, the way we would for basic commands, like sit, stay, come to heel.'

As I thank Jean and we end the call, I'm left with that final thought – it could take *years* before we have a 'normal' dog . . .

Our helter-skelter September continues. If Diane is not away in Cambridge or Frankfurt, I am off to Italy for one night to do some media training for a multinational or to the Scottish village of Wigtown for a book festival. But we've worked it out so that one of us will be around for Sophie each day, if not on a 24/7 basis, for overnights and as much as possible during the days. And each of us does manage to have some good moments with Sophie.

One Friday afternoon when I am travelling back from Italy, my phone pings with a message from Diane: 'Sophie just followed me down the side passage to the front garden! She's also chewing all kinds of stuff today. Very frisky.' Over that weekend when we're all together again, Sophie continues to be very playful, doing normal dog-like things like collecting shoes from the rack in the hall and bringing them to the living room rug for a good old chew. 'We may need to replace that rack with a shoe cupboard,' concludes Diane wisely at one point.

Unfortunately though, there is some bad news from poor Si – instead of calming down, his CRPS flare-up has got steadily worse – so much so that he is now in a wheelchair. Thankfully this is a temporary measure, until the pain subsides, but understandably he's been left feeling very low: 'I'm broken,' he tells us at one point. We both sympathise with him, telling him to rest up and to not worry about Sophie or about us until he's feeling much better. A short time later, however, there's a message from him with detailed instructions for the next steps in Sophie's harness training.

Keen to follow up on Si's suggestions we take up the harness work again with Sophie straight away, following his advice to the letter, but the results are mixed – sometimes she just doesn't want to engage with this strange game we seem so determined to play with her. The following day, an entry in my dog diary reads: 'Getting on perfectly well with Sophie but getting nowhere with the harness . . . She looks at me as though I'm bonkers.'

But over the coming week, on the days she is home, Diane makes several big leaps forward, getting Sophie to put her head through on the promise of a cuddle rather than a treat and then laying the harness on her back for quite a while. Then during the last weekend in September, when I am away in Scotland, Diane sends me and Si a series of photos which tell a very encouraging story. One shows Sophie wearing the harness – albeit with the strap under her belly not yet done up – and looking pretty comfortable. Other pictures show her with her paws up on the kitchen table, apparently having located some sausages; there's some too of her standing on her hind legs in the same manner against some bookshelves, as if she is in the process of selecting a book. 'Full of mischief – shoes, crayons, saucepans . . .' Diane writes. Finally, there's a shot of Sophie curled up in her big comfortable bed, with the caption: 'Tired out after making mischief all day . . .'

With the welcome news that Si is now back on his feet and doing much better, the month has ended on a high note. Progress with Sophie has slowed a little in comparison with the big changes we saw in August, but it has certainly not stalled. Every time we post a picture of her in one of her beds, we get thousands of likes and wonderful, heartfelt messages of encouragement, telling us how far we have come.

It does not always feel like that, especially when I consider how the big day when we go for our first walk keeps getting put back. But surely it will come in October – won't it?

Chapter Thirteen

The Fall

'Fall down seven times, get up eight.'

Japanese proverb

One day in late October, I arrange a call with two people I have been meaning to contact for a while. Ryan and Rebecca are the new owners of Bella, Sophie's sister. We last met her in the summer, rampaging around the scruffy garden of the bungalow, rented by Adrian at Friends Indeed. Bella's first British owners had given up on her after a day or so, apparently unable to cope with the fact that she had a bad bout of diarrhoea. However, in mid-August a young couple living in the same area as Adrian and Maria stepped up and agreed to take on the boisterous young dog.

When I ring Ryan and Rebecca, I immediately get the impression they are very comfortable around dogs. 'I've always had dogs,' says Ryan. 'Yes, we both grew up with dogs,' says Rebecca. I ask them what Bella was like when she first arrived, thinking back to when her terrified sister Sophie came into our home last December. They admit that she was a little nervous at first, and had an upset stomach for the first few days. But they took it in their stride, adjusting what they gave her to eat, and now, they say, she is 'pretty easy-going'.

While Bella appears to be wary of older men, she really likes to meet other dogs: 'If there's another dog around, she relaxes completely,' says Ryan. 'We can go to my parents' house – they've got two dogs – and she's charging around . . .' They have put Bella in the car and taken her on quite long trips without any problems and, as for going for a walk, that appears to have been fine from the start.

I persuade Ryan to turn on the camera on his phone, and we immediately get a glimpse of a very chilled-out dog. Diane, who has been listening in while preparing dinner, wanders over. 'Lovely, ooh they do look alike,' she says. I try to show Sophie to Ryan and Rebecca – and introduce her to her sister – but she is in a rather skittish mood and keeps running away.

The call ends with us all agreeing that it would be great if the two sisters could meet one day. Afterwards I reflect on what I have just learned, and how intriguing and even puzzling it all is. Of course I can't help feeling a little envious of Ryan and Rebecca and the very much easier time they seem to have had with Bella, compared to what we have experienced with Sophie. And yet from what we can tell the two dogs have almost identical life stories – except that Bella spent longer in the vet's father's barn in Romania before she was brought to the UK.

The more I think about it, the more I'm at risk of falling down the familiar rabbit hole of doubt about whether our whole approach with Sophie has been the right one from the start. Perhaps even now, ten months on, I should just pick her up, put her in the back of the car and take her for a romp around the park . . . ? But when I mention this to Diane, she reminds me of what Si has said before on this subject – no two dogs are exactly the same when it comes to temperament and personality – even when they come from the same litter and seem to have had very similar early experiences. And if we suddenly change tack now, tearing up Si's carefully crafted plan to get Sophie into a harness, we might well wipe out any progress we have made with her.

In any case, right now, picking Sophie up, bundling her into the car and driving off anywhere is quite literally a physical impossibility for me. A couple of weeks ago, I had a bad fall, followed by a tortuous battle with the NHS to get the treatment I needed – and I'm now potentially facing months of physiotherapy before I am back to normal. And the date of my accident? Almost unbelievably, it all happened on Friday 13 October – a day when my superstitious mother would hide under the bedclothes – something which on this occasion I would have been far better off doing myself! All this unfortunately seems to have pushed me a few steps further down the Parkinson's path of decline so that my tremor has become worse and my walking much less confident. And so it's not entirely surprising that the conversation with Ryan and Rebecca and the (remote) encounter with Sophie's sister Bella have left me with more questions than answers, and feeling unsettled about our approach once more.

October starts so well. Diane and I still have quite a lot going on, but not as much as in September, and it looks initially as though I'll have just one night away all month – which means a lot more time spent with Sophie and a chance to progress things on the harness front. And there's something hugely exciting marked up on the Coyle/Cellan-Jones' family calendar for Wednesday, 11 October – a trip to Windsor Castle for Diane's investiture as a dame.

The first weekend of the month is a low-key one, and Diane and Sophie can enjoy some quality time together – which means lots of high jinks and playful fun, and plenty of play bows and belly rubs. The following Tuesday, my jet-setting wife sets off to California for some high-level meetings about the impact of AI, so Sophie and I are alone for a few days. I take the opportunity to introduce her to a new toy we have bought her – a puzzle game where you hide treats in compartments with sliding covers and the dog then has to find them. Being a smart cookie, Sophie soon has it sussed, rattling and shaking the whole toy to force it to reveal its secrets.

We have an enjoyably quiet few days, mostly comfortable in each other's company – except when Sophie suspects that someone might have approached or even just walked past our front door, and starts barking furiously. I try to remember Si's advice not to reprimand her – since that will only make her more convinced that there is indeed something to fear. Instead, I walk purposefully to the front door, open it and pronounce cheerfully, 'Look, nobody there – nothing to worry about . . .' This definitely does work but by the time I've done it half a dozen times in a morning, my patience is a little frayed. And when someone does actually come to the door – the postman turns up with a package – the 'get-away-from-me' chorus of barks is so loud that I have to shut Sophie behind the kitchen-living room door.

At the end of the week there is one night, Friday, when Diane and I are both away – she is on an overnight flight home from California, while I am at a book festival on the Isle of Wight. Our daughter who, as I've mentioned, isn't on social media, will be staying the night with Sophie. But on Saturday morning in my Cowes hotel room, with no early morning tweet or Instagram update, I see that Sophie's online fans are getting restless. I request a photo from our young dogsitter and get something back that is poorly framed and shows Sophie's tail firmly between her legs. Oh, well it will have to do – I post the picture on Twitter and Instagram with the caption: 'For those asking, #sophiefromromania is in good hands at home and the Prof will be back from her travels soon.'

By that evening we are both back home, Diane's favourite TV show *Strictly Come Dancing* is on and Sophie seems relaxed. I post a video of her wandering up to the sofa, prospecting for snacks. Much of Twitter is speculating that she will soon be up on the sofa with us but at least one woman is not impressed with our 'parenting' skills, declaring in a series of comments that Diane and I 'simply don't have the time' to give Sophie or 'the commitment and stability' she 'so desperately needs', and concluding cheerily that, 'there has been no progression in months'.

I usually try to ignore these kinds of comments but they still get under my skin every now and again. Not because, as in this case, I believe there's any truth to the assertion that we aren't able to give Sophie the time and attention she needs – Lord knows, I have spent more hours in the dog's company than with Diane this year – or because we are going to change the way we live at the behest of someone we don't know from Adam who conversely knows virtually nothing about us or our circumstances. No, it is the line about no progress being made that gets to me, because even though it's hardly the truth, it touches on the ever-present doubts in my own mind about the avenue we've taken.

On Monday, I've a meeting with my fellow 'Parkys' at the pub in Notting Hill for another recording session of the *Movers and Shakers* podcast. While quite demanding, this is always fun too. I do find myself worrying each time about whether all six of us will turn up, whether the noise levels in the pub will be too high and whether our mostly unscripted ramblings will add up to something which makes for a decent podcast. And today's session has the potential to be emotionally draining, because there may be some very frank and perhaps difficult conversations. Of the two episodes we're recording, one will focus on our partners and how they cope with our Parkinson's, while in the other, we'll be talking to our kids about what it is like having a parent with a degenerative neurological condition.

The husband and wives of most of my fellow movers and shakers have turned up at the pub for the recording, and there are some heartrending moments as we discuss how this wretched disease has affected our relationships. Judge Nicholas Mostyn's wife, Liz, describes the terrifying moments when he is in the middle of a violent nightmare – his most distressing Parkinson's symptom – and tries to throttle her. Nick, while aware that this happens from time to time, says it is a shock to hear it described so vividly. Meanwhile Julie Mayhew Archer, asked about her husband Paul's forthcoming Deep Brain Stimulation (DBS) operation, falls silent for a while, and then reveals that she is terrified that he might not wake up from the brain surgery.

As Diane is away in Cambridge, I've recorded an interview with her the previous day at home, which we now play back in the pub. She admits that her approach to my condition is quite practical and robust – 'I love you more than I can say, but I wouldn't make a very good emotional support dog, would I? . . . It's more, "pull yourself together and get on with things" with me.' I tell her that I really like this approach, to which she replies: 'That's good – because I'm not going to change.' Throughout the interview Sophie has been watching and listening to us and at the end, Diane says she feels that things are going okay, '. . . and will be all the better when you can get the dog to take you out for a walk'. The tone is light-hearted but now, listening with my fellow podcasters to my wife's quiet common sense, I realise I have a lump in my throat. I think back over what we have been through – first my ocular melanoma, then my Parkinson's – and realise once again how strong she has had to be. An hour or so later, when Adam Cellan-Jones, my son, is being interviewed by Gillian Lacey-Solymar for the Kids episode, and echoes his mother's thoughts on not making a fuss, I feel even more emotional. Afterwards, when the three of us are next together and get a chance to discuss the two podcast interviews, we realise that this is by far the longest we as a family have talked to each other about Parkinson's.

But the challenges of my day are not over. A friend I have known for more than forty-five years is coming to stay the night – and I know this is going to spook Sophie. Sure enough, the moment Rob rings the doorbell, the barking starts. It continues as I sit him down on the sofa and make him a cup of tea, Sophie trembling beside me in the kitchen, convinced that this stranger is a threat to both of us. I feel my stress levels peak again – I thought owning a dog was supposed to be good for you?!

On Tuesday morning I rise early, wanting to have some time with Sophie before Rob comes down and the stand-off starts anew. She is a bit better today, calming down once my guest is sitting at the table and even giving him a few cautious sniffs. She then sees him off the premises with a few loud barks. The next few days are going to prove tricky for her – there will be more callers to the house, as well as which, on Thursday we'll have our first visit to the vet without Si.

Before that, however, there is a landmark date in our household – Wednesday, 11 October – the day we go to Windsor Castle for Diane's investiture as a Dame Commander of the British Empire. Diane has come back early from Cambridge on Tuesday night, and on Wednesday morning, perhaps to calm her nerves, she decides to do a bit of harness training with Sophie. She works wonders, getting as far as clipping the straps closed under the dog's belly, without any great fuss from Her Royal Highness.

Then we get into our finery, with the Dame wearing for the first time an 'occasion' hat – or in this case, what I'm told is called a 'fascinator'. 'Stupid thing!' she pronounces, not impressed – and we pile into the car with Adam and Diane's brother, John. I drive up the Long Walk to Windsor Castle, wait while our car is thoroughly checked by the security team, and then continue through the castle gates, past other cars of investiture guests until we reach an arch – where I am waved through and directed to a prime parking spot. 'Why are we getting the VIP treatment?' I wonder out loud – at which Diane confesses that she ticked a box to say I have mobility issues. Parkinson's has its uses after all.

Inside, the ceremony is immaculately organised, with each recipient of an honour and their family ushered separately into the throne room where the royal personage – in this instance, the Princess Royal – hands over the gong and then has a brief chat with them. We had speculated among ourselves earlier that a certain rescue dog might come up in the conversation but, while another of the investiture guests comes up and asks me about Sophie as we are waiting for the ceremony to begin, when the time comes Princess Anne sticks to economics.

After a few photos outside, we rush back home to West London for chocolate cake and champagne, and a proper family celebration with the grandchildren. But not sadly with Sophie – her constant barking at anyone who is not Diane or me is just too wearing for the assembled party, so we have to shut her in her new safe space, the front room.

When I wake up the next morning, the sights and sounds of yesterday – the grandeur of the ceremony at the castle, the laughter and merriment back home as we tease Her Ladyship about her new status and whether she is going to get a coat of arms – are still echoing in my mind. Checking my smart watch, I realise that I've slept longer than usual – by my standards anyway. Only then do I remember that another big day lies ahead, one of a very different kind – our first Si-free trip to the vet. By 6 am, I'm heading downstairs to give Sophie her regular fluoxetine pill but also a trazodone. I want it to kick in before our 9 am appointment but the cubes of paté are ignored for half an hour, while Diane tells me off for stressing about it: 'Sophie can sense your anxiety!'

At 8.30 am we need to somehow get a lead on her to get her into the car. Sophie is not impressed and there is a comic chase around the ground floor of the house. Inevitably, it is Diane who grabs her and bundles her onto the back seat of the car; there she sits cuddling our trembling dog while I drive to the vet's. By now, my stress levels are rocketing again, making my Parkinson's tremor more pronounced, as I wonder how on earth we are going to get Sophie out of the car and into the surgery to get her second round of vaccinations – which has to be given exactly four weeks after the first. Once we get there and park the car, however, everything goes far better than we could have hoped. The lovely vet comes out to the car to assess Sophie and then gives her the shots while she stands on the pavement, rather than insisting that she comes inside. On the way home, I am so relieved I almost burst into song.

That evening there is another encouraging development, with the first guest ever to manage to get on friendly terms with Sophie. Lyndsey is Diane's oldest friend from university and while she does not own a dog, she works with a cat rescue organisation and it turns out that some of the skills she has picked up there are transferable. So when greeted with furious barking, she responds by chucking some of the treats we have given her to Sophie while ignoring her. She does not look the dog in the eye or call out, 'Good girl,' but gradually the pieces of sausage are landing closer to Lyndsey. And after two hours, wonder of all wonders: Sophie approaches cautiously and starts taking sausage from her hand!

The following evening is Friday, 13 October.

I have been booked to babysit our grandchildren while Adam and Franny go out for dinner. I ride the Elizabeth Line train just one stop from West Ealing to Hanwell but when I get off, it is suddenly raining quite heavily. I am not wearing rainwear or carrying an umbrella and I stand at the station entrance for a few moments, wondering whether I should wait for the weather to improve. Then I tell myself it is only a five-minute walk, and a bit of rain won't hurt me, so I set off briskly down the poorly lit street. Within seconds, my face hits the pavement and I am covered in blood.

As I try to stagger to my feet, I realise I am tangled up with a branch which has fallen across the pavement. Some kindly passers-by stop to help, looking shocked by the state I am in. One of them tells me I need to get to hospital because my head wound will need stitching. I manage to talk to my phone and get it to ring Diane and fifteen minutes later she is there with the car, her face turning white when she sees how battered I look. In the meantime she has been able to call Adam and let him know what has happened.

Ten minutes later we are in the Emergency Department of

Ealing Hospital – not the place you want to be on a Friday evening, but thankfully at 7 pm the queue is relatively short. I sit feeling dazed, beginning to realise that along with injuries to my face and my teeth – my tongue keeps probing a jagged gap at the front of my jaw – my right arm is hurting quite a lot.

My progress through the Emergency Department is accelerated when, as I describe to the triage nurse what has happened, Diane helps me out of my anorak. Suddenly blood starts to pour from my right sleeve, leaving puddles on the floor – the first sign that I have a serious problem with my elbow. This leads to me being immediately dispatched through the doors into a treatment room. But if we think things will now move quickly, we are much mistaken. For many hours I am lying on a trolley, waiting to see a doctor. There are two visits to the X-ray department which I come to think of as a torture chamber as they manoeuvre my wounded arm into the right position to get a decent shot.

Finally, there is a verdict. It seems I have fractured my elbow and I am probably going to be staying the night and having an operation in the morning. By now it is 11 pm so I send Diane home. But by midnight there is a change of plan – I am going to be sent home in an ambulance and the surgery will take place after the weekend. There is still a lot of toing and froing in a casualty department now packed with patients. I have a plaster cast fitted and make increasingly impatient requests for information and painkillers from nurses sitting tapping away at computers – they are pleasant and sympathetic but tell me someone else is in charge of me and wander off to find them.

Finally, I am carefully loaded into an ambulance and ten minutes later – at 3.45 am – I arrive home.

The next morning, having had no sleep, such is my discomfort, I am a man with a mission. My elbow will not be fixed until

Monday at the earliest, but I can do something about the smashed tooth, which feels as though it is in three separate pieces in my jaw – if I pay enough, that is. As I make a series of phone calls from the kitchen table to emergency dentists, Sophie eyes me nervously. My arrival home in the middle of the night has unsettled her – who is this strange one-armed man?

Eventually I find a very obliging dentist who offers to open his surgery in Ealing. He removes every trace of the tooth efficiently and relatively painlessly, but warns me that in the long term I will need an implant – and that will come at a price which will put the hefty fee I am happy to hand him now in the shade.

Looking in the mirror when we get home, I am not a pretty sight – a plaster conceals a deep cut on my forehead, there is dried blood on my nose and lips and a great big gap whenever I smile. Although right now, that's a rare occurrence. But I feel good about having sorted out my dental treatment and am looking forward to going back to hospital and having surgery early next week so I can get on with my recovery. After all, I need to be fighting fit to continue Sophie's rehab soon. It does not work out like that.

On Monday Diane leaves at 7 am for work in Cambridge, having made my breakfast. This week she is going to commute daily as she cannot leave me overnight and even worries about how I will cope on my own during the day. Suddenly I am getting a bleak insight into my future as my Parkinson's progresses and I become less capable of looking after myself. Meanwhile, Sophie has been unsettled by this turn of events. When my friend Pola, who's a palliative care consultant based in South Wales, pops by for a visit she gets barked at for a tediously long time. She always has useful advice on navigating the NHS but we have to move to another room to make ourselves heard.

One Twitter follower, @DuxburyCarole, tells me: 'Be as

patient and kind with yourself during this recovery period as you are always with #sophiefromromania. A fall is a shock to the system even without any added physical injuries, and these things take time.' I think guiltily that I am probably being far from patient with Sophie at the moment. Meanwhile I am definitely growing impatient with the hospital. After a brief call from a junior doctor on Monday morning promising to get back soon about an appointment for my surgery, I am effectively ghosted. I try to ring, but without a contact name I find myself in switchboard hell, passed from one extension to another. I am beginning to learn something about communications within the NHS and how vital it is to have the name and preferably contact details of the doctor in charge of your case.

Then at noon on Tuesday, the hospital at last rings. They want me to come in for a CT scan so that they can have a good view inside the elbow before they operate. A kind neighbour drops me at the hospital, the scan is done quickly and efficiently, and I am soon back home. Then at 5 pm the phone rings again. It is the junior doctor who ordered the scan and she sounds concerned. 'Did you know you have an open wound and there's gas in it?' she asks. I haven't a clue what she means but she tells me I will need to come back to the hospital that evening, to be put on an antibiotic drip and prepared for surgery on either Wednesday or Thursday.

Later, it becomes clear to me that there has been a serious communications blunder at the hospital. I should never have been sent home early on Saturday with an open fracture – one where the bone has broken through the skin – or at least not without some antibiotics. But the discharge letter from the hospital made no mention of an open wound. And it's only now, three days after my return from hospital, that I notice that my hand has swollen up and that beneath the plaster cast my wounded elbow feels inflamed. The gas in the wound might indicate the start of a dangerous infection.

When Diane gets home, I pack a few things and she loads me gingerly into the car to drive me to the hospital. We arrive around 7 pm under the foolish misapprehension that I will be whisked in and put on that antibiotic drip pronto. No such luck. It is 9 pm before I am lying on a stretcher with a registrar inspecting my wound and replacing the plaster cast. We are in a cubicle which also houses the linen cupboard so there is a constant stream of medical staff coming through in search of sheets and pillows.

It is 1 am the following morning before they at last find me a bed on a ward. I am conscious of the crisis enveloping A&E departments across the NHS and the scarcity of beds, so I am philosophical about the long wait. What does worry me is exactly when I am going to be put on the antibiotic drip I was told was so urgent. I keep mentioning this to anyone who comes near me but get blank looks. After 11 pm I am told I can no longer eat or drink so that I will be ready for surgery in the morning. Finally, at 3 am, a cannula is inserted in my hand and the antibiotics began to flow.

Wednesday morning comes after a virtually sleepless night but I feel positive because at last my fracture is going to be sorted out . . . Or is it? I keep asking when a decision will be made on my operation but get no answers. Hope begins to fade, and then around 10.15 a doctor arrives and seems surprised that I had ever expected to be heading to theatre – after all, I have only been on the antibiotics for a short while. There is a huge sense of anti-climax but at least I can have some breakfast now and I'll be home by the afternoon of the next day.

On Wednesday night, the whole cycle begins again – nil by mouth after 11 pm, a few hours of fitful sleep, awake at 5.30 am eager to go – but with the same result. At 9.30 I text Diane: 'Still waiting for information. This place is driving me nuts.' Shortly afterwards comes confirmation – I have been bumped off the list. A ninety-four-year-old has come in with a broken hip and someone else has been badly injured in a car accident. It is hard to argue that they should not be given priority in theatre. Nevertheless, if I'd been kept in back on Saturday I would have been sorted by now.

Now this is all making me miserable. While my Parkinson's may not have caused the fall, my symptoms are being exacerbated by the pain and discomfort from my right arm, in which I am experiencing a tremor the like of which I have never seen before. Up until recently, I feel I have coped well with my condition – so well that I can forget I have it until my smartphone reminds me to take my pills. Now I fear I am going to emerge from this ordeal having taken a big step further along the Parkinson's path of progression.

It feels as if the fall has damaged me mentally as well as physically. I feel ten years older, shaky, indecisive, a patient waiting to be told what to do rather than a free agent shaping my own life. I try to explain some of this to the medical staff and at last they begin to listen. Suddenly, I have three doctors and a senior nurse around my bed weighing up my options. They could try again to get me on the operating list on Friday – now I am here, I favour this option – or they could send me to another much bigger hospital, Northwick Park, with greater capacity which should have a slot on Saturday . . .

They decide to go for the latter course of action, which at least means I get to go home and snooze in front of the telly with Diane and Sophie. But my ordeal is not over – I'll have to wait for a call on Friday afternoon from Northwick Park confirming that they can do my surgery. As 4 pm ticks past, then 5 pm, then

5.30 with no call, the tension becomes unbearable. Diane has been researching the possibility of going private and has tentatively agreed a Monday appointment with a surgeon in Hampstead. Now she wants to push the button. 'We can't go on like this,' she says, the stress of the last week beginning to show.

I insist we wait until we hear one way or another from the NHS hospital. Then just before 6 pm, my mobile phone rings. It is Ealing Hospital calling – apparently their colleagues at Northwick Park have been trying to contact me. In a final, supreme feat of miscommunication, they have been given only our home landline number – which we ditched months ago because it was only being used by scam callers.

But from the moment we manage to get through to Northwick Park, everything changes. We are told to turn up at the hospital near Harrow at 7.30 the next morning – and when we arrive, we find that I am first on the surgery list. Soon, I am meeting the anaesthetist and the two surgeons who explain in some detail what has happened to my elbow and the metalwork they are going to insert to fix it. At 2.30 pm I wake up, groggy and quite sore but mightily relieved that the operation has been done. A few hours later, Diane is driving me home and my recovery can begin.

I feel I have truly had the stuffing knocked out of me, not just by the fall but by the week of battling the NHS to get the treatment I need. And now I have been warned that I may have a couple of months of hard graft ahead of me if I am to regain something like the full range of movement in my right arm. That Sunday I write an entry in my Sophie diary but it is mostly about me: 'I am still very much an invalid – I need help showering and dressing. I have moments of feeling great and then not so good when the pain returns. But we (that's Diane and I – not the dog of course) go for a walk around the block at lunchtime, very slowly, and I feel more confident. Sophie seems to be still quite nervous around me and we need to rebuild her confidence – as well of course as mine.'

Over the coming weeks that turns out to be a slow, challenging job, for both parties. I am spending a lot of time alone at home with Sophie and that means long periods of her snoozing in one of her two beds, interspersed with frantic barking every time she suspects someone may be approaching our front door. When Steve, who does occasional gardening for us, turns up, the volume gets even louder.

However, when I post a video on social media of Sophie barking at Steve, there is a surprising reaction. Quite a few people point out that Sophie's tail is up – surely, they are saying, a positive sign which signifies that she's not afraid, but is in fact happy and just giving our visitor an overly enthusiastic welcome. When I reply that whatever her tail may be doing, Sophie is not happy, Si takes to Twitter to back me up: 'Tail wagging is a complex language. Not all necessarily friendly or happy. You need to view it in context and along with other body language. A slow bark, with tail held mid-way, may be just watchdog mode. Tail high, almost curled over her back, rapid bark and constant advancing and retreating means not happy, as Rory says – stranger danger!'

By early November I am a little more mobile, and can start doing book-related events again, though I travel mostly by taxi. And I've started walking ever so slowly to our local shops, although I'm still very tentative, scoping out the pavement ahead of me for hazards and nervously eyeing kids on scooters or people rushing to the railway station, in case they might bump into my right arm. Around this time Diane decides to go ahead with a four-day trip to Canada, having assured herself that I can now get showered and dressed without her help.

But my relationship with Sophie remains a little tense, like a couple after a row. Only when Diane returns from her travels does she perk up and show her playful side once more. Si, watching from Scotland, advises us to focus on getting Sophie more comfortable with visitors to the house, rather than returning to the harness work and getting her out for a walk: 'My feeling is that, as keen as Twitter/X is to see Sophie in her harness and walking the streets of West Ealing, it's not a priority in my head (though I'm conscious of its importance for Rory). I think the more pressing issue to focus on is the family and anyone Sophie is likely to encounter over Christmas and New Year.' I understand and accept Si's reasoning on this – especially since I realise that my damaged right arm, coupled with my anxiety about falling again, mean in any case that I am in no fit state to take a dog for a walk.

True to form, Si prepares for us a whole PowerPoint presentation along with a YouTube video on the theory and practice of getting dogs accustomed to visits from strangers. There are lengthy explanations about 'desensitisation' and 'counter-conditioning', but a slide with the statement 'A predicts B' sums up the basic idea. In this case, 'A' is the stranger arriving in our house and 'B' is the treat that Sophie is then given.

But, as Si stresses, it's crucial to get things in the right order: 'For a dog to have a positive response to the first event, it must predict the second. "A" must come before "B" – not at the same time or afterwards. So if a dog is fearful of strangers, the order of events must be:

1. Sees the stranger at distance.
2. Then receives a great treat and praise straight afterwards.
3. When the stranger leaves, the treating stops.

'It is tempting to try and "prevent" a reaction by showing your dog the treats up front, but this is a mistake. There must be a predictive relationship. Strangers predict goodies.'

Reading this and understanding the logic behind it is one thing; putting it into practice quite another. A few days later, at the weekend, we have a first attempt at the new strategy when Theo arrives for his weekly lesson with our daughter. I greet him at the door with a selection of cubes of cheese and slices of sausage to throw at the barking dog. Theo does his best but many of the treats roll under the dresser or fall too far from Sophie, and he can't resist uttering words of encouragement: 'There's a good girl, come and get it – what a brave dog!' Si has told us this is strictly forbidden – the visitor should throw the treats in an offhand manner, ignoring the dog and certainly not looking it in the eye. It is this studied indifference which proves to be the hardest thing to teach to visitors.

The following day Diane bravely tries to confront another issue relating to Sophie's wellbeing: her very long claws. If she had been out pounding the streets of Ealing every day for the past eleven months, she would have worn them down but as it is, she is slipping and sliding around the floorboards of the kitchen on her huge talons. Diane has bought some special nail clippers, we have given Sophie an anti-anxiety pill alongside her fluoxetine, and mid-morning, Diane settles herself down on the floor beside the dog bed. Sophie seems drowsy but the moment Diane produces the clippers, she is up and off: she is not having any of it. We give up and a bit later we book an appointment at the vet to get the claws sorted – though afterwards I realise that, now that I cannot drive or lift her, getting Sophie to the surgery is going to be quite an ordeal for Diane on her own.

Meanwhile, although my arm is still in a sling when I am away from the house, my book tour is back on with a vengeance. In one mid-November week, I am in Frome in Somerset for one night, invited by a local bookshop; the following night I am back in Ealing at a sold-out event to launch a new book festival; and the next morning I board a flight to Gibraltar, with Princess Anne, former Prime Minister Theresa May and a host of fellow authors on board.

We are all heading for a literary festival in the British dependency. After a brief detour to Malaga because Gibraltar International Airport is fogbound, the trip turns out to be tremendous fun. We go to dinner with the festival patron, the Princess Royal, and I give two talks to engaged audiences in a beautiful nineteenth-century library, one of the Rock's few memorable buildings. Best of all is the camaraderie amongst the various authors. I had been apprehensive about travelling with my damaged arm which is proving slow to heal but everyone is eager to help, almost competing to put my case in the overhead locker or escort me as I shuffle ever so slowly between venues.

But this frenzy of activity means I do not have much time for Sophie and our project to persuade her that stranger means treat not danger. Only one new person comes to the house in this period during the time I'm there myself – Jane, who lived next door when we moved in thirty-one years ago and gave us a warm welcome. She lives in Shropshire now but is back on a visit and is coming to my Ealing book event. She has been warned about Sophie and seems unconcerned about the mad barking that begins even as she approaches the front door. I sit her down with a cup of tea and a box of treats on the famous sofa in the sitting-room behind which, before July, our dog would have cowered silently if we had had visitors.

Now, as Jane tries to bombard Sophie with treats, the barking continues unabated. We are trying to have a conversation but it becomes impossible with so much background noise, so we admit defeat and retreat to the front room, leaving Sophie who we can still hear growling to herself like some bad-tempered old lady disgruntled at the state of the world.

A few days later, my life has quietened down a bit. I am home alone with Sophie, who is now in quite a chilled-out mood, snuggled up with her toys in her lovely blue bed. Reflecting that I should be grateful for how far we have come, I snap a photo to capture this moment of contentment, and post it on Twitter with the caption: 'So what's the plan this morning #sophiefromromania?' At first, I get the usual warm response from Sophie's hardcore fans: 'Tummy rubs and bacon please,' says one. 'We are taking for granted the lovely girl reclining in her bed when not so long ago it was behind the sofa – #progress!' says another, reassuringly.

As I scroll further down the feed beneath the photo, I see the profile picture of one of the most vocal critics, alongside a series of comments, coming into view. I pause and am about to read the content of these messages. But then, looking up from my screen for a moment, I see Sophie shifting in her blue bed to find an even more comfortable position. As I watch her settle down again with a contented sigh, I decide to stop right there. Since 13 October and my fall, it's been a very tough few weeks – but slowly we're getting there again, me and Sophie. I'm starting to get some proper mobility back and the fear of falling again is beginning to recede; the constant pain in my arm has subsided to a far less intense, dullish ache which bothers me off and on, but just for fairly short periods of time. And Sophie has made progress too – in her own way and at her own pace.

So I go back to my screen and scroll through the comments on this latest picture of Sophie. Once again I get that dopamine rush from the waves of love and approval with which most people respond to our dog. Right now, I feel I've never needed it more.

Chapter Fourteen

A Year with Sophie

'Love is patient, love is kind . . . [Love] always trusts, always hopes, always perseveres . . .'

1 Corinthians 13 (v4 and v7)

As a child, Christmas was always the highlight of the year for me. It meant escaping with my mother the cramped and dismal South London council flat where we lived and, most years, heading to the Birmingham home of my aunt and uncle, Bunty and Bill, and their three daughters, all a good deal older than me. There we would have a very traditional Christmas – a huge turkey and all the trimmings at lunchtime, finished in time for the Queen's Speech, then jovial Uncle Bill acting as Santa handing out the presents. I loved every minute of it and felt sad as I went to sleep that it would be another year before we could do it all again.

Even as an adult I retained some of that excitement as the festive season approached. We developed our own rituals, buying the Christmas tree a couple of weeks before the big day from a business set up each year in the local park, and decorating it with ornaments that Diane's parents had in her childhood. As soon as we had children, we decided that we would have Christmas in our house, welcoming close family to come to us for lunch. And Christmas was when I came into my own as a cook – Delia Smith's sausage rolls on Christmas Eve, and her timetable for turkey followed religiously as I prepared lunch on Christmas Day.

But as December dawns this year, I am not quite feeling the festive spirit. I am still dealing with the consequences of the fall which happened in mid-October. While my confidence is gradually returning and I have got a bit more flexibility in my right arm after some intensive physiotherapy, my range of movement is still a long way from being back to normal and I am warned that this arm may never be completely straight again. I make a joke of it, telling friends that my ambitions to bowl for England's cricket team are over because I'd be labelled a 'chucker', but the truth is I still feel disabled by my injury, moving very slowly when I am out and nervous in crowds that someone may bump into me. And there is a new ailment plaguing me. I thought at first that the itch on my right arm was just my wound healing but then a rash began to spread over much of my body. It is desperately irritating and uncomfortable, particularly at night when I just cannot find a position which protects my arm while allowing me to stay still long enough to fall asleep.

As I lie there revolving and trying to resist the desperate urge to scratch, one thought keeps bubbling to the top of my mind. We are coming up to the anniversary of Sophie's arrival at our home – so I know that I will be weighing up everything that happens over the next few weeks to determine whether we should see the last year as a success or a failure.

On the very first day of December we face another Sophie-related challenge. Having failed to clip Sophie's claws at home, we have asked the vet to do the job. My sore and itchy right arm is not up to driving or even picking up a 15kg dog so it will be up to my calm and collected wife to drive us through rush-hour traffic to the surgery. But first we have to catch our dog. My only real contribution to this is to come downstairs early and attempt to feed her the trazodone which should calm her down well in advance of our departure. For forty-five minutes, she studiously ignores it and the daily fluoxetine hidden in lumps of paté. Finally, with less than an hour to go she swallows both pills.

When the time comes for Diane to scoop up Sophie and carry her to the car it is not clear that the drug has had any effect – unless the chase around the ground floor of our house is a bit of playfulness rather than terror. But when she is deposited next to me on the back seat of the car, it becomes clear that this is one fearful dog. She trembles violently as we set off, so much so that I can see as well as feel her whole body shaking. But this is her fourth trip in our car to the surgery and after a while, the trembling subsides and she begins to show some interest in the world outside – the passing bicycles, the parents with toddlers in pushchairs, the occasional dog being taken for a walk. Perhaps, I ponder, she is starting to think it would be nice to be out there.

But such thoughts fade as we arrive at the surgery and now it is my heart pounding as I wonder how we are to get our dog to submit to a procedure that she has already shown she wants to avoid. Once again, I am going to be a helpless bystander – and what happens next leaves me lost in admiration for my wife and the young female vet. After Diane scoops her up and carries her into the treatment room, the vet asks if there is a danger that Sophie will bite her, in which case she will need to wear a muzzle. I say tentatively that she has never shown signs of aggressive behaviour and the vet seems satisfied. But then Diane acts as a kind of human muzzle, lifting Sophie onto the treatment table and clasping her head tightly while the vet deftly wields the clippers. I wince at the loud click as the sharp claws on each paw are reduced to a manageable length. Then we are done and with a huge sense of relief we are heading home.

When we arrive Sophie is at first reluctant to get out of the car, as if she has decided it is her new safe space. But when she does emerge, we take her into the front garden where she enjoys sniffing her way through a flower bed before ambling up the doorstep on her way to Sophie Central, the kitchen and living room where she can choose between two beds.

Overall, I feel this expedition has gone pretty well, confirming Si's often repeated opinion that we have come a long way over the past year. But another thing strikes me that I don't think he will agree with. Each of the four visits to the vet in this last twelve months has involved doing what Si calls 'taking Sophie over threshold' – exposing her to situations which frighten her. This is something he tries to avoid in all but the most exceptional circumstances, believing it is bound to set her back. Yet after her terrifying trips in the car to the vet, she has apparently either bounced back very quickly or suffered no side-effects at all. That sets me wondering whether we should try taking her on more trips in the car when there is no pressing need, perhaps to the park. Getting a lead or harness on would be the hard part but if we began to associate a car journey with something fun like a trip to the park rather than a scary visit to the vet, surely we could accelerate our progress towards a walk? (I don't quite dare ask Si about this at this stage.)

Our upward momentum continues through the first weekend of December, with Theo showing again that he is the star visitor of our 'stranger danger' training programme. He is enthusiastic and does not get discouraged when Sophie barks at him, perhaps because, as the owner of a boisterous poodle called Coco, he isn't too phased by anything our dog does. He is mastering the art of throwing cubes of cheese or sausage just in front of her and she now routinely pays him the ultimate accolade of a prolonged sniff – perhaps detecting the scent of Coco.

But if the dog is in good shape, our health problems continue to mount. Waking after another bad night driven mad by the itching of my rash, I end up paying £60 for a private video consultation with a GP, who prescribes an ointment that I have already bought over the counter at the local chemist. Meanwhile Diane, already tired and feeling the strain from trying to look after me, somehow pulls a muscle in her back. Quite apart from the pain, she is depressed that she will have to give up for at least a month the twice-weekly ballet classes which she says keep her sane.

I am sure Sophie senses the low mood which has enveloped the house and after her upbeat weekend, she appears down in the dumps again. I fear I am not great company in the days Diane is in Cambridge, especially as my skin condition continues to make it even harder for me to sleep than usual. In my nerdy way I sometimes use my Apple Watch to track my sleep, and the data from Monday night tells a sad story. While it shows that I spent nearly seven hours in bed from 11 pm until 6 am, for only three-and-a-half hours of that was I actually sleeping. I dozed for a brief time, then woke just after midnight and it took me more than an hour to drop off again. But this time after just twenty minutes, I was awake again and stayed that way for an hour and three-quarters. And so the pattern continued: short periods of sleep followed by long spells awake and eventually I gave up and stumbled downstairs to make a cup of tea. Poor Sophie looked bemused when I switched on the kitchen light and made it clear that, while I may be getting up, she intends to stay in her blue bed piled with toys and will be having a duvet day.

All week, with a brief spell of playfulness when Diane arrives home on Wednesday, Sophie is off her food and rather quiet – if she was human, you might wonder whether she was depressed.

And by Thursday I'm still not in the best shape myself, feeling wiped out after more nights of broken sleep and no improvement in my skin condition, and worried that I have let things slide on so many fronts with Sophie. What little harness training we have done has been all down to Diane, and with Christmas coming, we have achieved very little in the way of making our dog less afraid of visitors.

Luckily, things are about to take a turn for the better. It is time for another trip to the hospital for the surgeon to assess how my wounded arm is coming along. Slowly, is the answer, though I am more preoccupied with the infernal rash which is making my life miserable, and which hasn't been shifted by anything I've been prescribed. What I need is a powerful steroid which I can only get if I first see my GP – and my experience, like that of so many other people these days, is that getting an appointment for something not deemed to be urgent could take days or weeks. But this is where my surgeon comes in to save the day. He sends an email to my GP, saying I need to be seen – and, hey presto, the next day I am at the surgery showing off my rash. The GP explains that there are various strengths of steroid ointment and she is going to prescribe me one of the more powerful ones. And it works – within a couple of days the rash is receding, I'm sleeping better and my mood has lifted. Now I am ready for a big push to end Sophie's year with a major step forward – or that is my hope, at least.

It's the second weekend in December and, as we refocus our efforts on Sophie, Diane reminds me what Si has told us about the importance of play. Any real connection with our dog will only come when she is relaxed enough to allow us to stroke her, scratch her ears, give her a belly rub and enjoy a bit of rough and tumble. So as we try to get more playful with what is still quite an uptight dog, Diane discovers an unlikely method of connecting. Each morning, as regular as clockwork, she lies down on the rug in the living room to do the back exercises prescribed by her physio. At first, Sophie observes this new activity from a distance, as if to say, 'What on earth are you doing?' But gradually she gets closer, and one day, she starts pawing at Diane, then, when she is doing an exercise which has her lying face down on the floor, Sophie climbs on her back, forcing her to stop what she's doing and play. From then on, Sophie seems to see her new role as Diane's fitness trainer, urging her on and even on occasion joining in – although perhaps those social media fans who respond to a video clip I post by insisting she is teaching her the 'downward dog' yoga move are getting a little over-excited.

So the relationship between Sophie and Diane has become more tactile than ever – and occasionally our dog even gives me her paw, rather in the manner of a princess accepting the worship of an adoring subject. But if we are doing well with playtime, the picture is a bit more mixed when it comes to the reception Sophie gives to visitors to our home. Theo continues to make progress with her and each week her visits to the front room – where I am currently being taught 'A Foggy Day in London Town' – get longer.

But on a Sunday evening a fortnight before Christmas, there is a hostile reception for our neighbours when it is our turn to host the weekly get-together over a glass or two of wine. Each new arrival is greeted with some very loud barking and, even though the dog is shut in the kitchen-living room while we are in the front parlour eating cucumber sandwiches off the best china – well, a bowl of crisps anyway – Sophie can be heard carrying on throughout the evening. One of our visitors asks whether this is the reason we are not having our regular Christmas drinks do this year. This sets me thinking – we haven't had anyone round for dinner for months and even with family we have been keener to meet at their homes or on neutral ground. Is our dog making us antisocial?

But we do have one visitor who really seems to 'get' Sophie. Lily, who is a picture researcher and photographer from the publishers of this book, has called in to begin investigating how we can go about getting a portrait of Sophie to put on the cover. When she rang a few days earlier, I explained that if she was thinking she could turn up with a camera and just snap away at Sophie, she was going to get a surprise. But it turns out that Lily is the ideal person for this job because she has a very nervous rescue dog of her own.

When she arrives and Sophie greets her in the usual fashion, she knows exactly what to do. Lily is neither scared nor gushing, but simply takes some cheese from the box of treats I have prepared and lobs them in Sophie's direction in a rather offhand way. It is the natural reaction of most guests to try to coax the dog into liking them – 'Oh what a lovely girl, aren't you beautiful,' and so on – but Lily avoids even looking at her, and just keeps the treats coming. The barking does not exactly stop but is reduced to a grumble and a whine. I post a short video clip of this encounter, and one Twitter follower asks Si – or @sociabledog – for his view.

Here is Si's analysis: 'Lily does the right thing. No coaxing but throwing food within reach. Technically #sophiefromromania is "over threshold" and while the barking is a spontaneous response to the scary person, over time the behaviour could be maintained by virtue of negative reinforcement. (Scary person goes away.) Ideally we keep Sophie under threshold. As not possible, she'll eventually habituate and choose her safe distance. At that point the counter-conditioning will have a greater impact, & neutral (habituation) becomes "like".'

I have to read this a few times before I think I understand it – but then I realise I don't, so I ring Si. He says that Twitter is not an ideal place to explain things but what he was trying to say was this: '"Over threshold" means Sophie's fear response is triggered because Lily is too close – ideally we would have them meet first outdoors at a distance, but that isn't practical. As for "negative reinforcement", my point is that if Lily left straight away this would teach Sophie that barking makes the stranger leave, so it would be worse next time. But if she stays, what we hope is that Sophie starts to relax, finds a safe distance from Lily, and starts accepting the treats. If you can get that positive association between the person and food, then you're winning.' While I am a bit clearer now about the science behind fixing the 'stranger danger' problem, I'm not sure we will be able to put theory into practice in a hurry.

But a few days after her first visit, Lily is back and this time I escort her to a seat at the kitchen table. The barking from Sophie is as loud as ever at first, but eventually she appears to decide that Lily is at a safe distance and retires to her bed, where she continues to mutter and grumble to herself but we can at last hear ourselves speak. There is, however, more loud barking and a rather worrying lunge towards Lily as she leaves, so I remain anxious about how quickly our home will return to being a relaxing place for visitors.

As 17 December approaches, and with it the anniversary of Sophie's arrival, I begin to wonder how we should mark this milestone on social media where there is such a strong community of Sophie fans cheering her on and checking in faithfully for daily updates about her activities. Unlike in this book, I know that on social media I have sugar-coated our story a little, accentuating the positives and gliding over the moments of doubt and depression about a dog that has given me plenty of sleepless nights.

In the end I decide to make a short movie cut to music, with photos and video showing the story of Sophie's first twelve months. It begins with the image of the dog delivery van parked on our street, then we see a terrified Sophie in my arms on the doorstep, followed by a quick series of shots of her peering anxiously out from behind the red sofa. But very quickly the mood lightens, and she's romping around the garden, hanging out with me, Diane and Si in the kitchen and sleeping in her two fine beds. The final scene of the one minute and twenty-two seconds shows Sophie and Diane having a cuddle in front of the Christmas tree. So once more, I am giving the online audience a largely positive story – there are no images of our visits to the vet, for example – although there is a photo of me looking bruised after my fall, with Sophie hanging out in the background.

On the morning of the big anniversary, after preparing a big Sunday breakfast of scrambled eggs and bacon for me, Diane and Sophie, I post the video on YouTube, Instagram and Twitter. On Twitter I also post a thread with further photos summarising the events of the last twelve months:

> 'A year ago today a van arrived in the small hours bringing #sophiefromromania to our home . . .
>
> . . . the poor dog was absolutely terrified . . .
>
> . . . and for months spent most of her time behind our sofa . . .
>
> . . . but gradually with the help of the wonderful @sociabledog she grew more relaxed . . .
>
> . . . and playful . . .

. . .there is still a long way to go, but thank you to everyone who has joined us and supported us on Sophie's journey away from fear.'

The reactions come quickly and are heartwarming, as ever:

'Oh, my word. What a year it has been! So far travelled and further to go. You would never have imagined that, with all her terrors and trembles, #sophiefromromania would have captivated so many of us so completely.' @janeinpenn

'Bless her, she's come a long way. Just shows what love and patience can achieve.' @veronicareagan

'Ah, Team Sophie, what a year! It's been amazing to witness your journey together – thank you for sharing it here. I've loved watching Sophie fall in love with the Prof, become partners in crime with Rory & learn to be a pup with Uncle Socks! Happy Gotcha Day #sophiefromromania.' @Sarah_racewear

The critics, who have been so noisy of late that Diane has had to block several of them, seem most unusually to have fallen quiet. @Davethepostie has a question, however, and to my mind, not an unreasonable one: '. . . I'm all for rescuing dogs, I have a rescue myself and I've previously had rescues. Surely we can rescue dogs that are in our own country first before we import other countries' strays?'

What some are calling our 'gotcha' day (the day we first got Sophie) passes off quietly, with Sophie in a reasonably cheerful mood, but in the evening there is a reminder that a year ago we had expected a rather different kind of dog. Most years our daughter-in-law Franny's parents hold a Christmas carol party for family and friends at their house, which is about a mile from ours. Her dad, a gifted musician as well as a Brentford fan with a seat next to mine in the stands, plays the piano while her mum hands out sheets of carols – everyone gets to choose one to be sung, and a few brave children play recorders or sing a solo. It is lovely and always feels like the start of Christmas.

This year the festive event is back after a break for the pandemic, and we set off to walk there. But every time we have been to the party before Covid, Cabbage has come with us, and once there, would slumber under the piano, or patiently tolerate the attentions of exuberant toddlers. Of course there is no question of Sophie coming along – we have to sedate her just to get her out of our house, let alone into someone else's. So we leave her behind, meaning that she misses out on our four-year-old granddaughter singing, 'Away In a Manger' – with just a little help – while holding a candle. We have a great time but as we head home, I cannot help feeling a little sad that Sophie can't yet join us on family occasions like this.

It is time, then, to reflect on our year with Sophie with some of the people who have been with us on this journey or have watched it closely from the sidelines. Were we wrong to get a dog from Romania rather than find one at a British rescue centre, as our Twitter critic suggested? Should we have done something different after Sophie's arrival to try to deal with her fear? Did we choose the right path in deciding to move forward only at her pace? And what have I learned about myself from the experience?

I know that what we might call the 'dog establishment' in the UK is pretty hostile to the idea of bringing in pets from overseas. Not long after we got Sophie, the British Veterinary Association made clear to me their worries about the risk of importing diseases such as brucellosis, but when I talk to Adam Clowes from Dogs Trust, he is more concerned about the 'blind date' nature of many of these imported pet transactions, the stress of the journey and the lack of post-adoption support for the new owners. He explains that if we had got a dog from one of their rescue homes, we would at the very least have met it and possibly had it to stay for a trial period before making a long-term commitment: 'The ability to meet and bond and have some information about the dog before they arrive is what I would say is really important. And also, understanding the type of dog you need for your current lifestyle.' Whereas with Sophie all we had to go on was a ten-second video clip and the few warm words of the website description of her.

As for the added element of stress for pets being transported from other countries: 'The journey the dog goes on – there is no time [for it] to decompress before it goes into the new home.' I ask him what Dogs Trust would do if I got a dog from them and a month in, it was still living behind the sofa. He says they would offer to take it back or if we wanted to persevere, they'd give us further support. He believes, however, that the whole scenario is unlikely: 'I would hope that we wouldn't hand you a dog that lived behind the sofa for the first month, because we would have said that maybe she's not quite ready for a home environment just yet.'

I seek feedback on Sophie's first twelve months from those directly involved, and speak to Adrian of Friends Indeed. While he doesn't explicitly say it, I sense that he thinks our approach all along hasn't been the right one. When I call him to get his thoughts on how things have panned out with the dog he brought us from Romania, he starts comparing Sophie with her sister. After a brief unsuccessful stay with one set of owners, Bella has settled nicely with Ryan and Rebecca. Between the two homes, Adrian and Maria looked after her for a few weeks. He says that at first she was very nervous, rather like Sophie, but they took an altogether different approach to getting her walking: 'We got her out – we didn't wait for her, as you did, as Simon advised you,' Adrian tells me. Like her sister, Bella was very nervous at first but they forged ahead: 'If the dog doesn't come to you, you have to go to the dog and we just put the harness on her without asking her if she wants it or not.' On her first two walks with their other dogs, Bella appears to have dug her heels in, much like Sophie when I tried to walk her on the first day. After a few steps, Adrian recounts, they took her home. 'Of course we didn't force her, we didn't push her too hard . . . But then the third day she'd learned from the other dogs, so we managed a short walk with her to the park.'

Within a week, according to Adrian, Bella was enjoying walking with the other dogs. But, he says, he and Maria can simply not afford to wait months and months for the dogs they take on to acclimatise. He concludes by giving me his view on dog psychology: 'I would also say they need a leader, they need somebody to inspire them, they need somebody very confident.' It's a philosophy I suspect Si would see as rather old-fashioned.

All this makes me reflect again – which I've done so often before – about the fact that we have only been able to move at Sophie's pace because of Si's generosity with his time, his willingness to drop everything to come and help us. If we had not found each other via social media, who knows what we would have done? I think we might have tried to force the pace at an early stage or even perhaps given her back to Adrian for a while.

I suppose the reason I'm mentioning all this is that I am not sure that all the praise we get online from Sophie's fans is justified. Although all the positivity and encouragement they offer is greatly appreciated: 'Unbelievable how far she has come with your love and patience. Wonderful to see,' says @miller.jackie. 'To see her sleeping in her own bed after all that time sleeping behind the sofa says it all,' says @cheryll_m_g.

When I speak to another Friends Indeed dog owner, who has closely followed our story – my friend Sadaf – she too is full of praise for how we have handled Sophie, despite the fact that she took a different approach herself with her dog Cookie. 'I think you've been incredibly patient – and knowing you as I do, I think I can safely say you're not always the most patient of people,' she says, and we both laugh, remembering incidents when we were working together as producer and reporter in the pressure cooker of TV news and I was, perhaps, not totally even-tempered. 'Actually, to be honest,' she continues, 'I'm quite astounded at how patient you've been, Rory, and I am sure it's a lot to do with Diane's influence. You have both just put Sophie's needs and her apprehension and her fear first, above your own desire to have a quote, normal, unquote dog.'

Sadaf says it is obvious that Sophie has bonded with Diane but she has comforting words for me: 'I think she loves you both and she's comfortable in your home, which is now her home.'

My final conversation about Sophie's year with us is with the man who has had more influence over her, and us, than anyone – Si Wooler. He has been telling me from the start that it is not unusual to find a rescue dog that is reluctant to engage with the outside world, and that we just need to be patient. But I am struck by his admission, which he only now verbalises, that, of all the cases of fearful dogs he has handled, this one has been the most challenging – 'I can't think of a harder one . . . She's a very delicate creature – setbacks can be really significant for her.'

But as ever he is keen to reassure me that, stepping back from the day-to-day ups and downs, we really have made huge progress, particularly in the five months since we got Sophie on fluoxetine. As ever he understands my impatience, but insists once more that if we try to go faster than Sophie is willing to move, we will only achieve the opposite: 'This is about a proven, evidence-based methodology that says, this works faster. And all the evidence and all the research says it works faster. And so, saying to the dog, "Right, I'm going to put your lead on because *I* want to put you on a lead," will be detrimental to the whole process.'

Of course, something which Si has had to put up with for months – and lately at a higher pitch than ever – is the criticism on social media from those who believe he has been leading us down the wrong path. Some of the comments have been truly challenging, questioning his professional competence and personal integrity, and Diane and I have had to block a couple of the most vociferous critics. When I ask him how he has coped with it, he is honest: 'It can be pretty corrosive when it gets really toxic and personal – it's so difficult.' But then in typical Si fashion, he tells me that he tries to keep it all in perspective, '. . . because you realise you just have to tell yourself that actually, it's a very, very small minority'.

After a year as therapist-in-chief to a Romanian rescue dog and her owner, what then, I ask him, does he think about the whole idea of importing dogs from abroad – to which he replies, 'I don't have any views on it in terms of whether I think it's a right or wrong thing to do . . . I just don't think it's helpful for somebody to say they shouldn't have got the dog – they have got the dog: so, what are we going to do about it?'

But Si does have this advice for those preparing to welcome a rescue dog into their homes: 'Be aware that it's a lottery. It is by no means certain or even likely that you will get a "problem" dog – and in any case, a problem could well be ours not theirs.

Dogs usually adapt and find ways of dealing with a problem, even if that means hiding away.' I ask myself, not for the first time, whether we have been the problem all along.

We sail past Sophie's anniversary and into Christmas. It is a quiet one – but that suits us just fine with a dog that is increasingly comfortable with us, but not so much with visitors. Last year the Christmas tree appeared to be a source of stress for our new arrival, who sent it lurching into a bookcase one night and then hid behind the sofa for quite some time. This year, however, she is snuggled in her big cosy bed in front of the tree which she eyes with some curiosity. Then one evening I am upstairs when I hear Diane yelling, 'No Sophie, stop it!' I rush down to find that our playful pet has decided that it is fun to chew the Christmas tree ornaments – not a great game, especially as some are made of chocolate, which can of course be lethal to dogs. We take some comfort, however, from this latest example of normal doggy mischief, as we do from her penchant for grabbing shoes from the stand in the hall, tearing out their insoles and arranging them neatly on the living room rug.

On Christmas Day we are going to our son's house for lunch, but beforehand our close friends and neighbours pop round for a drink. Despite the fact that they're regular visitors to our house, they are greeted by a prolonged bout of full-throated howling from Sophie. But luckily when they retreat to the front room, she quietens down, with just the occasional not very festive grumble to herself for the remainder of their visit.

As with the Christmas carol party, Diane and I feel sorry to have to leave our dog behind when we head off at noon to the festive family lunch – exactly the kind of event which would once have been incomplete without Cabbage. But even in the last few days Sophie has taken to following us to the door as we leave – and do I detect for the first time signs that she misses us when we go out? We are back by 5 pm and for the rest of the holiday period, the three of us are at home together nearly all the time.

There's no doubt that Sophie is gradually thawing out – playing more with us, happier to sit close to us and be stroked, sometimes even putting her front paws on the bottom step of the staircase as we stand above, willing her to come up to our nice warm bedroom where her third bed sits waiting next to the radiator. So far she loses courage each time, and heads back to the safety of the living room. But after a year which has been harder than I could possibly have imagined, full of worries about this strange little creature and concerns about my own health, I suddenly realise that I am feeling two strong emotions, and I do not think they are anything to do with the dozen Parkinson's pills I take each day.

The first is hope, and it has been sparked by a conversation with Si before Christmas. He has finally found the right medication and his CRPS has gone into retreat. This in itself is very welcome news, as we have both been concerned on his behalf. The next thing he says is that if it's okay with us, he is planning to come down early in the New Year and stay for as long as it takes to get Sophie used to the harness and ready to go out for a walk. Oh yes, Si, that is very much okay.

And the second emotion is love – love for a dog called Sophie, whose life started so badly: dumped by the side of a road and left to die, then transported across Europe and handed to terrifying strangers in a place where for a very long time she only felt safe in a dark, narrow space where nobody could get to her. Over the past year she has puzzled me, worried me, maddened me and given me any number of sleepless nights, But she has also taught this increasingly grumpy old man the value of patience. I have at last begun to realise that it is no use trying to browbeat her into becoming the kind of dog I want her to be, one whose tail begins to wag furiously at the mere suggestion of a walk.

I remember something that Sadaf said to me about not fixating on a walk when the important thing is that Sophie loves us: 'That's the main thing, even if she never gets out. The fact is that you've given her a home and she's comfortable and happy there.' Of course, I would like to take Sophie out for a walk to our local park, have her accompany me along the clifftop path on Cardigan Bay, throw a ball for her to chase on the beach. I am still confident that will happen but for now the sight of her curled up in her bed, surrounded by her toys, snoring gently, tells me all I need to know – Sophie has come home.

Epilogue

One frosty Sunday morning in late February, after a wretched night when I have slept for perhaps two hours, I come downstairs at 6.30 to get ready for an adventure. I put the kettle on to make a cup of tea for me and Diane, take my first four Parkinson's pills of the day and get a block of paté out of the fridge. I cut three small cubes from the block, insert Sophie's daily fluoxetine pill in one, a trazodone anti-anxiety booster in another, and then, along with the third unadulterated cube, put them in her dog bowl.

I place it near Sophie's bed where she is having a big stretch and while I am making the tea, she snaffles the paté. Good – in half an hour or so the trazodone should kick in, making her a calmer dog. I take Diane her tea, and we discuss the plan she formulated the night before. By 7.15 we are downstairs with coats and shoes on. I peer outside and realise that there is a hitch to our plan – our car parked at the kerb outside our house is covered in ice. I set about clearing the windscreen, spraying it with de-icer, turning on the car's aircon system which (of course) always makes things worse before they get better.

Before I have finished the job, Diane shouts from the front door that she is ready and I need to install myself on the back seat. She comes out carrying Sophie, who has a harness on with a brand new red lead clipped onto it. The dog is then deposited on the back seat next to me, visibly shaking, not with the cold but through sheer naked fear. As Diane does some further work on clearing the windscreen, I try to comfort Sophie, giving her a scratch behind the ears and handing over a couple of dog treats. I work out that this is just her fifth trip in our car and the previous four have all been to the vet, so perhaps it is not surprising that she is so frightened. But this time we have another destination in mind – a park just a mile away where we will attempt something that I have been dreaming about ever since Sophie arrived in our home.

At the beginning of January Si comes to stay, recovered from the bout of CRPS which had put him in a wheelchair, and raring to go. He tells us his mission is to get Sophie out on a walk, or at least get her harness on – and he will stay as long as it takes.

But teaching Sophie to accept the harness – and the two of us to become more adept at putting it on – proves unexpectedly hard. One week passes, then two, then three, and we seem to be in the familiar pattern of two steps forward, two steps back. But in the fourth week Si has a breakthrough, getting the harness on and a lead clipped to it while Sophie is in the garden. Even though she then stands rooted to the spot for twenty minutes, we decide that this is mission accomplished – for Si at least – and at the beginning of February he heads home.

Now, after the excellent work of our patient behaviourist has taken us within sight of the surface of the moon, it is up to us to land the craft and take the first step. But still it takes time for us to gather confidence – at first we struggle to reproduce what Si has achieved in getting Sophie comfortable with the harness.

We inch forward when Diane is at home, grind to a halt when she is away.

Then, one evening in mid-February over dinner at the Royal Opera House where I have taken Diane to the ballet as a birthday treat, we have a long chat about where we are at with Mission Walk. Somewhat to my surprise it becomes clear that she now favours the kind of decisive move that I have been thinking about – just bundling Sophie into the car and taking her to the park. But as it is Diane who is more trusted by our still very nervous dog, and far more adept at putting the harness on, it is she who will decide when we push the button.

Nothing happens straight away, but on the last Saturday in February we have a great day, wandering into the front garden with Sophie in her harness trailing a lead clipped to it. She's nervous, yes, scurrying back indoors when people walk past our house, but she is also inquisitive, popping back outside and sniffing the air as if eager to explore.

That evening Diane tells me the time has come – tomorrow is W Day, we are going ahead with Mission Walk.

In the back seat of the car that Sunday morning, as I stroke our poor trembling dog, I calculate our chances of success as we approach the park. They don't look good. We could have started with a walk from the front door, however we remembered the day of Sophie's arrival when she was put on a lead and just dug her heels in and refused to budge. Although she is getting better at going into the front garden, she is still incredibly jumpy about anything happening in the street and bolts back inside at the slightest excuse. By taking her to the park and presenting her with a new environment without a safe space to retreat to, we hope that her natural curiosity will trump her fear and she will begin to explore. But it seems far more likely that she will just freeze.

After one wrong turn we realise we don't know the route to the car park because we have always walked to this place, not driven. But finally we spot the cul-de-sac we need and moments later, nerves jangling, we are pulling up in the empty parking area. Without stopping for a moment to gather herself, Diane gets out of the driving seat, comes round to the back door and clips a second lead onto Sophie, this time on her collar. We have heard stories of nervous dogs wriggling out of harnesses, so we want to be absolutely sure she can't bolt – although I have also attached a tracking device to her collar so that we can find her if she does escape.

But that seems a very remote possibility once Diane lifts our still trembling dog out of the car and puts her down. As expected, poor Sophie just freezes. Thirty seconds go by, then a minute, and she seems to be saying, 'I'm going nowhere.' And then quite suddenly, her nose is in the air and she is having a sniff. A short time later she moves a few feet to a row of trees bordering the path and apparently finds something utterly intoxicating in the undergrowth in which she proceeds to bury her nose. The next thing we know we are heading across a frosty expanse of well-kept grass – and yes, I can barely believe it – we are actually walking!

Or rather, Diane and Sophie are walking, stopping every few yards for our dog to have another sniff, and I am following them with my phone, trying to capture something of what, to us, feels like a historic moment. As they continue on their way, the pace isn't always smooth or uniform – while at 7.30 on a Sunday morning, the park is still very quiet, every so often the odd runner appears, and Sophie stops each time, looking slightly panicky.

Now I take over the leads, grabbing them ever so tightly in my left hand – which has now become more reliable than my right. We set off again in staccato fashion, stopping and starting, but making reasonable progress. It feels so good to be walking a dog again – it is now more than two years since I walked Cabbage, very slowly, around this same park and over the last fourteen months with Sophie, there have been times when I have lost hope that this day would ever come.

I hand the two leads back to Diane and soon we are facing another big unknown – finding out how Sophie will react to other dogs. For months on end, well-meaning people have been saying that all she needed was another canine chum. But when some months ago we'd cautiously invited Sadaf's Cookie, and Rex from two doors down, to come and hang out at our front door they hardly got an enthusiastic welcome. But now, when a dog and its owner hove into view, Sophie turns towards them looking interested rather than scared or angry, which seems encouraging.

Then, as Diane stands in the middle of a patch of grass, two energetic black dogs appear in the distance, off-lead, with their woman owner some way behind. One of them ambles over towards Sophie and stops at a safe distance. Then suddenly, in a heart-stopping moment, the other one races straight at our dog and tears past her. Sophie wheels around in what seems like a panic, and then both dogs approach her. This all feels like a very tense, possibly even dangerous situation and as the dogs' owner approaches, Diane – who has remained remarkably calm as always – explains to her that we have a very nervous rescue dog on her first ever walk. But suddenly I see that the three dogs are all having a sniff at each other and although there is a brief growl and lunge from Sophie when one of them gets a bit too forward, this isn't alarming, it's just normal dog behaviour.

After this excitement, we have another five minutes gently strolling back towards the car park. Sophie is a little calmer on the way home as we both tell her what a good dog she has been, but once we arrive and get her out of the car, she can't wait to head through the front door.

Diane and I, however, are exuberant – the morning has gone better than we could ever have hoped! As I start preparing the usual Sunday breakfast of scrambled eggs and bacon, with a special portion for a brave dog, I feel as though I have taken off a pair of lead-lined boots and can move again. It is only now that I can finally admit, after so many months, just how much I have been yearning to have a dog that will walk with me – and how painful it's been to wait so long for that moment.

This is beyond a doubt the biggest step forward in Sophie's story so far, and my normal instinct would be to tell her legion of social media fans the news straight away. But this time it feels right that we should first break the news to the one person without whom this would never have happened – Si. Diane taps out a message on our WhatsApp group: 'A big day, Si! We popped Sophie's harness on with no trouble, put her in the car and drove to the park – where she walked on the lead and even said hello to 2 other dogs.' With it she sends a picture of me from the back with arm outstretched as Sophie leads the way on our first ever walk together.

As ever, Si is quick to respond, messaging: 'Oh my word! That's fabulous news!'; he signs off with five handshake emojis. Then he wants to know whether she looked playful or cautious with the other dogs, so I send him my video of the encounter with the two black dogs.

He is bowled over: 'Bloody well done, both. That's absolutely made my decade. Nerves of steel, Diane!'

But still we don't put the news on social media, allowing ourselves to just savour the moment and let its full significance sink in. Just before lunchtime, Diane tries to take Sophie through the front door but after a few hesitant steps on the pavement, she takes fright when a neighbour comes out of their house, and rushes back inside. No problem – we know that in the right environment she will enjoy a walk again.

It is only after 9 pm that I check in on Twitter and Instagram and post two photos of Diane and me in the frosty park seen from behind with our dog. I add this caption: 'At 0730 this morning the Prof and I put #sophiefromromania in the car and took her to a local park for her first ever walk. More details tomorrow.'

Even that late, the message gets a huge reaction – before long we've clocked up tens of thousands of likes. Early on Monday I follow up with longer posts on both platforms, explaining in more detail what we did, along with a video clip of the incident with the two black dogs. A wave of unbridled joy and love breaks over us . . .

> 'Thank you so much for taking the trouble to document this. You know how invested thousands of us are in this beautiful girl's progress. You're brilliant, all of you. So happy for you. Be proud.' @katynott53

> 'Absolutely brilliant. Teamwork makes the dream work. Granddaughter off to tell her teacher about this exciting development. You're breaking all our hearts, Sophie. What a brave girl!' @Lesley35042161

> 'Actually crying reading this. So proud of you all for sticking to the plan. @sociabledog – congratulations on your students!' @Catheri24284230

> 'Such an emotional sight, from the dog who spent weeks and weeks behind the sofa to first trip in the park, this is a massive step.' @jennykensit

We are of course overwhelmed with gratitude to these people who have joined us on this journey. But, in my glass-half-empty way, I think back to previous breakthrough moments – such as the first time Sophie took food from our hands or put her head through the harness – and how they were often followed by months where we made no progress or even went backwards. Will it be the same this time?

The answer is a resounding 'no'.

After a couple of days when Diane is away and I try but fail to get the harness on, the three of us make a second successful trip to the park on her return. Then we start walking Sophie from the front door, at first just to the end of the street, then around the block. Within a couple of weeks we are doing two walks a day, a couple of times a week taking the car to the more distant park, but mostly heading from the house up the tree-lined streets to a familiar destination.

It is hardly big enough to be called a park – just a rectangle of grass, really, about 400 metres by 100 metres – but it has a special place in my heart. This is where I took Cabbage every day during the first Covid lockdown for the daily half hour of exercise we were permitted. Back then I took a picture each day and posted it on social media. The photos were dull but the ritual felt comforting to me and, it seemed, to many others.

These days Sophie and I are often in this little park, usually before 7.30 in the morning. She has begun to approach me after I have had a cup of tea, and then she'll sit patiently as I fiddle with the straps of the ultra-secure harness and attach two leads. As we leave the house and head along the quiet streets, she can still be very nervous – terrified one morning by a group of builders unloading a van; startled on another day by her deadly enemy, the postman, blocking the pavement with his bright red trolley.

But once we get to the park she seems to relax and is surprisingly keen to interact with both dogs and humans. Gradually, I am beginning to rebuild the network of dog owners I knew well enough of old to nod to in the park – some from the days of Cabbage; some new. Many know about Sophie and are considerate in how they let their dogs approach her. But gradually we are all relaxing because this is a sure sign that the dog that hid behind the sofa for months – that would refuse food for a couple of days when Diane was in Cambridge and shy away when simply being shown the harness – is now happy. As we head across the grass to greet another dog, her tail is up and wagging furiously.

Sophie has taught me another life lesson – in the immortal words of the old hit by Diana Ross and the Supremes that I keep humming:

'You Can't Hurry Love.'

I had so desperately wanted a happy ending for Sophie – and for this book. But now it strikes me that I have got something even better: a happy beginning to lots more adventures with our brave little dog, Sophie from London.

Acknowledgements

It was barely a month after Sophie's arrival in our home that my agent Elly James emailed me to say she was getting a lot of calls from publishers wanting to know whether I was planning a book about our painfully shy rescue dog. At the time I was knee deep in the final draft of my memoir *Ruskin Park* and the idea of starting on something new seemed daunting. But in her usual calm and efficient way Elly helped me craft a proposal, arranged a series of meetings – the first time I've been wooed with dog treats – and organised an auction that went without a hitch. Elly's colleague Heather Holden-Brown, the legendary founder of the HHB agency, had wanted me to write a book about our previous dog Cabbage, and was as ever hugely supportive.

How fortunate I now feel that Square Peg and its publishing director Marianne Tatepo came out on top in the contest to publish *Sophie from Romania*. Marianne had a clear vision for this book, focused on a message of hope, and in the dark days when we seemed to be getting nowhere, her optimism and her belief in the power of Sophie's story kept me going. Her colleagues Emily Martin, Leah Boulton, Fiona Brown, Lucy Upton and Mia Quibell-Smith – Team Sophie, as they dubbed themselves – all gave the impression that this was a very special book to them.

After I completed the first draft, the arrival of a fresh pair of eyes in the form of Susan Feldstein was a great boost, helping me to see where the story needed expanding and where less would be more – and persuading me to be more open about the emotional rollercoaster our shy dog was taking me on.

Special mention must go to Lily Richards, picture researcher and photographer, who turned out to be the perfect person to work on the cover. Lily has a very timid Romanian rescue dog of her own and, warned by me that Sophie would bark at her in terror, won her trust over three long visits to our house. She and brilliant designer Yeti Lambregts conjured up a delightful cover, despite the best efforts of our star to avoid the limelight.

My friend Lindsay Shaw, another person adept at wooing Sophie with judiciously thrown treats, did great work researching the history of how the dog became man's – and more often woman's – best friend.

But without two people this book would not have happened. Si Wooler, our advisor and now our dear friend, taught us to move at Sophie's pace and was as much my therapist as hers. And Diane, showing a patience that often eluded me, worked tirelessly to win our dog's trust. Her calm and loving presence showed Sophie that she had nothing to fear and that she had at last come home.